Building

Better

Bridges

Building Better Bridges

A guidebook to having difficult conversations that can save our children

Clint Davis

PRESS

To request permissions, contact the publisher at clintdaviscounseling@gmail.com

Hardcover: ISBN 979-8-9887037-0-9
Paperback: ISBN 979-8-9887037-1-6
Ebook: ISBN 979-8-9887037-2-3

First paperback edition November 2023.

Edited by Sarah Wilson
Cover art by Nathan Treme
Chapter heading images by various artists

Garrison and Mitcham Press

PRESS

Dedication

To my wife and kids, I love you more than the moon and the stars.
To my best friend and brother CJ, you are a better bridge that I needed.

Table of Contents

Building Better Bridges

Acknowledgments

To my wife Jacie, for fighting for me and with me through our own healing journey. Without you none of this would be possible. You make me a better man, husband, and father every day. Well, mostly every day. ;) I love you. Now and Always.

To my two boys, I did this all for you. I did not want to wake up when you are 15 or when you are adults and know I could have tried to do something that would make your world better and realize I didn't do everything I could. You both are such special boys and will be such special men. Thank you for learning and growing together with me. Thank you for both making my heart 2 sizes bigger. Thanks for loving me even if I am imperfect and even if you "love mommy more."

To my family, thanks for all the imperfect growth and healing that has taken place over the years in all our lives. I know it is messy and difficult at times, but the lessons have been invaluable. Thanks for supporting me in your own unique and special ways. I love you all.

To my friends and loyal supporters, you know who you are. You have been such an encouragement through this process. Each one of you has played a pivotal part in me getting over my fears and insecurities. Y'all are the absolute best.

To my staff and workmates. Thanks for all the hard work you do to help keep CDCIW going and allowing me the space to reach more people. You are an amazing group of human beings!

To my O.G. Editor, Sarah. Thank you for painstakingly going over this book with me in a way that had just the right blend of personal and professional balance. Thanks for letting my passion come through and for challenging me to be my best. I truly couldn't have done this without you. God knows what He is doing.

Clint Davis

i. What is This Book and Who Is It For?

You would not have called to me unless I had been calling to you,
said the Lion.
-C.S. Lewis, *Chronicles of Narnia*

Hey, there. It is my firm belief that you have picked up this book because there is a purpose and a plan for your life. Whether or not you set this right back down or only read a part of it, you are meant to do great things, and so are the children who surround you. I hope these pages can play a small part in that.

You may be wondering if this book is for you. Here are a few questions to answer those thoughts:

Have you suffered from abuse in the past? This book is for you.

Do you want to keep your child safe online and in public? This book is for you.

Do you want to understand practical tips for having difficult conversations with your child or children in your life? This book is definitely for you.

Have the changes in technology, the internet, and social media wreaked havoc on your children, family, or friends? This book is for you.

Are you a teacher, leader, or mentor for children and teens? This book is for you guys, too.

Do you find yourself trying to search the internet for helpful information, but you don't know where to go to find a balanced perspective? This book is for you, and I hope it helps your search in a big way.

Building Better Bridges

Are you wondering why you have such a difficult time navigating conversations surrounding sexual health or sexuality in general? This book is for you, and you aren't alone.

Do you want to know the why's, how's, and what's of our brains, our culture, and our children? This book is for you!

This book is written for *anyone* trying to navigate the world right now. Parents, grandparents, foster parents, and all other forms of caregivers. Though many of the messages here are for parents, this book is also helpful for people without children. We are all humans who have grown up in a world full of toxic messages, suppressed feelings, and generations of neglect, trauma, or abuse. We all have an inner child trying to understand what we've been through and how to live or parent in this new world. In one way or another, and based on the best research and statistics, the issues we will talk about in the pages of this book affect us all and those we love.

I know that the things you are about to read are some of the major issues of our time and signify a turning point in human history. As such, there is a lot to cover here. In the following paragraph, I will try to summarize the thesis of this book and to describe the experiences I had that brought me to write it all down. (No pressure, eh?)

We are in a world-wide crisis, physically, emotionally and spiritually. Over the past decade, I have seen a steep decline in areas that matter the most: intimacy, face to face conversations, healthy living, work ethic, and unity. Unfortunately, I have seen a rise in a focus on external things that don't bring us peace. Things like click bait news, outward appearances, numbers of followers on social media, and an obsession with things that bring comfort and pleasure. Many writers, podcasters, and speakers around the world will say, "We are at our best." In some ways this is true, but they say this because people are living longer, medicine is readily available, we have the best human rights, fewer poor people than ever before, more resources, more entertainment, and more comfort than ever before. If some of these things are true, then why do the statistics show us that anxiety, depression, suicide, and addiction have risen so high in young adults, teens, and children? ***I believe that we are missing some root causes and drivers to this mental health crisis.*** I also believe that as parents we can help minimize these negative experiences in our children's futures and help those suffering recover from the unintentional damage already done. I know if you are reading this, you want to make changes and are looking for guidance and help in this strange and difficult new world. I'm a father myself and am going through this same journey with you!

We can do better when we know better. In order to know better, we have to have conversations and discussions that might require some bravery. We have to learn about our children in a holistic and integrative way. We have to be resourced and equipped, and lastly, we have to get past our own pain and negative coping mechanisms to make positive changes for future generations. Many think that the internet, social media, and the smartphone are to blame for most of the problems of today. I will show you that this is true in many ways, but it's not the whole story. I will attempt to show that research points to immense changes that have happened in the past 15 years across the globe and not all for the better. What I am hoping to do with this book is show you that there are a few hidden problems that have always been there for children and teens. They were there in your childhood and in mine, and it is time to address them. We have to bring them out of the darkness and into the light. These issues have been mostly hidden or kept secret for a million different reasons. The internet, social media, and phones have only exacerbated those problems and allowed them to happen more often and more intensely. Peoples' hearts are not more broken than they have always been, but our ability to spread that brokenness like wildfire has dramatically increased. I know that if we can wake up and make some radical (but simple) adjustments in our families and our communities, we have a chance to save our kids and our children's kids, for generations. I hope by the end of this book that you see some of the reasons things are happening and that you feel resourced in how to actively start making a difference with your children or the children you are in community with. I will attempt to zoom in and out on these issues from a macro systemic perspective then down to a micro level, right into your living room. It will be a wild ride, but I know you are brave enough to make the journey!

Recently, I was able to do a Ted Talk on some of the content in this book. After doing that event and having hundreds of people reach out to me, I finally got the courage to put pen to paper (fingers to keyboard, really). If you are interested in listening to that before reading, please take 8 minutes, and go to YouTube and just search "Clint Davis Ted Talk." This video content will be covered in chapter 7, but the talk will really set the stage for the entire book. The discussion I have there is just the tip of the iceberg of the issues close to my heart, and after doing the talk, I realized the deep and pervasive need for a "How-To" manual of some sort. How to approach our kids about sex in the 21st century, how to know when we should have that conversation, how to deal with this new and unique onslaught of technology. Above all, we will look at how to make changes in our family, and just as importantly, *why* we should. I will try to address some of the millions of how-tos that we haven't had to deal with before now, and give you a great place to begin.

I am living this out with you, after all.

I know what it's like to be a parent or caregiver for a child and not have time to listen to endless podcasts or read 15 books. I know we need one central source to answer our burning questions, instead of piecing together self-help articles and advice from well-intentioned friends and family. I get emails and phone calls every week from friends asking me "what do I do about x, y, or z." It usually goes something like, "Hey man, so this thing happened with my kid and I have no clue if it is normal or not? I feel so uncomfortable. What should I say?" 8 out of 10 times it is something healthy that we just do not talk about, but sometimes the behavior or situation might be a red flag to more. The common thread is that we were not taught how to handle these issues, and so we are terrified to address them or even admit that they happen.

However, these "unique" issues represent problems we face universally. It does not matter what your politics, religion, ethnicity, or country says about these issues, they must be addressed, and no one is immune. So because of years of these questions and concerns personally and professionally, I figured it would be helpful to put as much as I could in one location. To be honest, I was only going to write like 50 pages, and then it just kind of went and went and landed here hundreds of pages later.

Clint Davis

This book is the result of my career-long piecing-together of all this research done on your behalf. I have tried to summarize and condense the best parts of many books and research articles I have read, while adding personal stories and first-hand clinical evidence and experience. I have painstakingly tried to write in a way that is not attacking, not judging, and not patronizing. I am sure I will step on a few toes, but I think a little toe-stepping is what we need right now. If it wakes us up and saves our kids, hopefully you will thank me later.

Also, I absolutely did not get here on my own! God has guided me every step of the way. All glory and honor to Him.

Though I received support and guidance from many sources, I want to dedicate this book to all the clients and survivors I have worked with over the past decade or more. It has been an honor to walk with you and hold space for you to heal and process the darkest parts of your life. Every one of you helped to write this book. Your bravery, stories, and vulnerability have helped bring me encouragement and given me the courage to write this book. I hope it brings you joy and purpose to see our work together bring healing and resources to so many. If you are reading this, I love you and am so thankful for our time together. Those sessions had meaning beyond comprehension.

This book is also dedicated to anyone who has been abused, neglected, or taken advantage of in any way. Despite what you feel or have been told, you are not alone. In spite of all the minimizing and excuses our culture and families do, I want you to know your experiences are valid. Trauma in all its forms touches more of us than you can imagine. I want you to hear these words and let them touch your heart. It was not your fault, and you didn't deserve it, no matter what you did, what you said, how you dressed, or if you felt physical or emotional pleasure. You were designed to be protected, guarded, and nurtured, not abused or abandoned. You were never made to be neglected or left to figure out your sexuality, sexual development, or internet safety all on your own.

I am not sure what went wrong or what you went through, but there *is* hope for you and your family. I have experienced healing for myself and seen it for many others. People who felt they were past the point of no return have found recovery, healing, and become beacons for others in darkness. God can – and does – use a little good to overcome a lot of bad.[1]

This book is also for all of us parents who feel we have messed everything up. It is not too late for any of us. None of us is perfect, but I know we can stop the cycle for our kids and future grandchildren. I refuse to look up in 10 or 20 years and have to apologize to my boys for knowing better and being too scared to act. I hope this book motivates you in the same way. We all have forgiving, healing, and restoring to do!

Lastly, this book is dedicated to the people out there fighting the good fight. I hope that this book validates your already courageous and amazing work. Many of you I have referenced throughout these pages, and some of you I have not. Regardless, I am forever grateful for you paving the way. Rising tides raise all ships.

****

At any point throughout your reading, you can stop and seek out your support system. If while reading this you recall an unaddressed memory or if an experience is brought to the light that you had previously ignored, justified, or accepted, I pray that you will find courage to address it and face it. Maybe make a phone call to that trusted counselor, pastor, or friend, and tell them what happened in a short and simple way. Get help today because there is no need to continue suffering alone and in silence. You deserve peace and freedom right now.

I truly understand what these feelings are like. It took me over 25 years to address my sexual trauma and early porn exposure, and I am still working in therapy and in my marriage to recover from the damage it did to my mind, body, and spirit. This road is long, and it is difficult. But I will tell you now – the fight for freedom is worth it. It is worth it for our own hearts and the hearts of those we can help with our stories of healing.

I know my goals for this book are lofty - creating healing in our families, setting all new boundaries, learning about how our brains work in this

---

[1] "The light shines in the darkness, and the darkness has not overcome it." John 1:5 (ESV)

new world. That's big stuff. But, as one of my favorite office managers says, "'You miss 100% of the shots you don't take.' - Wayne Gretzky - Michael Scott"
IYKYK.

So, we are embarking on a journey together to try to find a way forward. The truth is, very few roads are paved for us. The great news is we all have a choice after learning new information. We have two choices really. We can respond or do nothing. The choice is yours, and mine, and all of ours. Recovery or prevention are our two options in the battle for our hearts, minds and souls. Our children deserve better and so do we!

One more time, I want to repeat. This book is likely going to take you on a difficult ride. Pace yourself and take notes. There will be a question section at the end of each chapter for you to do some processing or even having some new discussions. I will also have lists and breakdowns for resources, apps, books, conversation starters, etc, in the "Appendix" sections at the back of the book, so that you can get support in real time. But first, I will speak briefly to who I am, the childhood traumas I experienced, and the career experiences that led to this work.

ii. Who Am I and Why Should You Listen to Me?

We have been to the moon, we have charted the depths of the ocean and the heart of the atom, but we have a fear of looking inward to ourselves because we sense that is where all the contradictions flow together.
- Terence McKenna

I hesitate to write my own story and advice on these pages, because, like many people, I have minimized my own experiences and pain just to survive. I also know that in the year 2023, I cannot possibly please everyone or say everything in the way that everyone needs to hear it. I feel inadequate and afraid to put this all out here, but I know I must. So I step out in faith that God will use it for others, and hopefully for you too. I also don't want anyone to experience shame or guilt, especially my parents. Like many of our parents, they did the best they could with what they knew and the few resources they had. Ultimately, I don't want this book to be a simple autobiography about me. This is *our* story, not mine alone. I realize my perspective is that of a 40-year-old, caucasian, Western raised, American male. Much of the perspective and research is from a Western American culture. I accept I cannot write this book without bias and without some stereotypes or blinders. I tried really hard to get a wide variety of professionals and friends to read this, give me feedback, and add to it, to eliminate as much bias as I could. I'm sure I will miss things, but I hope at a minimum this can open conversations and lead to more people adding to those conversations. I hope the facts can speak for themselves.

The purpose for sharing my own experiences is to show people that even ministers, clinicians, and professionals have their own struggles and stories. We are not set apart from suffering, and neither are you. I also want people to see how God was present the entire time, in every detail, and He continues to use my experiences to help other people find healing. I want you to know that this can be your story too. If you are a Christ follower, you have been given the ministry of reconciliation, no matter what you believe about yourself or your abilities.

I know that not everyone reading this is of my faith. Whatever your faith background, I hope that this book can still help you in your parenting journey, open your eyes to universal truths about us as humans, and that by the end, you can see and accept just how loved and valued you are. No matter what you have been through or done, you have a mighty purpose on this earth.
I will be vulnerable and tell you my story because stories are powerful, and because I hope mine gives you hope and a reason to keep reading. For some, this story will sound familiar and for some, parts will be foreign. I hope the common thread of humanity shines through. This is a general overview to help lay the foundation for the content of this book and what perspective from which I am writing. I try to leave out the gory details. It is not helpful in my opinion to try to use trauma for shock and awe, but I do want you to understand a little bit about the human writing these pages.

My story starts when I was just a young boy growing up in the country roads of Deville, Louisiana, population 1,208. Picture any small country town from any movie with one traffic light, and you've got it. People knew everyone's last name and could ask things like, "You Greg's boy?" or say, "I know your Granddaddy from church!" It wasn't exactly Mayberry, but you get the picture. We went to Big Island Baptist Church, where everyone there was grey-haired and loved the Lord. My grandfather (PawPaw) was a deacon in the church, and my grandmother (Neicy) was the church clerk. They served their entire lives in this tiny church. I grew up singing hymns about the wonder working "pow'r" of the blood of Jesus. It was a small start, but there are some wonderful memories and people there. Shout out to all the Devillian's still out there! You are the salt of the earth.

The childhood I experienced was the last of its kind. The last before the internet changed the world, before devices were in everyone's hands, and before the door to a wide variety of entertainment and depravity fit in our back pockets.

Building Better Bridges

Instead, we rode our bikes around the neighborhood, stayed out until the streetlights came on, and spent days camping outside and playing in the woods. Not a single parent knew where anyone was until dusk. We did not have nets around our trampolines. We call these the good old days. I know we romanticize this. I understand the reality that many of us wear rose-colored glasses when we look back on our pre-technological lives. Bad things did happen. Abuse, trauma, exposure to pornography and adult content – all of these happened and more, but the way it happened, the amount it happened, and the exposure to it all was light years behind today's average childhood. ***Our parents' margin for error was much wider than ours is today.***

My family went to church every Wednesday and Sunday, plus the additional church camps and conferences. My parents believed in God and the redemption of Jesus, but unfortunately they divorced when I was 8 years old. Like many parents they were not equipped or educated on mental health, body safety, or the dangers of the internet. I mean, goodness gracious, they were just 20-year-old babies when they had me. They had their own trauma and neglect to recover from! I am sure the same could be said of your parents. Needless to say, things did not go well. Sexual trauma, exposure to adult content, and inappropriate interactions with other adults and teens were all commonplace occurrences for me and the children around me. Many of these experiences I never shared with anyone. I did not know how to, why I should, or if anyone would help. If I did try, I was met with silence and a lack of resources or support. This wasn't anyone's fault, but it internally placed the blame and responsibility on myself. Like many others, I suffered in silence and shame for fear of getting anyone in trouble or calling attention to myself. No one at church talked about these things so I felt like I was alone in my experience. All the kids knew this stuff was going on so we assumed so did the adults. It was not every second of every day, but over the course of a childhood it sure was impactful. Let's just say, the silence was deafening.

As I grew up, I could spend the night with friends and family members whenever I wanted. We didn't have supervision, and there were none of the rules or awareness or guidelines that you will find in this book. Many parents today think this is still acceptable, even with all of the changes we will discuss. It is not. These things really are "that big of a deal."

Before puberty, kids should be innocent and lack sexual exploration for the most part, but when they are exposed to sexual content, things escalate. Simply playing house or doctor suddenly becomes risky. This doesn't mean I or the other children were trying to be sexual on purpose, just that we were curious. Children are not wrong for playing out things they have seen or experienced...that's what learning children do. They see a superhero cartoon, they put on a cape and pretend to fly. They watch a movie about a princess, they dance around in dresses and call for tea time. What is wrong is a child seeing or experiencing inappropriate things as children which negatively warps the playing in their mind. In my own childhood, it was the response from the adults that stuck with me. I remember getting yanked out of a closet when me and another child were playing doctor. I remember being very scared and ashamed for whatever we were doing. We got in trouble and lectured, and then it was never addressed again. That experience taught me that deep down in my mind I was bad, bodies were bad, and that I was deeply wrong for exploring. I know that might not have been the intention of the adults, but that was what I learned to believe when there was no clarity or real discussion. Sound familiar?

God bless my Mom and Dad. They either didn't know how to respond or didn't know that things were happening. I'm sure like most parents, they were just doing the best with what they knew. Heck, they might not even remember, but I definitely do. One of the more traumatic experiences I had was with another child over the course of a few months or years. I honestly don't recall the timeline anymore. I know it was before and during puberty. Things are fuzzy and blurry now, but trauma therapy does help with that. Because no one taught me about my body and my boundaries, or prepared me for puberty and how to protect myself from others, I experienced many confusing, damaging, and shameful things. I remember not understanding or knowing why my body was changing or responding differently or why it would feel good or uncomfortable. These were completely normal developmental things, but I felt confusion, surprise, and shame. You have to understand that allowing children to shower together, sleep in the same bed, and stay up late watching Cinemax and HBO was bound to lead to disaster, especially when we do not prepare them or teach them appropriate boundaries. Over the months leading up to and through puberty, scary, exciting, embarrassing, and traumatizing things happened for me, and for many of the people I counsel. Like I said, this is not just my experience. Those images and experiences are still burned into my mind. 20 years of therapy has dimmed them, but they are not fully gone. Whether through playdates, campouts, or at summer camps, I had many more troubling times. It might have happened to you as well, in some form or another. These events shamed me and deeply impacted my life from then on. I, like many of you, and many children today, thought I was the only one going through these issues. I thought I was uniquely broken and messed up. Well, I wasn't, and you aren't either.

As if all that wasn't bad enough, in the early 90s, the world wide web started bursting into everyone's homes. By the time it hit our house, I was 13 or 14. Raging hormones, curiosity, and early sexual trauma got me into a lot of trouble. You see, the thing that minimized the damage for many of us was that the computer was in the living room, and everyone used it. Access was limited because it was out in the open. It was also dial-up internet. I am certain the loud *pshhhkkkkkrrrkakingtshchchchc-ding-ding-ding* can still be heard ringing in outer space. We couldn't get into too much trouble because nothing loaded quickly, and there was nothing speedy about it. Regardless of its speed or immediate accessibility, the internet entering our homes gave birth to many children's addictions and exposure to adult chat rooms and adult content. AIM (AOL instant messenger) had some *really* weird people on it. For the first time, porn was available for children to consume and be aroused by. I overheard my older teen neighbors and babysitters talk about things they had seen or done in person and eventually online, and this fueled my curiosity and normalized toxicity in my mind. This is another red flag. These kids who were 5 and 6 years older than me were traumatized and oversexualized. They were my mentors and educators on many subjects like drugs, alcohol, sex etc. It is important to know the exposure level of the people and kids your children are being surrounded and influenced by. We need to know how to prevent these things.

Between sexual trauma and exposure to the internet, I also just faced a general lack of protection from adult movies, violence, and adult content. I had cable television in my room and can still remember trying to watch the squiggly lines on Cinemax in the hopes that I could catch a peek of something. (The lines were squiggly because we didn't get those channels.) Today, children have unbridled access. The squiggly lines are gone.

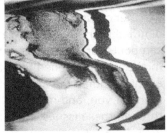

I mentioned I have two sons, and I shudder to think of my young boys being exposed to the things I saw at their age. It would absolutely crush my heart. Even when our family sits down to watch some of my "favorite" Disney movies and childhood films, we have to immediately shut them down. I'm floored at what used to pass as "kid's shows." Between the early sexual exploration, the child-on-child interactions during my puberty, and the dawning of the internet, I was an internal mess before the age of 15. I didn't know it at the time. Neither did my parents. What I have learned through years of personal counseling and through counseling others is that my story is not unique or uncommon and in many cases is rather mild. Does this story or experience sound familiar to you? I'm betting it does, but I hope this lets you know you are not alone. Your experience isn't anyone's fault, but rather a cultural and societal problem we all missed.

Unfortunately, our parents didn't know the degree to which seeing sex, drugs, and violence would affect little kids, and in many ways the culture did nothing to prevent it. I still sometimes search release dates for movies like *Child's Play* or *Friday the 13th* to remind myself that my dad (love you, dude) or some other adult took me to see those films in theaters when I was under 10 years old. I remember being in grade school and watching a sex scene in which Jason Vorhees, from Friday the 13th, cuts a lady in half with a stop sign. *Ouch.* How about those Chucky movies? I couldn't sleep for weeks because of *Child's Play* and that horrific doll. That movie came out when I was just 6, and I had seen all three Chucky movies by the time I was 10! It was totally common and normal for kids to see or hear these things on a regular basis. I have heard countless stories from both men and women about their childhoods and how adult books, music, and film shaped their view of love, life, and self. Again, these things were and are "that big of a deal." For the first time ever, sex and violence in mainstream media silently affected an entire generation. This is just what technology and entertainment do:

enters and affects our brains, sometimes without us realizing its damage. The changes in technology and the way we consume media create a double edged sword, bringing both great advancement and horrible risk.

For the majority of people it was not unusual to find *Playboys* or not-so-wholesome VHS tapes in some family member's closet, next to the toilet at a friend's house, or right out in the middle of the living room for God and everyone else to see. Of course, everyone "read them for the articles."
(Sure, Cousin Eddie...we all believe you.) I have also heard several stories of little girls and boys finding their mom's Danielle Steel book or a harlequin romance novel and the impression that it left on them. We can never be too careful about what we leave around for our children to read or pick up.

The insane thing about all of this and what continues to shock me, is that all this exposure *pales* in comparison to what children can see in 2023, instantly and right in the palms of their hands, for hours at a time.

Incidentally, I survived the Voorhees stop sign shock and the Chucky doll nightmares of my childhood. As I navigated highschool, dating, and forming my identity, shame and confusion were always present. I had no idea how to date, what sex was, what was appropriate to ask or do with girls, or anything about their anatomy. There were no conversations in church, at home, or at school, except "don't do it" or "do all of it." There was not much of an in-between. This is another huge problem we still have today. Helping teens navigate these years is so vital to giving them a healthy future in marriage and in society. Teaching consent, respect, how to manage hormones, and about the opposite sex has to be a priority.

I eventually graduated from high school and joined the military. I did not have the best grades and no plans for my future. My parents brought me to an Army recruiter, I joined the Louisiana Army National Guard and went to basic training. The recruiter told me things were really calm and that we hadn't had a war in a long time. He explained that I could go to college for free and just do one weekend a month with the National Guard. Boy, did he lie. The second week in basic, as I sat on the rifle range learning to shoot my AR-15, we got the call that our country was under attack: the date was September 11, 2001. Like most traumas, these memories stuck with me and shaped my life. Many Americans reading this can remember exactly where you were at the time you heard the news. After returning from basic training, I was quickly shipped off to a war in Afghanistan at the ripe age of 20. What an experience that was. I returned home and tried to start college, but battled many emotional struggles. Just a couple of years later, Louisiana suffered one of its most devastating natural disasters in Hurricane Katrina. My unit was activated to respond, and I barely survived my time in the living hell on earth that was the Superdome. (That's a book in and of itself). During the 6 years I served, I spent more than half of them deployed to war or a natural disaster. In the middle of all of this, the trauma from my past followed me, and it all started to pile up. At one point in 2004, I had a full-blown meltdown. I was using whatever and whoever to cope with my pain. My world was shattering, and I needed help. I remember calling my mom, and she rushed home from work. I can still recall the feeling of the carpet between my fingers, as I laid on my back in our living room panicking and crying uncontrollably. I remember going to a Christian Counselor who helped me stabilize, and I began the long journey of figuring out what had happened and what I was going to do with it. We will all reach moments like this. Moments when all of the pain of our past and unrecognized trauma comes calling.

In the following days, weeks, and months, the Holy Spirit made it clear to me that I was going to use my life to help others, but first I needed to get some education and some support in understanding my own experience. So, I decided to leave the Army and to buckle down at school and in my own counseling. I had several mentors that stepped into my life and guided me along the way. I highly recommend that painful but amazing process. I eventually decided I was going to study to help people, just as my counselor had helped me.

After exiting the Army, I got my Bachelor's in Psychology from Louisiana Tech University and went across the country to California to get my Masters in Marriage and Family Therapy from Fuller Theological Seminary. I wanted to make psychology and theology make sense together, but I also wanted to learn how to help people with different beliefs or values than mine. To be able to counsel them without doing harm or forcing my beliefs on anyone.

I hope to achieve the same thing in this book and to give valuable tools to people from all faith backgrounds. I hope you won't shut the book because you have religious trauma or a history with toxic Christians who showed you the wrong version of who God is.

During my time at Fuller, I was able to do EMDR therapy and find some healing from my past trauma, my parents divorce, and some of the things I had experienced in the military. This healing led to more healing in my relationship with my girlfriend, who became my fiancée, who is now my wonderful wife. My story would be nothing without her and the enormous impact she had and has on my life, but this isn't the book for that. I would like to acknowledge our healing and growth is still ongoing and a beautiful mess. Learning to be a husband has taught me how selfish I am and learning to be a father has taught me how much God loves me. Much, much more, but I am sure you get it.

After graduate school, God, in His infinite wisdom and through His wonderful plans, brought us back to Louisiana to start my work as a counselor. At the start, I did many odd jobs trying to survive and served in many ministries that taught me so much. The main one that changed my views and helped me in the area of sexual abuse and assault was The Hub: Urban Ministry and its off-shoot program, Purchased: Not For Sale. Both of these programs were founded by Cassie Hammett and are still going strong today! The Hub is a ministry that started out helping people in poverty and homelessness at its "Lovewell Center" and then added an outreach ministry that then turned into a full blown, inpatient housing ministry for women and children rescued out of human trafficking.

In my years at the Hub, as Director of Recovery, I worked with some amazing people to write programs, gain resources, and work as a counselor with women and children who had been in trafficking most of their lives. At the same time, I was working for a Children's Home helping abused and abandoned children learn to cope with and recover from childhoods filled with trauma and neglect. As you can imagine, or maybe you cannot, I heard hundreds, if not thousands of stories of heart-breaking abuse, neglect, and trauma that to this day can haunt my darkest dreams if I let them. A few of those sessions contain experiences I still can't believe are true, and no horror film can capture the terror of those stories.

It seemed that in all areas of my life where I worked as a clinician and attempted to help people find healing and restoration, a common song played over and over again. A terrible dirge of sexual abuse and trauma, all happening before puberty even began. I found sex and violence were a part of so many children's lives, but nobody was talking about it publicly or even acknowledging it! Not my professors, not my peers, and not my pastors.
I spoke to countless people. Nearly every single person I talked with had been sexually abused or traumatized by a peer, parent, or neighbor. Many of them had been exposed to hardcore pornography on some level, and been exposed to adult content in books, films, or magazines. It had become so normal and people were so numb that they wouldn't even acknowledge it as a problem, let alone realizing it may have been traumatic. They would insist that it certainly wasn't influencing their lives now. Cough, cough. It was, and it is.

I started to take notice of the number of people mentioning these experiences, and I was astonished to find that it wasn't just victims of human trafficking or dramatic abuse cases, but also the average client in my private practice world or in my community Bible studies. I thought I might be biased because I work with "hard cases," but I have come to realize my story is very common, and I started to realize that none of us are uniquely broken. Human beings are funny that way – all unique and yet so similar and connected by universal experiences and feelings.

What's more, this strange thing started to happen when I shared my story and the testimony of what God had done and was doing in my life and the lives of my clients. More and more people found freedom and started an incredible journey of lifelong healing in their own lives. Some of those people give credit to God and some to themselves, but either way healing started! *It seemed like I was giving a voice to the same things that they had kept hidden and quiet their entire lives.* I have continued to struggle and recover in some areas, and I am sure getting to where I want to be will be an ongoing process. So, I want to remind everyone that all of our journeys are different, and that's okay. Be kind. Be patient. Keep an open mind and heart.

I want to encourage you that you can help other people even if you haven't gotten all the healing you want or are fighting for yourself. Sometimes healing comes in the form of therapy, sometimes in the form of conversations over coffee, and sometimes it comes from a direct and profound experience with God. Due to my own desire for healing and for the conviction to help others that the Lord put on my heart, I began to search for resources and answers.

As a therapist, I started to read and study everything I could on trauma and the brain. I eventually got trained in prolonged exposure therapy, EMDR (Eye Movement Desensitisation and Reprocessing), and also got my certification in sex addiction therapy from the international Institute of Trauma and Addiction Professionals (IITAP). I read *The Body Keeps the Score* and many other amazing books. I listened to podcasts, speakers, and read journal articles seeking direction and guidance on how to help others that had been through similar things. The resources were limited, but I did my best to soak it all up.

These experiences have continued to bear fruit in my life, and God continues to be kind and gentle in revealing my own flaws and areas of growth. In recent years, the combination of research, clinical work, and personal experience came together to show me the severity of this issue of sexual trauma and abuse and how it spans across the globe, though it feels especially acute in American society. Sexual trauma, exposure, and abuse remain at the core of almost every story I hear when it comes to symptoms like porn addiction, affairs, drug and alcohol abuse, and many of the psychological struggles I see in my clients and their families. As my staff has grown, been trained, and worked with people, this continues to be their experience as well. This has helped me to formulate the thoughts and solutions that you will read in this book. All of this has further opened my eyes to a new term, "childhood sexual neglect," that I defined in my Ted Talk and will unpack in later chapters.

Lastly, in March 2017, I branched out on my own and started Clint Davis Counseling, which eventually evolved into Clint Davis Counseling & Integrative Wellness. What started out as just me has grown into a team of credentialed and passionate professionals. In addition to the 25+ mental health professionals that span across 5 offices and 4 cities, we have physical therapists, doctors, chiropractors, dietitians, and other providers from different modalities who make up our integrative wellness team, who have become partners in this attempt to bring holistic treatment to the world. For all of us at the clinic, our faith in Jesus is a priority, and although we don't just work with other believers, the love and grace He has shown us is a hallmark of how we want to serve and love our clients. He brought reconciliation to the world, and we want to bring that to our wonderful clients regardless of their background, culture, religion, or financial standing. We are still learning to work as a team and see our clients holistically and treat them as such. I am also growing and learning as a clinician, a father, and a husband. I have a long way to go, but I tell you all of this to help you understand why I am so passionate about having this conversation within the short pages of this book and to show you that there are resources and people available to help you. I also want this to be a story about how good and gracious God is and how much He can create purpose and meaning in your life as well.

I know that my story is unique in some ways and totally common in others. I know that many people will have strong opinions about some of the things in this book. I have experienced quite a few of them already in my short journey. Whatever your story is, I want to try to communicate the information in this book in a therapeutic way that shows both truth and grace. This next chapter will hopefully set that up nicely.

iii. Caveats and Disclaimers

At the heart of science is an essential balance between two seemingly contradictory attitudes--an openness to new ideas, no matter how bizarre or counterintuitive they may be, and the most ruthless skeptical scrutiny of all ideas, old and new. This is how deep truths are winnowed from deep nonsense.
-Carl Sagan

Despite my experiences and expertise, I want to be clear from the outset that I do not have all the answers, and sometimes information doesn't immediately lead to transformation. I hope that this book will lead you to more conversations and even start a journey of healing for you or your family, but I don't think that this book will be the answer to *all* the problems we face in these areas. There are many other resources I will put at the end of this book and throughout that have helped me on my own path, and even more that I mention on my podcast, *Asking Why*.

I hope you will do what is best for your family, in your culture, and with your particular morals and beliefs. I will share some of my beliefs, but that doesn't mean I want to project those on to your situation. I do not know what you are going through or what your exact situation is. I like to take things on a case-by-case basis and try not to overgeneralize. As much as I would love to write a how-to manual that works for every person, our lives and hearts and minds are different. So instead, this serves more as a conversation starter, an attempt at drawing back the curtain on things we need to hear, and a set of practices that hopefully help us do better in the future. I hope it is a lens to see through. So feel free to modify these practices to fit your life. Just be aware that the things that feel the hardest or most awkward just might be the most important to discuss.

I want you to learn how to put into practice some of the challenges ahead by being the most authentic version of yourself but also being willing to take action.

At the end of each chapter, you will find a set of questions to help guide discussions with your children, family, or peers, and that will likely inspire thought-provoking reflection in your own heart. You are welcome to skip them, but remember, this is much more than a book of detached information and will act as such if you let it.

If you get halfway through or to the end and you feel lost or stuck, reach out to us at my clinic, call a therapist in your area, go speak to a minister or religious leader or trusted professional. Just have *someone* in your community help you walk through this difficult process, because isolation is not the way to do it. Being immersed in a healthy community can save you so much heartache and pain.

Last disclaimer. This book may be triggering in various ways. It may cause you to recall memories, details, or events that you have forgotten or purposely suppressed. It may shine light on situations you thought were innocent and now realize were harmful. It may reveal that you did something when you were a child that now you look back on with shame, disgust, or regret. Whatever may come up for you, God can handle it.

You are loved, valued, and worthy of healing and restoration. You are not alone, and you are certainly not the only one going through this. Do not let your triggers determine your freedom!

The first several chapters will sort of be a fire hydrant of information. Information about how our families have evolved in the last 300 years, what different childhood developmental stages look like, how our brains have been rewired in today's technological world, and what it means to have trauma. Hang in there through some of the research and science because I can tell you, it will open your eyes to your own brain, your child's, and how to get some of the growth and help you are longing for.

Building Better Bridges

One of the biggest caveats I can give that will be crucial to remember through the rest of these pages relates to neurodiversity in children and adults, as well as those who live somewhere on the autism spectrum.[2]

I am 100% certain that some of you reading this book will have children with all kinds of different gifts and struggles related to brain structure, and you likely have your own as well. I have had parents ask me what to do with kids who don't register what they are doing or don't pick up on social cues, parents who have children with attention disorders that make them more likely to fidget in unhealthy ways. I understand that all of our kids are different, and each one of them needs different methods of communication, understanding, and processing information in a comfortable and safe way that speaks to their own brain. I'll say it as the book goes on, but I want to remind you up front - do not hesitate to do things a bit differently than I have prescribed if your child responds in a different way. At the end of the day, you have to know your child well enough to know that he or she will need specific things that the other children in your family or community will not. Parenting and raising children is so difficult, because with each child their unique needs, personality, and circumstances may change the way you have to apply parenting skills. Parenting is also complicated by how our children become different people year after year. This is why community support and a village mindset is so valuable.

If you have a kid of your own or you mentor children who will struggle with these conversations because of neurodiversity or other challenges, here are a few tips and tricks I suggest and that have been suggested to me by parents:

    - Write down the conversation, and leave it for them to read in
    their own time.
    - Record a voice memo, and leave it for them to listen to at their
    own pace.
    - Have the conversations in tiny chunks over the course of
    several years.

---

[2] Shout out to these folks because your brain is fascinating and different, and you have skills many of us will never have. I hope you can find confidence in your differences, not shame or loneliness!

- Increase supervision and limit exposure earlier and more cautiously due to their particular needs.
- Have them read the books to you or on their own like *Good Pictures, Bad Pictures* or *God Made All of Me.*[3]
-Do an activity like shooting basketball or playing catch, and have conversations while moving or doing the activity.

You can also create picture cues for children who are hearing impaired or anyone with communication delays. For example, give them a picture of a body with a green check mark or a red X. You can also give them safe and unsafe pictures of strangers and family members. Helping them to visually label who and what is safe is vital. Keep it simple. You might want to address one body part or safe person at a time over a longer period.

Some of these tips might work with any child, but it is important not to use them to avoid having difficult talks or for the benefit of your own comfort. Try to use them only if the child needs special accommodations or support. As a heads up, here are a few points that I will cover moving forward:

- The statistics and research regarding children and adults in America are staggering as you will see in the following chapters. Sadly, these statistics are only getting worse, with little to no explanation of why. I hope to cover the whys and paint a vivid picture of what is going wrong and what we can do to prevent it.
- The young adults and teens who are creating and forming the next generation are overly sexualized, traumatized, and mentally unhealthy. These teens and young adults are going to be the ones shaping culture and shaping our world, and if we do not help them, I truly fear the collapse of society as we know it.
- These teens and young adults are also going to be the ones mentoring, teaching, and leading our younger children. If they do not recover from the damage of the last decade, then the

---

[3] I will mention these works later in the book, as well as in my resource list at the end. Thanks to the amazing men and women authors out there seeking to help our kiddos!

risk of our younger children falling into the same perilous circumstances is high.

- Our younger children do not know the dangers, red flags, and protective skills required to keep themselves safe online or in person. They are being raised by parents who are stressed out, overworked, under-supported, and who have their own unresolved traumas, unrealistic expectations, and broken lenses through which they see the world.
- Our kids are being raised in a system that heavily focuses on behavior modification, grades, performance, and achievements and does very little to educate and equip them on emotional intelligence, Biblical literacy, building belief structures, or cultivating problem solving skills.
- Most concerning of all is that children are being given devices and access to the world earlier and earlier with no preparation, education, or support systems in place to do damage control. We are normalizing unhealth and toxicity because we are desensitized to all these things ourselves.

These points might sound very serious to you and in fact are quite serious. We have the right to feel some level of fear surrounding these things, but we also have the right to feel a great amount of hope. The chance to change is in our grasp, and the steps to get there might be difficult but are not complicated. Don't lose heart, and let's get going. Trust is difficult to earn from readers, so hopefully these caveats can help build a bridge between you and I before we get into the heavy topics!

Just a couple more things before we move on, I promise.

As you begin reading these pages and putting them into practice ask yourself: What are my foundational beliefs? What are the things that are core to how you live life, how you treat your spouse, and how you raise your children? I would go out on a limb and say that those values or beliefs should be solid and well-defined for your family before any of my other advice makes a lick of sense. I will not dictate to you what those values should be for your household, but I will also not lie or shy away from using my core beliefs to structure this whole shabang. Our beliefs, whatever they are, will shape how we treat the content to come, and we should do our best to make them firm and stable for our kids and peers.

As for me, I am going to be coming from the perspective of someone who attempts to treat people like Jesus would treat people and walk in love, joy, peace, patience, kindness, goodness, faithfulness and self control.

In these pages, I will not shame you or beat you over the head with the Bible. The main purpose of this book is to use the most amazing science and research to show a pattern in our parenting and in our culture that is destroying our children and our society. I personally believe that the Bible aligns with the things I share here, but I know that for many people that will turn them off or shut them down. Therefore, the basis for most of these things is rooted in research, real experiences, and a 20 year career of clients who have taught me so much. Though I believe in the inherent truth of the Bible, you won't hear me use much of the phrase "the Bible says to do this." The scriptures are sufficient for salvation and Truth and so many things about how to live, but it is not something you can go to for specifics when your toddler is throwing a tantrum, you are learning how to breastfeed, or when the nightmare of sleep training comes into play. It does not have a lot to say about social media or the practical tools to keep our kids safe on devices.

I want to acknowledge that people have been harmed by twisted scriptures and religion. I want to make sure I do not do that with this book and I hope you will give me that chance.

A word to my non-believing friends:

I appreciate you giving this book a shot. I want to deeply apologize to you for any abuse, mistreatment, or shame that you have faced at the hands of those that claim to be Christian. We are all imperfect humans, and you didn't do anything to deserve that mistreatment. I hope that for the sake of your own healing or the protection of your children that you will be able to look past that and hear the research and information I have to offer. Information that I sincerely hope can change lives.

I will in some ways be expressing my personal beliefs in God, Jesus, and the Holy Spirit throughout these pages at times. I fully understand and respect that people will disagree with some of the things in this book, and maybe even some of my Christian readers might raise their eyebrows. If that is the case for you, I ask that you don't throw out the baby with the bathwater. There are amazing pieces of research and experience here that I think are useful for anyone of any faith. The message of Christianity that you will hear echoed in these pages is simply a reflection of my own imperfect understanding of the teachings of Jesus and how I apply those truths to my parenting and live them out in my life.

At the end of the book, there is a more in depth conversation between me and my editor where I lay out my beliefs more explicitly. If after reading this content you decide you want to read more about what I believe and how it impacts my parenting, you can find that discussion in the "Q&A with Clint Davis" section. Thank you for allowing me to share with you in any capacity, and I feel strongly that there are things here that every parent anywhere could use to improve their communication with their children!

I want the information to reach many families and I would hate for it to not get into your hands because you have differing beliefs than I do. I hope that I can remain authentic to my faith in this book without cramming anything down your throat or throwing it in your face.

A note to my fellow believers:

I am so grateful you chose to pick up this book. I hope to call us to revival. Not one of those superficial, over emotionally-based revivals. Not one that is chaotic or unorganized. A revival that is clear and precise that will change our families and help us to change those around us. A revival of our hearts, minds, and bodies that will lead us ahead into the darkness that is ever encroaching with tools and help. There are adversaries seeking our destruction, and the spiritual warfare surrounding us is real. We must remember that our battle is not against flesh and blood, but against the evil forces that war around us and in us at all times.[4] A revival around sexual health is so needed by us and so desired by God! I've heard it said that the devil is a creature, not a creator. All he can do is twist the clay God creates. Well, when it comes to our view on our bodies

---

[4] "For we do not wrestle against flesh and blood, but against the rulers, against the authorities, against the cosmic powers over this present darkness, against the spiritual forces of evil in the heavenly places." Ephesians 6:12 (ESV)

and sexuality he has twisted it up! The great thing is that what Satan and evil forces twist up, Christ redeems and restores!

The unfortunate thing for the American Church is that the stats are the same inside and outside of the walls.[5] We have become so comfortably numb in our congregations that in many ways we look wildly similar to every other person out there. We forget to shine a light on darkness, but instead hide the darkness in the closet and nail it shut.

The things that I will address in this book have been swept under the rug for far too long, and many of them have crept into our homes and organizations under the cover of darkness and manipulation. What we avoid as "awkward" might be hurting our families, churches, and friends more than we ever realized.

The Bible tells us to "Enter through the narrow gate. For wide is the gate and broad is the road that leads to destruction, and many enter through it. But small is the gate and narrow the road that leads to life, and only a few find it."[6]

Right now, I fear many of us are on the broad road. Our lives simply do not look different enough when it comes to how we practice marriage, parenting, social media, finances, sexuality, and a laundry list of other things. If we as adults or parents or leaders are sneaking through the wide gate, how do our children or peers have a chance to enter the narrow way that leads to life?

We are all so traumatized and neglected in our own lives that we just want things to be easy and comfortable. Trust me, I get that, and I take the easy way sometimes too. When we have lived a life full of pain, betrayal, or brokenness seeking a little comfort makes all the sense in the world! But we are looking for comfort in the wrong places and the wrong things.

---

[5] Stanton, Glenn. "Divorce Rate In The Church – As High As The World?," *Focus on the Family, 2011.*
[6] Matthew 7:13

So let's get back to the basics and find our way back to the narrow road. Let's get back to being considered weird and strange. Because I will tell you now: normal does not equal healthy.

People often come up to me at conferences or come to my office and say, "I just want a normal life" or "a normal marriage." I will tell you what I tell them. "No, you really do not want that." Normal is unhealthy. Normal is toxic. The "normal person's" mental, physical, and spiritual state is on the edge of a breakdown.

The only thing holding most people together is their ability to continue to put on a mask, to delay the inevitable through wealth, personal comfort, and empty entertainment. At some point, those things will not sustain us, any of us, and we'll crash. I believe we have arrived at this breaking point or will be there very soon.

Normal is not healthy, so let's be different. Let's be okay with being weird! Minority status in the areas this book covers should be a coveted position. It will tell us we are on the right road.

That being said, I have *incredible* hope for the future of the church. We have always rallied in times of suffering or persecution. We have always been the light of the world. We are called to be a city on a hill. We are to be the salt of the earth. We have been given the ministry of reconciliation. I hope that this book will show you in practical ways how to get back to those things again and redeem what has been taken from you and from all of us.

Thank you for giving me your time, your energy, and your hard work on these tough things. I do not think you will be disappointed.

Clint Davis

Part I:
How We
Got Here

29

1. The Roots of *Parenting*

Parenthood is about guiding the next generation,
and forgiving the last.
-Peter Krause

I didn't know this until recently, but parenting is a relatively new concept. Well, at least the *word* parenting. Merriam-Webster cites the word's first use occurred in 1918, in its simplest form meaning, "the raising of a child by its parents."[7] A graph of the *usage* of the word parenting, however, reveals that it didn't gain much ground until the late 1960s, as we can see in this graph showing the use of "parent" vs. "parenting" in America's body of literature from 1600 to 2019, with parent on top and parenting on the bottom.[8]

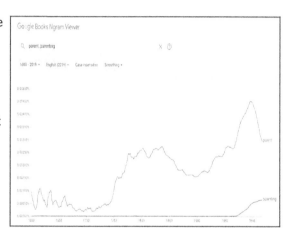

Other than providing cool knowledge for *Jeopardy!*, this signifies a couple of things. It reveals that parent as a noun is a word we obviously used for centuries, but parenting, in a psychological sense, has only become a priority in recent decades. In the past, what was high on the priority list was survival. For centuries, children were a utility. In poorer or rural families, they had to work the land, contribute to the household, and pull their own weight for the sheer survival of the family. Even in richer or royal households,

[7] "Parenting." Merriam-Webster.com Dictionary, Merriam-Webster, https://www.merriam-webster.com/dictionary/parenting.
[8] Google Books Ngram Viewer, "Parent, Parenting," 21 May 2023.

Clint Davis

children were either asset or liability, male children bearing the burden of future kingship. But let's set the royals aside for now. Unless you are in line for a throne, in which case...I hope you can semi-relate to the rest of us.

For hundreds of years, families often had many children. As recently as the 1800s, the average family had 7 children in one household. Compare that to our current average of about 1.5, and we can see things have changed pretty dramatically over the last 220 years.[9]

There are lots of reasons for this change, but the effects are still very consequential. Families needed multiple children to work their land, and due to disease and a lack of medicine, children were lost on a painfully regular basis. How mom and dad talked to them, nurtured them, or emotionally supported them was secondary to what mom and dad had to do just to keep them alive. There was also a decline in children being birthed as our culture industrialized and birth control became available, along with women's rights and the rise in divorce. The last two major factors are the breakdown of the nuclear family and the rise of infertility in both men and women. This is not a judgment of any of those things, just to help us think about how and why the numbers have changed. With death not knocking on everyone's door and access to healthcare for the average family, we had the capacity to begin to study how adult lives affect their children for the first time.

For most of history, the study of psychology in children was non-existent. Our ancestors weren't studying how children were affected by the world, their environment, or their biology. Child psychology and the study of child development first began in the mid-1800s with Charles Darwin, and by 1891, an American psychologist G. Stanley Hall established the first Pedagogical Seminary devoted to child psychology. Then in the 20th century, there was an uptick in Child Psychology scholars: we know names like Freud, Klein, and Jean Piaget. I won't bore with you pages of clinical scholarship from those guys. The point I am making here is that

---

[9]https://populationeducation.org/resource/historic-average-number-of-children-per-u-s-family-infographic

31

the understanding, study, and support of children's psychological well-being is truly in its infant stages (Ha…dad joke intended).

Only in recent years have we been able to study the brain, body, and mind in a way to better understand childhood development, discipline, and how to best meet a child's emotional needs. Many early psychological and developmental studies were based on an A+B=C model. We learned that A) what we do as parents affects our children and B) the experiences they go through impacts their brains and their resiliency to hardship. *In this equation, though, we focused on rudimentary behavior modification instead of looking at root causes.* At this stage on our psychological journey, the connection between trauma and the brain wasn't even a thought yet. We didn't know that babies can have trauma in the womb or that we pass down epigenetic changes through generations. Scripture actually speaks to this, but that is for another conversation.

It wasn't until 1984, that the word PTSD got recognition in the DSM (*Diagnostic and Statistical Manual of Mental Disorders*). So ideas like how trauma happens, how to define it, and the effects it has on children and the systems they live in all the way into adulthood, are essentially brand new concepts to us.

We are still trying to figure out how to be good parents and keep our children safe, all while building resilient adults who can handle the conflict, difficulty, and suffering that life will bring them. The questions this brings up for me are things like: Have we become less resilient? Was there always trauma? Why are kids and families so fragile today? What can we do to build more resilient children who live in a world that has increasingly more difficult and toxic things to combat? I feel I could write a dozen books on parenting and its history, but let's tackle one at a time. Let me mention three crucial things for today's parents that are foundational.

I. Behavior Modification is Causing Problems

Due to a lack of education on the science of how humans work, how family systems work, and how children develop and are wired, a focus on behavior change has been in the driver seat of almost every part of western society. The court system, the educational system, the prison and judiciary systems all focus on behavior change without taking a hard look at the causes of those behaviors. These systems have often valued behavior change over heart change. Let's face it. If we cannot measure it, we cannot get funding. How are we going to create systems that deal with humans and have long term positive outcomes for humans, when we do not even know how these humans develop and what is the ideal state in which they thrive? Reformation, restoration, reconciliation, and rehabilitation should all be a part of these systems, and I hope we are moving in this direction. The truth is that the science and research was not available when we were creating these systems. Heck, even religions often focus on performing the right behaviors to please God, be enlightened, get to heaven, or be a good person. Christianity, at its core, is not works based. The Bible teaches that people cannot *earn* God's love, nor can we lose it. God's love is a free gift of grace. God *is* love. We are worthy of love because God loves us. For example: Imagine your child ran up to you and said "Look, mom/dad, I built this lego! Don't you love me??" We would hopefully laugh and say, "No silly, I love you because you are my child, not because you performed or earned it." I hope that no matter what background you have, we can all agree that children should not have to earn the love or security of their caregivers.

Unfortunately, without realizing it, many of us did not grow up this way, and even worse, lots of people are still parenting within a primarily behavioral framework. We should not live our lives trying to please God so He loves us or blesses us, but we should recognize that God loves us and because of that unconditional love, we will go and do good things in His name. Good behaviors will flow out of the love in our hearts. Our behavior or performance should not be an indicator of our worth and value as human beings. We are human beings, after all, not human doings.

I am not saying that our behavior and the behavior of our children does not matter. It does. We have to teach them how to function in society, in relationships, and in a classroom or work environment. This is about diving deeper into where our behaviors come from and finding more effective and enduring ways to change them. In Dr. Mona Delahooke's book *Beyond Behaviors,* she puts it this way: "...think of behaviors as the tip of an iceberg—that part of an individual that we readily see or know. The tip reveals answers to "what" questions about a person. Just as we can see only the tip of an iceberg, while most of it remains hidden underwater, we can observe childhood behaviors with the understanding that the many factors that contribute to them are hidden from view."[10]

Dr. Delahooke and many others have done lots of amazing work trying to help parents understand the science and the biology of children and their behaviors. As parents, one of the most important things we can do is look deeper than our children's performances and behaviors and instead become curious about why these things might be happening and what our children are trying to communicate to us. I have been to many conferences that teach about how to support traumatized children who are in foster care or who have been severely abused. One of the best trainings out there is at Texas Christian University. It is called TBRI or Trust Based Relational Interventions. When I worked doing in-home counseling with youth "at risk for out of home placement," it was an incredible thing to learn and try to bring to our community. In these training sessions it seems like parents and professionals understand why you should look past behavior and towards root causes and the children's deep-seated needs. There are obvious reasons and excuses for the innocent child to behave in an extreme way when they have been abused, but sometimes it seems that "regular" children don't need such special treatment or have any excuse. I always leave these training sessions thinking, "why do we only need to be patient, kind, understanding, or therapeutic with these *unique* kids?" Why do we understand that we should not hit a child who has been hit before, but we think it's okay to hit children who have not? How about we just treat all children this way! Of course children who have trauma have unique circumstances, but in reality, if we start parenting in a way that takes the child's development and emotional needs into account instead of a sole focus on performance or behavior, all children will learn to thrive!

Given our heavy focus on behavior modification and our early understanding of children and family systems, it is no wonder we have focused on behavior more than hearts and minds. This has led to adults

---

[10] Delahooke, Mona. *Beyond Behaviors,* PESI Publishing and Media, 2019.

and society as a whole taking a very shame-based approach to parenting and even the ways we criticize parents daily. This heavy focus on behavior is not good for the kids or the adults. I don't know about you, but I struggle to feel like I'm providing my child with everything that they need and deserve. I feel like I lose my temper too often, I am not patient enough, and that everyone around me is going to judge me if my child is not standing in line, eating all their food, listening, or "respecting all the adults." I often feel the internal weight of not being good enough, that my children do not have enough, and that I am not setting them up for success in the future. Surely I am not the only one, right?

There are infinite blogs, Instagram stories, and posts from social media influencers about the newest psychology, parenting methods, and "the secret to raising a good kid." There is a constant rush of voices telling me how I should improve, things I am missing, and situations where I am totally failing as a father. However well-intended such content might be, it all just leaves me (and us) feeling lacking. I saw a post recently of a mom and dad with 5 kids showing me how they do their "morning routine." This family prepares to go running. They get all 5, yes 5, of their children in roller skates, on skateboards, and in a baby carrier. They load the carrier down with 50 extra pounds to make the run harder, and then they proceed to do a 3 mile run, followed by a work out in the park, while their kids "worked on their own skills" with hockey and basketball. I laughed so hard thinking about how it is tough for me just to get my two boys to go to the library and get a book without touching everything, needing to poop, yelling about something, begging to go back home, or crying because they are starving because they did not eat enough breakfast an hour earlier. Maybe, just maybe, some people actually live a life like the magnificent family of seven running at 7 am. Maybe this encourages you to be better and do more, but for the rest of us, these types of posts or expectations can be so overwhelming and shaming. If we are *really* honest, most of these things are not real. They are for followers and advertisers to market products and content.

The other major problem is that many of us grew up and are raising children in the first generation to have entertainment and comfort as the norm instead of as a luxury. Some of us grew up in a time where our parents could have nurtured us more, but they didn't know how, didn't have the resources we have now, and were never shown why it was important. There has been a huge shift in the past 40 years, and we are all stuck in the in-between. Our parents might not have had the tools and resources, but we do. We just have not learned to use them and don't know where to find them. This lack of tools on our parents' part, as well as their own need for healing, left us with wounds and scars that have never healed. We then went on to have children of our own, also without the proper tools, and we have created this cycle of shame and inadequacy. Because of this we can constantly feel like we are failing at this parenting gig or that we are out of our depth when it comes to having certain emotional or difficult conversations. How are we going to build better bridges made out of steel and iron, when our bridges were made out of straw? How do we make sure our bridges continue to grow more sturdy and durable, instead of burning them down?

Let me give you a couple of examples of how a heavy focus on behavior modification leads us to parent shame:

Have you been here before?
I'm in Target, and my child acts out – my response is based on "everyone is thinking I am a bad parent."
Our family is out to eat, and the kids are throwing a fit for everyone to hear – bad parents.
I am failing as a parent because my son can't sit in class for 8 hours without chewing pencils, talking, causing a disruption or my daughter is playing with her hair and "talking too much." Bad parent.

Or how about here?
My daughter won the game, and my son got the highest grade in the class! I must be doing something right!
I want our kids to be amazing at sports or violin or singing because that makes me and his mom feel like we have done a great job. Between our genetics and our parenting skills those home runs are because of us!!

Although many people don't come out and say these things (I mean some do), you get my point. On and on this cycle goes. Most everything is geared to have some reflection on the parent. Good or bad.

Clint Davis

We have created a cultural and parental nightmare of narcissism. I am not saying that we are all narcissists, but when *everything* our kid does reflects back on us, then that means we base our worth and value on our child's behavior, for better or worse. I am here to tell you now, once and for all that this is simply not true. We need to heal our own wounds so that we do not need our children to serve as our confidence or make us whole.

Our children are living, breathing *others*. God created them separately from us. We are given them for a small time on this earth to figure out who they are and walk alongside them until they can walk or run on their own. Yes, they have a little bit of mom and dad in them, and we love to claim it when they do something awesome. We see it in their behaviors or mannerisms. We claim them when they are talented, kind, or good looking. We deny it when they act like little psychos. You know how it goes - one parent says, "Come get *your* child!" They do something good and they are "just like ole Dad," but they do something stupid and it is "Well he's your son!" Of course they carry some of our traits good and bad, but for the most part, our kids are going to grow up to be different from us, and that is a good thing.

Before I share a personal example that will lead me into important thing number 2, let me say this:

I am not a perfect parent. I am sometimes impatient. I have lost my temper, and I have raised my voice at my children. I will say however, so far in their lives, I have never shamed my kids. I haven't called them names. I haven't put them down emotionally, and I have never harmed them physically. I try to remember that their behavior is not always a reflection of my parenting skills. All in all, they are turning out to be incredible boys, but by no means are they perfect either. When I am focused on convenience or outcome, I tend to question if any of this parenting knowledge and philosophy I'm implementing is wrong. If I have patience, however, and play the long game, things usually work out in the wash and I'm like, "I do know what I'm doing!" Before you roll your eyes and think I'm bragging or that you can't possibly relate to me, let me tell you the story.

37

II. **When Healthy Children Lose Their Minds**

A few weeks ago, my oldest son (8), wanted a snack, some water, and to pee for the 100th time at bedtime...you know the drill. I have calmly and emotionally helped him through this 30 minute episode, and he's still hungry. We have deep breathed, counted sheep, and gotten all the wiggles and giggles out. Unfortunately, he has been sick, he's tired, and did I mention he's hungry and just wants another snack? What he really needs is to go the F to sleep. (F stands for "frick" in our house haha) Anyway, I tell him to go back to bed, and he ends up yelling and screaming at me, threatening to hit me, trying to hit me, and finally devolving into a full meltdown outside in our backyard.

I am standing there frustrated, with my hands on my hips, and through tears, my baby boy is saying, "I hate myself, I am an awful kid, I deserve to go to hell, I want to kill myself." Can you imagine the gut wrenching blow to my stomach hearing those things? These words are some of the most painful a parent can ever hear their child say.

Now remember, I truly have *never* said anything like this to him. I haven't been perfect, but for the large majority of the time I have showered him with therapeutic positive regard. I have helped him breathe, given words of affirmation. Heck, we even have a calming corner in our home. I have taught him about the grace of God since day 1, and in my opinion, I have knocked this gentle-ish parenting thing out of the park. Yet here he stands, hot tears running down his precious face, saying horrible things about himself. What happened? Where does this come from?

It was at this exact moment that I realized that no matter what I do, no matter how much effort I put in, even if I could be the *perfect* parent, I can't do it all. To some degree, my boys will have to work out their identity, their emotions, their salvation, and their faith on their own. They will get attacked by the voices of the world and the voices in their heads. Sometimes they will choose to believe the lies of a broken world over the love of their imperfect earthly Dad.

So I want to tell you that A+B does not equal C. Not everything our children do is a reflection or a response to my parenting or yours. This revelation can be overwhelming, but also massively relieving. Now, this doesn't mean, of course, that we should just phone in our parenting and take a totally hands-off approach. We ought to be active participants in our children's lives, modeling and shaping them into their best selves, but when they fail or succeed, it is mainly about them and who they are becoming. It is not about us. The better we understand our unique child and what they need the more their behavior and outcomes won't seem so important or critical. I hope this helps explain some of the huge swings we see in culture when it comes to "creating good kids." There are many different philosophies of parenting, so try to relax and enjoy the ride. Author Stephen James has a quote about this that I love. "So the question we need to be asking as a parent is not 'How am I doing?' as in looking for a grade, but 'What am I doing?'"[11] In the book *Parenting with Heart* by Chip Dodd and Stephen James, parenting is described as "a giraffe ice skating." It is awkward and difficult at times.

III.   Shame is Not the Solution

This might be one of the most important conversations we have, and I wanted to have it before we dive into the heavy content, because the goal and purpose of this book is to inform, *not shame*. To challenge all of us, but not to condemn.

As you read, you may realize you have missed a lot as a parent in some of the areas we are discussing. You might even have royally messed up, and you know your child suffered because of it. I want you to know **it is ok**. You can start fresh today. It is not too late. This applies to all parents no matter the age of your child! Every rupture has the chance for repair, but only if we take that opportunity. The amazing news is that repairing relationships often makes them stronger than ever. Whatever has happened with you or your child is not always your fault. In fact, finding fault might not always be the right answer. Sometimes the only way forward is to *know* better so you can *do* better, but dwelling on past mistakes likely won't help anyone. This is even for parents of adult

---

[11] This quote comes from James' book co-written with Chip Dodd, *Parenting with Heart: How Imperfect Parents Can Raise Resilient, Loving and Wise Hearted Kids.* I highly recommend this book if you want a deeper dive about parenting overall.

children. Our kids, no matter what age, are longing for reconciliation, healing, and connection. They have been desiring it their entire lives.

If fault is found, the proper response is to take ownership, apologize, and make efforts to show you will not make the same mistakes again. If you are a grandparent reading this book or a parent who missed out on many of these tools, take some time to realize you probably suffered as well. Take some time and heal. Then go and apologize, and try making a new start. Ask for forgiveness and just be patient. If you need to seek support or validation for your own hardships, do that with your pastor, friend, or therapist. We must not expect a hurting child to carry our burdens, even if they are legitimate. Supporting us emotionally is the job of our peers, friends, and mentors, not our kids. Reconciliation cannot happen if our behavior does not change. Remember your behavior is a reflection of the heart first and foremost, and the heart is the thing that needs to change to rebuild trust in adult relationships.

I will admit facing these big feelings and hurdles can be daunting, especially if it seems like too much time has passed. I will tell you, though, I have never met a client that said it was "too late" for an apology or healing. If we can be willing to make a difficult first step, I can only imagine the ripples of positive change that can impact generations down the line. I challenge you to push past your own fears, inadequacies, and shame. Stop making excuses and putting up barriers. Humble yourself and healing can and will come, one way or another!

If, while reading this book you realize that you did not get a lot of the things you needed growing up and that your entire existence is based on performing to receive or earn love, I want to tell you that this can change as well. You can change those habits and beliefs. You can heal and restore a relationship with your inner child that is vibrant, full of confidence, and joy. Now is as good a time as any to start this beautiful, messy journey of heart change!

That addresses a few things regarding parents. I say all these things now, because as we go, we will get into difficult topics where it can feel like we have failed as parents. Maybe we have made mistakes and need to make changes, but I plead with you not to be too hard on yourself because there are many variables going on here. Up next, let's dive into some of the biological factors affecting our children.

Reflection & Discussion

1. How would you define parenting? What does raising a child well mean to you?

2. If you are a parent, do you find yourself focusing more on what you say to your kids or *how* you say it? Why?

3. If your focus has been on changing behaviors, how do you think you might expand that mindset?

4. What values are the most important to you - moral, spiritual, or otherwise?

5. Think back to moments you have felt ashamed. Was that a helpful experience, a hurtful one, or both? Talk it through.

Clint Davis

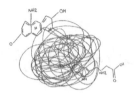

2. Hormones and Chaos

Children are human beings to whom respect is due, superior to us by reason of their innocence and of the greater possibilities of their future.
-Dr. Maria Montessori

So far, we have talked about me, you, and our parents. We have broken down the origins of parenting as a concept, and we have set up some of what we will face in the pages to come. Time to delve into the children's side of things.

Because we don't often research all this ourselves and because it is massively helpful, I want to very briefly cover some things about our children at different ages. Who are they from a biological, sociological, and psychological perspective? I am sure some of you picked up this book to get practical tips, but this part - the part about science and the roots of parenting and trauma - is crucial for everything that is to come. Otherwise, telling you what to do won't help in the slightest and I want you to have the highest possible chance at success and confidence.

Once again, these stages are just brief summaries with very simplified information. Discuss more with your therapist or pediatrician, especially since many children are different, possibly neurodivergent or fall somewhere on the spectrum. These attributes are what *most* likely happens at particular ages, not what happens all the time. There are many pieces of literature that dive deeper into this topic that I highly recommend.[12]

---

[12] Anything by Drs. Dan Siegel and Tina Bryson are my *absolute favorites*. I also suggest *Habits of the Household* by Justin Whitmel Earley and *Beyond Behaviors* by Mona Delahooke. All these are great if you want to read more on how to navigate the chaos of children in your home.

Building Better Bridges

Years 0-5

Intense and rapid right brain growth is the hallmark of these early years. This means that children are emotional and artsy. They focus on fantasy and games. They are adventurous, impulsive, and they cannot regulate their emotions. They have very little growth of their prefrontal cortex (executive functioning), as well as very little left-brain growth. Which means they are not very logical. They don't understand morality or right from wrong, and they have no idea what erotic sexuality means. They throw fits, tantrums, and usually don't sleep very well.

One of the major errors I see people make in this stage is to have unreasonably high expectations and to parent from a place of exhaustion and fear. Dr. Daniel Siegel and Tina Bryson explain in *No Drama Discipline,* that this stage is about connection and coregulation.[13] I'd highly recommend reading Siegel and Bryson's other works as well: *The Whole-Brain Child* and *The Yes Brain*. All three of these works are incredible resources on this same topic.

Years 5-12

These are the years leading up to puberty and high school. This is when the left brain and more of the prefrontal cortex starts to form. Children begin to learn and understand logic and morality. They realize they shouldn't hit their sibling, and over the next few years, they learn why not. Ideally that learning does not come from someone hitting them and then saying, "Now, don't hit." This always makes me cringe as a clinician. Please try not to do this. These little ones are starting to put things together and can start to have logical conversations, but that does not mean they are logical. They will make many errors, and it is our job to teach them how to start forming an identity. This is the first time they have ever been the age they are. Let us give them grace and guidance, not shame and disappointment.

Autonomy and self-regulation are a priority in this period. Children will want to do things for themselves, even if it takes time and is messy, and

---

[13] As defined in their book, Siegel and Bryson define coregulation as "The process through which children develop the ability to soothe and manage distressing emotions...through connection with nurturing and reliable primary caregivers" (*The Whole-Brain Child*)

we ought to let them learn and make mistakes. They need healthy boundaries, but they also need room to grow and express their highly erratic feelings and emotions. Healthy risk taking is also an important part of life. Piece of cake, right?

This is when discipline starts to come into play instead of just redirection. Discipline means "to teach." When we understand what our children are capable of learning and what lessons they are able to grasp, it will save us much frustration and heartache. They still need connection, attunement, and help regulating, but they also need to learn how to self-regulate at times and as they get closer to puberty, how to govern themselves a bit more. It is all about balance and modeling at this stage.

The common mistake I see here is forgetting they are still technically babies. They are tiny humans who still need help navigating their big world and especially the areas of development and puberty. I suggest reading other books or listening to podcasts to learn more helpful tips and advice on parenting these growing kiddos. If you are a church goer, it is important to meet with your community and find helpful parenting resources that take into consideration the science behind child development. After all, science can point us to how God has wired us and created us. Why would we miss out on this important bit of knowledge? This does not contradict the scripture. It simply helps us to apply it.

Stages of Childhood Development:
the breakdown

0 - 5 years

Rapid right brain growth that leads to high emotion, creativity, love of fantasy and games

Very little logic use or understanding of morality, right vs. wrong, or erotic sexuality

Will exhibit fits or tantrums and have trouble sleeping

Begin to learn logic and morality

Prioritize self-regulation and autonomy ("I want to do it myself"

Parents should focus on balance and modeling behaviors

5 - 12 years

Hormones kicking into gear and amygdala growing - leads to mood swings and lots of fear/anger responses

Many synapses firing and new connections forming

12 - 18 years Imaginary Audience or Personal Fable

Years 12-18
To answer your question, no, this age range still won't have a fully formed prefrontal cortex, and on top of that, their hormones are on hyperdrive. One minute, their boyfriend is

45

the best thing in the world, and the next he is the worst human on the planet, and it's tears falling and all hands on deck. They walk into the bathroom confident and walk out of the bathroom with a panic attack about their grades, friends, their future spouse, or about the tiny rip they got in that brand new shirt that no one can even see. They have pimples, braces, and their limbs and torsos haven't caught up with each other. It is also in this wonderful time that their amygdala is growing more than any other time in their life. The amygdala is responsible for our fear and anger. That answers some questions, eh?

Children's brains at this age are firing and connecting more synapses together than any other time, all while their bodies are changing and shifting, and their hormones are raging and changing. Sounds like a good time to me. Not confusing or stressful at *all*. We all think the baby and toddler years are hard, but the hard just shifts over time.

Lastly, the thing about this age is that kids have two possible narratives playing in their heads. 1) The Imaginary Audience: everyone is always looking at them and making a judgment of some kind, or 2) The Personal Fable: they are the center of the story, everything revolves around their decisions, and those decisions will haunt them for the rest of their life. Doesn't all this sound like a truly fun time? And now with the digital age, some of that is actually true for the first time in history. Children really do have an audience out there. But, we will get to that later.

If just reading those summaries makes you stressed, I included a simplified chart to make it as simple as possible. Also check out *Brainstorm* by Dr. Dan Sieigel. It can really help you to understand what is going on in relationships with teens and their developing brains.

None of these little humans understand from day one how to manage their emotions or how to regulate their bodies in times of stress or crisis. Yes, even the teenagers. That regulation is our job and privilege. Our job is to have recovered from our own childhood wounds so that we can be a stable, reasonable, and mature shoulder for our kids to cry on. It is up to us to create a model that they can look up to for the good and bad parts of life. We have (for the most part) fully functioning brains, and children have under-formed, baby brains.

Clint Davis

As adults, we allow ourselves to have long days, stressful events, and bad moods. Are we giving our kids space for the same? Are we teaching them how to respond with kindness and grace even when their emotions are on fire? I know in my practice I have seen many parents who yell, scream, argue, and fight, but they won't allow their children to be children nor are they modeling how to *respond* instead of react. Their expectation is for their child to act like a fully functioning adult, while the adult, at times, acts like an angry toddler. If you tell me you haven't seen one of these lovely "adult toddlers" in the wild, I will know you don't do the grocery shopping in your house.

This applies to our teens, as well. We are legitimately asking 18-year-old *kids* to make decisions about the rest of their lives when just last week they had to ask permission to go to the bathroom! Frankly, our expectations are sometimes unreasonable, and our current system is setting many of our kiddos up for failure. This doesn't mean we lower our standards, but it does mean that understanding their mental and emotional capabilities at various stages is vital. I hope that this quick section is a jumping off point for you to understand what is really going on inside your child. If we spent half as much time researching the workings of our children like we do a new iPhone or vehicle, we would be way ahead of the game and not so frustrated or discouraged.

A quick reminder on discipline that can apply to all these stages: the root word here is *disciple*, which means "to teach or instruct." It is invaluable to remember to have in mind a specific lesson you are trying to teach and to make sure that the child is learning that particular lesson. If they cannot learn the lesson you are trying to teach them, we must adjust expectations and standards for the child. For instance, if you are trying to teach a 3-year-old *why* they should obey, they likely won't be able to learn that lesson yet. You are wasting time, energy, and probably losing your mind.[14]

If we are asking so much of our children and likely not using all the tools in our arsenal, what do we do? **What do our children really need?**

---

[14] For more help and specifics on disciplining ideas, check out *No-Drama Discipline* by Daniel J. Siegel and Tina Payne Bryson or *Beyond Time-Out* by Beth A. Grosshans and Janet H. Burton!

What are some tools and resources to change the paradigm? There are a couple of modalities that I find extremely helpful! When it comes to treating root causes in marriage, parenting, and in life, I love to use Terry and Sharon Hargrave's "Restoration Therapy"[15] model for many of my sessions and in my own life. Their model shows how violations of love and trust construct a cycle of pain that bleeds into every part of your life. The goal is to teach you how to replace pain with peace and engage in healthy behaviors that come from healthy belief systems.

I have used Restoration Therapy and would encourage you to find a therapist trained in something similar. I know as a parent that providing "love and trust" might seem obvious, but let's get a clear picture of what that looks like practically. I call them the 4 A's. Some of this I got from a friend of mine and just added my own spin! Thanks, Rickey![16]

The 4 A's

Affirmation: Our kids need us to tell them the truth about their identity, worth, value, and security. Affirm who they are and that they are safe. Let them know they are special, unique, worthy, beautiful, and amazing. How we define that will be different depending on background and religious beliefs. I believe children are made in the image of God and that their worth and value is internally based on God's love for them. It does not matter their external, biological, or social features. They are all beautifully and wonderfully made.[17] They need to hear that from an early age and throughout their childhoods. Their security cannot be based on performance, pleasing others, or taking care of the emotions of the adults in their lives.

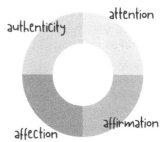

Affection: They need hugs and kisses from both parents. Shower them with kindness and play. Snuggle up and enjoy

[15] You can find more training and information on this incredible therapeutic technique at restorationtherapytraining.com!
[16] Rickey, you are awesome, and I appreciate your mind, brother.
[17] "I praise you, for I am fearfully and wonderfully made." Psalm 139:14

those young and innocent years. Show them what safe and secure touch means. Enjoy it! It goes in a blink. This is an area that I believe many of us missed out on and need to relearn what healthy and safe touch even looks like. Not all children love physical affection, but there are ways to connect and show affection without touch. Connection doesn't always have to be physical, especially if a child has had trauma or neglect.

Attention: They need quality time. They need real, phone down, eye-to-eye quality time. Playing or doing something that they enjoy while you learn why and how they do it, brings them so much joy. And what is so cool is that you can bring them into the things that you like, to give them a glimpse into your soul as well. Find balance in learning to know each other as you both grow together! You must also spend time doing things that they enjoy. If they like hockey, play hockey. If they like to play with dolls, play with dolls. If they like nerdy books, read those books with them. Not all quality time has to be spent talking or having deep conversations. Sometimes just taking an afternoon drive or sitting next to each other while you play is enough.

Authenticity: Children don't need a perfect parent, nor are they expecting you to be one. Please remember this throughout this book. Not a single one of us is perfect. Your kids simply need you to be a safe place. Not manipulative, passively or outright aggressive, or erratic. They need to know they can trust you and know what they are going to get from you 8 out of 10 times. Consistency over perfection, every time.

In fact, they need to know that you mess up too, and you can share your mistakes and flaws in an age-appropriate way as they grow.

Authenticity means modeling how to make mistakes, apologize, and how to fail in a healthy way. I'll give you an example for this one: when my son is disobedient, we sit down and talk. I have him explain to me what he thinks happened and what went wrong. I ask him if he was disobedient, and he agrees that he was (sometimes) and that he knew better. At 8 years old, he is just starting to understand morals and how his actions impact others. I usually tell him that being disobedient or defiant affects our relationship by damaging trust. I then say something like, "That's okay, buddy. Daddy was disobedient today too, and we all make mistakes." There may or may not be consequences, but the message I want him to hear is that **unhealthy behaviors are not okay, but he is not unique in making mistakes.** He is not bad in my eyes or God's. His behaviors are a symptom of a heart problem, and I care more about his heart than anything! He is certainly not alone in his inability to behave perfectly. So, I show him love, and I point him to Jesus. You might point your children to something else, but the principle is the same. We can teach our children the proper expectations without shaming them or isolating them in their mistakes. Healthy psychology would tell us that basing our children's worth and security on their ability to earn love or "salvation" is going to end badly. This is why understanding their development and what they need is a combination for success. As a reminder, I don't always do this right. When I yell or show frustration I have to use that rupture as an opportunity for repair! This builds trust and a sense that we are all growing together. No one is above making mistakes in our house.

There they are: the 4 A's. Simple enough, right? Or maybe it's stressful for you. Despite how simple or overwhelming this information may feel, I hope that discussing childhood brain function and the various stages of emotional development can help ground us and emphasize the importance of our role as parents. The importance of being their safe and loving guide in a world that is often neither safe nor loving is huge. We can do it imperfectly and as awkwardly as we need to, but we have to do it! You can do this. Parents are some of the bravest humans out there, and we are all facing some brand new obstacles and challenges in our 21st-century families. Lastly, I hope this chapter helps you set appropriate expectations for yourself and your children that are achievable and understandable so that you don't lose your mind or give up! We all need grace and so do our kids!

Reflection & Discussion

1. Regarding the 4 A's, what was your experience in childhood? Did you get affirmed, receive affection and attention, and did you experience authenticity? Whether yes or no, how did that impact you?

2. If you are a parent, are you employing the 4 A's in raising your kids? How so?

3. Have you faced any parenting frustrations that might be explained by the various developmental or neurological stages?

3. The (Real) Modern Family

The family is the seedbed of all problems,
and the seedbed of all solutions.
-G. K. Chesterton

"Clint," I hear you thinking, "If parenting from a developmental and emotional lens is the answer, and behavior modification is not the best way to make my kid a decent human, then what do I focus on?" To that thought, I would respond, "The heart." Focus on their feelings, emotions, and the deep beliefs we instill in their hearts and minds.

As I said before, scripture shows us that God is in pursuit of our hearts, not our behaviors and actions. The state of our hearts will often determine how we act in the world. Don't hear me say that our behaviors don't matter. They definitely do. Especially if those behaviors are harmful to ourselves and others. What I mean, first and foremost, is that a heart which has been nurtured and healed will most likely produce corresponding behaviors.

Our entire society has been built by humans who don't understand this concept. Like I pointed to earlier, almost every system in place focuses on behavior changes over heart changes. Look at our prison system, educational system, court systems, and even most religions. They all tend to focus more on behavior changes than internal growth. We have to dig deeper with our kids and focus on long term effects and root causes, not the quick fixes that produce immediate "results" which will fade shortly after we are no longer there to dominate and control the situation. Even our healthcare system, at times, is more concerned with symptom treatment than finding out what is causing our problems. What we focus on in our own homes and families will shape what flows out and what our society values.

Clint Davis

There is an old Cherokee proverb about two wolves that I love, and maybe you have heard it before:

A young boy came to his Grandfather filled with anger at another boy who had done him an injustice. The old Grandfather said to his grandson, "Let me tell you a story. I too, at times, have felt a great hate for those that have taken so much, with no sorrow for what they do. But hate wears you down, and hate does not hurt your enemy. Hate is like taking poison and wishing your enemy would die. I have struggled with these feelings many times."

"It is as if there are two wolves inside me; one wolf is good and does no harm. He lives in harmony with all around him and does not take offense when no offense was intended. He will only fight when it is right to do so, and in the right way. But the other wolf is full of anger. The littlest thing will set him into a fit of temper. He fights everyone, all the time, for no reason. He cannot think because his anger and hate are so great. It is helpless anger, because his anger will change nothing. Sometimes it is hard to live with these two wolves inside me, because both of the wolves try to dominate my spirit."

The boy looked intently into his Grandfather's eyes and asked, "Which wolf will win, Grandfather?" The Grandfather smiled and said, "The one I feed."[18]

Which Wolf Are We Feeding?

Research shows some bleak data about the average American family. Let's call them "The Smiths."

The Smiths are failing at cultivating the hearts and minds of their children. They spend less than 5 hours *a week* face to face with their children. The research also reveals "The Smiths" are spending around 16.2 hours a day looking at a device or screen instead of the eyes of a friend, child, or loved one. In the next 60 years, that daily 16 hours will add up to more than 40 years of looking at a screen.[19] If all the research

---

[18] This version of the parable comes from San Diego State University School of Social Work

[19] Lee, Craig. "Screen zombies: Average person will spend 44 YEARS looking at digital devices — and that's before COVID!," *Study Finds, 2020.*

about trauma is true, it is no wonder an entire generation or more is looking to escape their pain and problems into a screen full of dopamine and entertainment. Are you satisfied with this? How will this shape our future?

Pastor John Mark Comer, in his book *The Ruthless Elimination of Hurry*[20], paints a bleak picture of how much time our society wastes on binging a series, flipping through TikTok videos, and mindless scrolling on social media.

Let's all admit. 16.2 hours a day of this nonsense is a lot. A recent study found that the average iPhone user touches his or her phone 2,617 times a day. Millennials put the number at twice this.

That statistic might be hard to believe, but think about it. What is the first thing you do when you wake up? Grab your smartphone. I'd like to believe we are opening the Bible app, listening to something uplifting, or consuming something educational in those first precious minutes of our day, but likely we are not. We are checking in on social media, looking at work emails, or absentmindedly reading daily news updates. News updates that increase our stress hormones and throw us into fight, flight, or freeze mode. Not a great start to our day. We used to read shampoo bottles and magazines while we were on the toilet, but now we spend countless minutes on our devices. How many reels and memes are there about husbands getting lost escaping to "use the bathroom." This didn't happen before phones.

What floors me about our phone addiction is that it actively hurts us, and yet we can't seem to break away. Social media tells us we aren't cool or pretty enough; work sucks our energy and often still leaves us feeling empty; and the news seeks only to remind us of the bleakness that we can't overcome. ***The overload of content we are consuming seems to burden our hearts and minds, rather than uplift and inform us.***

Sadly, for most of us, I am sure very little information that we ingest on a daily basis is uplifting, helpful, or even truthful. Think about all the movies, podcasts, books, or music you listen to. What are the main

---

[20] Comer definitely provides a wake-up call, but I highly recommend this read to anyone willing to take a closer look at their wasted time.

messages that these things are teaching you or your children? Christian or not, we all face massive damage from our online habits. Garbage comes in, and garbage goes out. Ask yourself these questions. What are these messages telling me about my identity? Does what I am ingesting match my ethics? Does it match my religious beliefs? What am I feeding my heart, mind, and body? The truth is that many of us are feeding the wrong wolf. We have what feels like infinite knowledge at our fingertips, *and yet we watch senseless videos that drain our confidence, energy, and joy. We spend more time with strangers than we do with the living, breathing humans in the same house with us.* Our pal Mr. Comer also mentions some pretty sobering statistics regarding how we use our phones. Here is a summary of what he writes. "The average American spends 705 hours a year on social media. He remarks that if we would set down our phones and dispense with so much useless scrolling, we could read 200 books a year with all the time we gain back. We all complain about being too busy or never having time for things, but think about it. If we could learn to put our phones down, we could replace the 20 minutes of candy crush with praying for everyone in our family. If we replaced one hour of Netflix with reading, we could get through the entire Bible in just six months.[21]

Our society is changing faster than ever before. Church attendance is plummeting. We are having fewer children, and we are having them much later in life. We have fewer close friends than ever before, and we often live far from our biological family. Obviously, Covid played a part in all of this and has changed us in profound ways, but that would be a book all on its own. The one thing I will say is that the pandemic threw a lit match on the bonfire of anxiety and isolation in our children (even in many adults) that was already burning and sent them running deeper into TikTok, Snapchat, online gaming, and even pornography, like no time ever before. Pornhub alone had an 18% *increase* in viewers during the pandemic. They post all their statistics for the public. Just be careful when Googling.[22]

---

[21] Comer, John Mark. *The Ruthless Elimination of Hurry,* Waterbrook, 2020.
[22] Silver, Curtis. "Coronavirus Searches Spike On Pornhub As We Self-Isolate With Porn And Toilet Paper," *Forbes*, 2020.

Building Better Bridges

In addition to consuming so much toxic sludge, our kids have learned that this junk sells. Division, conflict, and sex is what goes viral. I hope everyone shares this book and these resources, but the reality is good and complex things get less attention.

I get asked at conferences, churches, and events to explain to teens why they won't all be famous by going viral. They expect to be able to go out and get a job making six figures all while becoming influencers, traveling, and accruing millions of followers. Somehow, they expect to achieve these things while handling staggering social anxiety and undergoing an identity crisis with every new day. This is not all their fault, but it is their current reality. I pray these teens and young adults rise up and find ways to make these advances in technology work for them. I have hope that they can use their tools for good and that they will blaze that path. This will only come with learning to have boundaries and control their screen time usage instead of it controlling them. They are an amazing group of young people so I have hope they can do it!

Unfortunately, we also have a generation on our hands who believes that everyone is out to get them. No one is on their side, and if anyone disagrees with them, they feel hated and have to worry about "cancel culture" or "doxing." If you are like me, you might take a pause here to look up those terms.

I hate to say it, but a lot of this is due to unintentional neglect on the part of unrecovered, unhealed, traumatized adults who didn't get the "4 A's" in their own childhoods. We must face this truth without letting our pride get in the way or flaring up in anger. It is not an indictment on our parents or on us but an opportunity to change our mindset and improve our strategies. It is not this generation's fault that they have been set up the way they have. They are raised by people who were not raised, and those people were raised by people who were not raised, and the cycle goes on backwards to many generations. Except now there is something new at play: we all have smart devices and the internet, and our children are running to these unstable sources for guidance through this unsteady life.

If you are anything like me, those truths are hard to swallow, and they are big and nebulous. How can I – just one parent – stand against giants like social media toxicity, dangerous internet exposure, and my child's constant search for identity?

First of all, I promise to try and give as many helpful answers as I can. Getting to those answers, though, requires knowing the right questions and background information. So, I hope you will stick with me while we trek our way through these things. Second of all, the many giants your kids will face have a source. We have information and science out there that can really clue us in to where these big feelings and fears are originating. We can also find the tiny stones of solution to knock those giants on their face and cut their loud, abusive heads off. So, let's freaking do it.

Dopamine vs. Serotonin

The silent war being waged both against and within our kids is a spiritual one, but there is another war raging over their brain chemistry. There are many great books that more deeply cover brain chemistry in all its facets – *The Coddling of the American Mind*, *Dopamine Nation*, and others – but for our purposes here, let's keep it simple.

Dopamine is a chemical that is highly addictive, touching just 5 receptors in the brain, and triggers pleasure in the brain.[23] It is responsible for our incessant desire for more of what makes us feel good. Sound familiar? Dopamine isn't all bad, but in high doses it is a major problem for today's humans, especially our kids.

Dopamine is a part of the reward system of your brain, and it is responsible for the feeling you get when you eat ice cream, watch porn, do drugs, sky dive, play video games, or push an app on your phone.[24] You get dopamine from positive and healthy things as well, but not at the same levels. Unhealthy and impulsive things tend to dump too much dopamine in the brain giving us a "dopamine high." For example: Every

---

[23] Bhatia A, Lenchner JR, Saadabadi A. Biochemistry, Dopamine Receptors. Updated 2022 July 18

[24] Trevor Haynes wrote a great article titled "Dopamine, Smartphones & You: A battle for your time" that expounds more on how dopamine gets triggered by certain social media reactions.

time you get a notification on your phone, a dose of dopamine hits your brain and instantly makes you want that feeling *again*. The problem is, due to our sinful and selfish nature, we have trouble regulating our desire for dopamine. Children especially.

Serotonin, on the other hand, is triggered by acts of long-term satisfaction. This chemical touches 14 receptors in the brain and is not addictive.[25] You release serotonin when you exercise, eat green vegetables, serve someone else, have a conversation over lunch, or participate in yoga, jiu jitsu, or meditation. Serotonin helps heal our brains and brings us good feelings that last a lot longer. It regulates mood, digestion, sleep, wound healing, and much more!

In the past two decades, our children have had more access to those instant dopamine hits than ever before. Due to the changes in culture in the past 50 years and the speed at which we consume entertainment and information, we have lost our ability to delay gratification.

Maybe you have seen it before, but a perfect visual of delayed gratification comes from a 1972 study that came out of Stanford. In the experiment a marshmallow gets placed in front of a child, and each subject is told that if they can wait ten minutes without eating their marshmallow, they will get a second one. You can guess what the majority of children do. This small, but revealing experiment has been conducted countless times with the hilarious results posted online. If you have young children, give it a shot, and see what you learn!

Eat me now!!

Mmm...don't I look yummy?

What it tells us, though, is actually quite serious. ***Our ability to wait, even for just a few minutes, is dwindling fast.*** In follow-up studies, the researchers found that children who were able to wait longer for the reward tended to have better life outcomes as

---

[25] I don't just know infinite brain facts! This info comes from a great paper cited here: Moncrieff, J., Cooper, R.E., Stockmann, T. *et al.* The serotonin theory of depression: a systematic umbrella review of the evidence. *Mol Psychiatry* (2022).

measured by SAT scores, body mass index, what level of education they attained, and several other life measures.[26]

This means that learning to defer our rewards and delay those dopamine hits will lead to a life of success – emotionally, physically, and spiritually. Well, that is if you measure success on things that matter and not material wealth, status, educational achievements, or any other external sources. This doesn't mean those things are not good, just that we need to redefine success for our children in order for them to thrive![27]

For the Christians reading this, the focus on long-term serotonin and the putting off of addictive dopamine is something that we can find throughout scripture. Our belief is in the return of the Messiah, Jesus Christ (arguably the longest serotonin waiting game out there). We await His return to restore a new heaven and a new earth and bring an end to all suffering and pain. As followers of Christ, as we wait, we are called to serve the Lord and sacrifice our pleasures and temptations in the here and now, and our rewards will be great in heaven. We are not to be pleasure seekers, but kingdom seekers. Sure pleasure isn't bad and God wants us to feel it, but when it is the goal trouble happens in our souls and in our bodies. We are to help those in need, give generously, and do our service in secret, without putting on a show. God also tells us to save ourselves for marriage sexually in the knowledge and hope that it will bring glory to Him and safety and security to our marital union. He wants us to delay immediate gratification and stop chasing dopamine highs and instead wants us to trust that His plans will lead to joy and peace that surpass all understanding. So many things in the Bible are related to waiting - waiting on the Lord in faith, waiting for our true joy to be fulfilled, and serving while waiting on the day we reach heaven.[28]

Regardless of your beliefs, the facts are the facts.

---

[26] One such researcher is James Clear, and you can find his wonderful article here: https://jamesclear.com/delayed-gratification
[27] Asking Why podcast episode 62 is on this exact topic titled "Reframing Success" if you want to check that out.
[28] This paragraph references several scriptures. Here is the list of them if you want further reading!
Revelation 21, Galatians 5:13, James 1:27, Matthew 6:3-4, 1 Corinthians 7:2-5.

Building Better Bridges

I don't share this to say that Christians are fabulous and have mastered the skill of delayed gratification. Quite the opposite. I share to say that God is perfect in his knowledge and wisdom, and what we are seeing today shows just how right He was to command these things. Our hearts weren't built for an endless dopamine rush.

What we are seeing is a world of people doing exactly what suits them at each moment. Cultural trends like YOLO, You Do You, Follow Your Heart, Live Your Own Truth, Trust Your Gut – all these narratives tell us to get all our pleasure now while we are here. No thought to the future or the afterlife. Not to mention that this everyday chasing after enjoyment and fame is crushing our mental health and damaging our bodies long term.

The battle we must fight for generations to come is to teach ourselves, and then to teach our children, to defer reward. This means we have to be able to put the phone down and go outside, learn to say no to certain food and drugs, stand up against rampant consumer culture, and guide our children to do the same. They need to develop their own will power, resiliency, and self-dependence in order to be successful in the world, a world that is still changing daily.

The world we live in now is hard enough, and if it continues on the trend we see, the time to take action is now. I have children who I love, and I love to see them happy. I still know it is my duty to limit these dopamine surges and remove the things that cause them. Instant gratification and rewards are easy and meet an immediate need, but they are detrimental to the long-term success and survival of our species. I want the joy of my children to come from within, from the Lord...not from every passing cultural pleasure.

I find it mad that children today are set up for failure and chemical alteration by having everything available at the click of a button or the swipe of a screen in their tiny hands. When I grew up, we had Saturday morning cartoons, named as such because Saturday morning was the only time that cartoons were available. If I missed an episode of *He-Man* or *Ninja Turtles*, I had to wait a week. Today my boys wake up and say, "Dad, I want to watch Paw-Patrol season 4, episode 9." This automatic fulfillment of a desire builds no resiliency, a resiliency typically grown and fostered through waiting and anticipation. There is no difficulty to get through to get a reward. Gaming systems are very similar. It is not the cartoon or gaming that is the problem, it is the mechanisms in which they are being delivered. One day I bought my oldest son a regular, old-school Nintendo. It was 8-bit and had something like 200 games built in. He was so excited. He played the ninja turtles game for about 15 minutes before he threw the controller down and asked to go play outside instead. I was surprised. The thing is, he lost 30 times within that 15 minute window and never made it out of the first level. He was frustrated and wanted to quit because it was taking too long for him to win. In today's video games or shows or social media, there is very little serotonin released, but rather a ton of dopamine being dumped into children's brains. They literally build these games to be as addictive as possible and set them up to be like a video slot machine. It should be no shock why our children are locked into them for hours on end and that when they are asked to shut them down and do something else they have a meltdown. It is called withdrawal.

Over exposure to dopamine is a major issue and can do serious damage to the brain. One of the more recent things psychologists have learned when it comes to brain chemistry is that after a while, our brains stop producing dopamine. This is covered well in the book *Dopamine Nation,* if you are interested in a deeper dive into the scientific side of this topic. <u>Warning - it is a highly explicit read.</u>

So, if we have run out of dopamine, why would we continue to go back to porn, food, and an endless social media feed? What the research shows is that people think they are chasing the dopamine high, but all they are really doing is avoiding withdrawal. This is one of the major issues I have with exposing our children to instant gratification: **they become pleasure seekers and pain avoiders.** This is why every generation seems to be more dependent and less resilient in many areas socially and emotionally. Being a parent is tough, and it is hard work. I understand. We still have to be willing to teach our kids the hard things in order to set them up for emotional wellness and future independence.

Help your children to see that earning the reward over time and making sacrifices will feel much better and last longer than the empty pleasures the world offers every minute of every day. Just think of the internal strength you can build in your child, so that when things don't go their way or trials and setbacks come their way, they will have learned how to endure difficulties without falling apart or giving up entirely.

"How?" you ask. Well, start with simple things like limiting technology and screen time, putting boundaries on gaming and social media use. Make a chore chart and have them earn money to buy extra toys and wants. Earning rewards and working hard for them will build resilience and confidence. Let them fail from time to time, when the consequences are not too high. Lastly, let them take healthy risks like camping, starting a fire, or licking a battery. (No one has died by Duracell, I checked.) Kids will never want to do the things that are difficult, but they will be so proud of

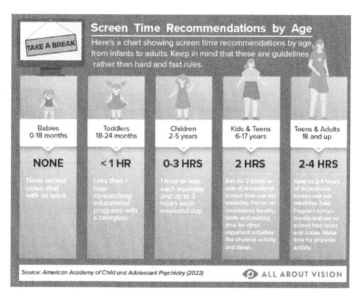

Screen Time Recommendations by Age

Here's a chart showing screen time recommendations by age, from infants to adults. Keep in mind that these are guidelines rather than hard and fast rules.

TAKE A BREAK

Babies 0-18 months	Toddlers 18-24 months	Children 2-5 years	Kids & Teens 6-17 years	Teens & Adults 18 and up
NONE	<1 HR	0-3 HRS	2 HRS	2-4 HRS
None except video chat with an adult.	Less than 1 hour co-watching educational programs with a caregiver.	1 hour or less each weekday and up to 3 hours each weekend day.	Aim for 2 hours or less of recreational screen time use per weekday. Focus on maintaining healthy limits and making time for other important activities like physical activity and sleep.	Keep to 2-4 hours of recreational screen use per weekday. Take frequent screen breaks and set up screen-free times and zones. Make time for physical activity.

Source: American Academy of Child and Adolescent Psychiatry (2022)   ALL ABOUT VISION

themselves when they do! We have to stop being a generation of parents who use screens as babysitters and are terrified for our children to have to push through and persevere through tough things.

Okay, I hope I have set you up to understand the questions we should be asking. Questions like what is parenting, who are my children, and how do I protect them from the world that tries to prey on their hearts and mental health. The chapters that follow will be a mix of research, my clinical training, personal experiences, and action steps that hopefully help you to feel more equipped and less frantic as you face raising a physically and mentally healthy human. The graphic above is the recommended screen time by age, as shown by the AACAP.

This next chart shows the systematic consequences if we allow too much screen time:

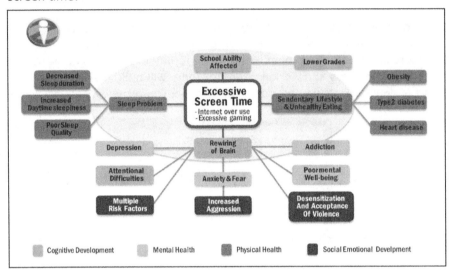

Despite what your own children might sometimes believe, I am certain that we all want our children to enjoy life and get both dopamine and serotonin. Their brains are wired for the joy, happiness, and enjoyment that these chemicals produce in us. We just have to learn to strike a balance between what is enjoyable enough to keep them engaged while also not *so* stimulating so as to grip their brains and imprison them for life. Every kid is different so their balance needs to be assessed. Some call this the Goldilocks test. We want the entertainment to be "not too hot and not too cold." If your child has already been hijacked by the dopamine bug due to a lack of knowledge on your part or due to convenience and circumstances, here are a few tips to help them withdraw:

---

[29] Image comes from a helpful article by Yuhyun Park - cited below:
Park, Yuhyun. "How much screen time should children have?," *The Digital Economy*, World Economic Forum, 2016.

Building Better Bridges

1. Find something that is engaging for your kids that they enjoy, but that they do not obsess about or throw a fit when they have to move on or put it down. For instance, a book can be engaging and sometimes a page turner, but usually kids don't freak out when they have to stop reading. The level of dopamine and pleasure just is not strong enough.
2. Give their brain time to reset. Dopamine triggers pleasure, but the cravings are usually short lived. Take 5-10 mins after taking away the screen or shutting off the game. Engage with them, and be patient. Then make them leave the space where the trigger is or move the trigger from their vision.
3. Create safe spaces where books, board games, colors, blocks, or writing materials are all that are available. Make sure that they cannot see the dopamine fueling monster.
4. Try not to make drastic changes at first. Slowly remove the object of obsession and conflict. If it is a video game, for example, maybe find something that is family friendly and cooperative, educational, and fun. Pick a gaming console like the Wii or Nintendo Switch (without using the handheld monitor) or even the old school Nintendo or Sega Genesis and limit the time to under 30 mins per session. It might not be as "amazing" as Call of Duty or Grand Theft Auto, but children should not be playing those games anyway. (That is another entire book's worth of discussion.)
5. Create opportunities for boredom. Our kids *need* to be bored. If you can push through the 5-15 minutes of whining and complaining, before you know it, they will be outside, building or playing in dirt, talking to a friend on the phone, pretending to be a princess or a dragon, or making up some silly games using potty words and fart noises.

And you know what? Let's face it - we as adults need a plan to detox as well. Will you start today and give your brain a chance to recover?

Reflection & Discussion

1. How much time do you spend on your phone? How do you feel your screen time affects your mood, your heart, or your relationships?

2. Did the pandemic affect your personal screen time and the screen time of your kids? How so?

3. What healthy risks are you letting your children take? Or yourself, for that matter?

4. What new thing have you tried in the last 6 months? What new thing do you want to try?

4. How to Talk to the *Right* Brain

The single biggest problem in communication is the
illusion that it has taken place.
-George Bernard Shaw

Earlier we touched on hormones, development, and what is happening to our children at what age, and maybe that was all the science-y stuff you wanted to read. Well, we are going even more Bill Nye in this chapter, but I think you will resonate with it (with or without a Master's in neuroscience lol).

I felt compelled to add this discussion because this info is so vital for understanding how to effectively communicate with others, especially your children. In reality, this entire book is from this perspective. I am trying to use the knowledge I have about brain science, human development, and trauma to keep you calm enough to retain the information, while emotionally stimulated enough to care. I'm also trying to keep it simple. These should also be our goals when talking about difficult things with others, which we will definitely do as we go through this content.

As we live, work, parent and build relationships with anyone, it is not enough to know what to do, but how to do it and why we must do things certain ways. This section is going to be a very basic overview and very simplified, but hopefully it will give you a good representation and visual of the brain and how it works when it comes to information storage and communication, as well as giving you some steps and examples. The brain is very complex, but for this concept let's imagine that our right brain is inspiration, music, art, feelings, and imagination. Our left brain is logic, math, language, and facts. Don't let your eyes glaze over. Hang with me.

 The prefrontal cortex or the executive functioning part of the brain is the mature adult part. I like to think of it as sophisticated and wearing a little bowtie. The prefrontal cortex is responsible for empathy, morality, intuition, attunement, body regulation, and fear regulation. The right brain first starts growing somewhere from 0-4.5 years old, and then the left brain starts coming online after this. The prefrontal cortex slowly develops over time and rapidly increases during adolescence. It doesn't fully develop until 25 years old and some say as late as 28. This is of course affected by trauma, genetics, and culture. There are many more parts of the brain that are developing and affecting you and your child, but for now just stick with these.

As parents, if we understand that the brain develops in specific ways, then we can know that most children need help doing the work of the prefrontal cortex as they grow. They need adults with fully developed and mature brains to model behaviors and help them emotionally practice what they are not scientifically capable of doing yet. If we want them to actually learn and retain the life lessons we teach, we must be able to teach them in a developmentally appropriate way.

Say you want your 3-year-old to know they should not hit their sibling. Based on their brain development and emotional ability, they cannot learn the moral lesson that hitting is unhealthy at this age. Science tells us that at 3 years, they will most likely hit because they are trying to communicate and have not developed a robust and healthy way of doing so. This behavior obviously should not be allowed, but our job would be to redirect them and give them other avenues to communicate their needs. If we punish them for hitting at this age because we believe they will learn that hitting is *morally* wrong, we are wasting our time and energy, as well as theirs. We will then be sorely disappointed that they continue this behavior, and we will feel that our child doesn't respect or trust us. This, in turn, will lead to negative feelings and lies attacking our brains about ourselves and our parenting. All this is just unnecessary chaos.

Building Better Bridges

Understanding child development and some of the science about the way children's brains function will give us what I basically call parenting superpowers. Understanding what children can learn at what stage will allow us to teach our own kids lessons they can actually absorb and leave them with feelings of trust and love and confidence in us.

If you want a child (or another adult for that matter) to be able to learn from you as you attempt to apply and execute some of the principles and conversations this book will put forth, then that means they have to feel safe and calm. Their nervous system has to be regulated, and certain parts of their brain need to be deactivated or soothed. This will be especially helpful knowledge as we talk about trauma and abuse that our children might face.

Here are a few of the important parts of the brain at work in ourselves and our children, culled together from my psychological background and continued research.

When people are emotionally upset, the brain activates a complex network of structures and systems that work together to process and respond to the emotional stimuli. Here's a general overview of how the brain works in this context:

1. *The Limbic System*: The limbic system is a group of interconnected structures in the brain that are involved in emotional processing and regulation. When a person experiences an emotional stimulus, such as a threat or a reward, the limbic system becomes activated, sending signals to other parts of the brain to initiate a response.
2. *The Amygdala*: The amygdala is a small almond-shaped structure within the limbic system that plays a crucial role in processing emotions, particularly fear and anxiety. When the amygdala detects a potential threat, it sends a signal to the hypothalamus, which activates the sympathetic nervous system, triggering the body's "fight or flight" response.
3. *The Prefrontal Cortex*: The prefrontal cortex is a part of the brain that is involved in decision-making,

problem-solving, and impulse control. When a person is emotionally upset, the prefrontal cortex may become less active, leading to a decreased ability to regulate emotions, make rational decisions, and control impulsive behavior.

4. *The HPA Axis*: The HPA (hypothalamic-pituitary-adrenal) axis is a complex system that regulates the body's response to stress. When a person is emotionally upset, the HPA axis becomes activated, leading to the release of stress hormones such as cortisol and adrenaline. These hormones can have a range of effects on the body, including increased heart rate, blood pressure, and respiration, as well as heightened awareness and focus.

5. *The Reward System*: The reward system is a network of structures in the brain that are involved in processing pleasurable stimuli, such as food, sex, and social interactions. When a person experiences positive emotions, such as joy or excitement, the reward system becomes activated, releasing dopamine and other neurotransmitters that create feelings of pleasure and satisfaction.

Overall, when people are emotionally upset, the brain activates a complex network of structures and systems that work together to process and respond to the emotional stimuli. These processes can have a range of effects on both the body and the mind and can shape the way that people perceive and respond to their environment.

Understanding how the brain and body connect is so important. Our parents might not have had this information, but we do, so let's use it!

No man, woman, or child can learn if they are emotionally upset, dysregulated, or if they feel unsafe. This means if we want to have tough conversations with our family that lead to change and improvement, we have to know how to keep them calm or get them calm when they are upset or when these talks need to occur. This also means *we* have to be regulated and calm first! It is for this reason that I titled the chapter *How to Speak to the 'Right' Brain*. This is not scientifically accurate, but I find it helpful that when you are going to communicate things that are difficult, you must imagine that you are speaking to the emotional side of the brain first and foremost. It is helpful to remember that the right hemisphere is emotions, feelings, fantasy, etc., and people need to feel safe with their emotional side before the logical side is ready to learn or listen. Even adults need help with this! So how do we do that? How do we get people to listen to us and hear us when things get intense and emotional? If you have a spouse or a child, you know first hand how difficult this can be.

I like to imagine there is an arrow that is surrounded by light bulbs, blinking and pointing to the "right" brain.

Veterinarian and trauma therapist Hilal Dogan, in her article "This is your brain on trauma," discusses some things that are helpful. According to her work, brain imaging studies show that trauma tends to get stored in and activate the right hemisphere of the brain, and the logical left side gets deactivated or shut down. We have to speak calmly, kindly, and communicate understanding to calm down the right side of the brain. When we do this, over time and slowly, the emotional flares will calm down and the logical left brain will come online.[30] Then and only then is our child or spouse ready to listen and learn. We have to do the work of the prefrontal for them. We have to be the filter for their big emotions if we are to get them to listen and learn from us! We have to help co-regulate. We have to help them feel attunement and connection before they will be ready to trust what we, as parents, are saying, much less put anything we are saying into practice. This is a whole body and brain way of thinking and communicating. Again, it is way more complex than this, and there are some amazing books out there on the inner workings of our brains, but I find that parents just want to know the basics and what to do. There is a really cool and simple way to teach the different overarching parts of the brain using a tool called "The Hand Model of the Brain.[31] To find the full article and full-size image depicting this tool, just look up "flipping your lid - Total Health." Additionally, I did training through Natural Lifemanship Equine Assisted Psychotherapy, and I learned about Dr. Bruce Perry's amazing Neurosequential Model of

---

[30] "This is your brain on trauma" - Hilal Dogan, BVSc, CCTP (DVM360.com)
[31] The image of the hand model from Total Health in West Berkshire is my favorite of the infographics on how to explain the brain to our kiddos or adults!

Clint Davis

Therapeutics." This method is a "developmentally informed, biologically-respectful approach to working with children, young people, and adults who have experienced early adversity, trauma, and neglect" that is also extremely useful. It has a great breakdown of the actual parts of the brain and how they function during emotional moments. Check out his book, *What Happened To You?* for more in depth info into this tool![32]

I love the brain and could go on and on, but let's press ahead. I said there would be steps, and people love steps so here are my simple but practical steps to de-escalation and open communication. I wish I could have come up with a good acronym, but my military days of endless acronyms are long behind me. One quick thing to remember. These steps are a lot like the stages of grief. They are not to be rushed through in one sitting. Sometimes with kids or spouses, they do not need us to fix, teach, or give suggestions in the moment. Sometimes they just need to be heard and seen. So do not feel like you have to go through every step every time, but at least doing the first 3 is very important.

1. *Connect* - you must be connected to who you are. First and foremost your identity and safety must be firm. You must be in your own body and emotionally ready to take on scary and difficult things. This allows us to open our hearts and minds to the other person, without needing them to be okay or waiting for them to validate us. This starts in the womb. Babies move to grow and safely attach to their mother. There are some awesome videos of this online you should check out! Whether 8 years old or 80, movement provides fundamental connection - from womb to grave. Babies and children need physical movements to regulate. Sometimes tapping, rocking, or moving from one foot to the other can help a child connect to their body or yours! If you have a safe relationship with your child, hold them and soothe them before moving to the next step.
2. *Validate* - it is important to speak to your child in a way that lets them know their experience, fears, and emotions are valid. Try saying things like, "I believe you experienced

---
[32] https://naturallifemanship.com/build-a-connected-brain/

71

x, y, or z," "I hear that you are sad," or "I see that you are frustrated." These are ways you can validate without agreeing or trying to go straight to facts and logic.

3. *Empathize* - being able to put yourself in your child's position and truly try to feel what they may be feeling allows you to move them from chaos to order. Showing empathy does not mean agreeing, it means you show the emotional connection and attunement to help them feel seen, heard, and understood. Compassion may be an even better word here. Try this: "If I were you, I'd feel that same way," "I can see how you came to that conclusion or made that decision," "Wow, that's really difficult," or "I have made that same mistake or had those same thoughts and feelings." Empathy alleviates shame and de-escalates the nervous system and the brain's protective mechanisms. This is talking to the right brain in both senses...the *right* side and the *correct* side.

Moving to some steps for the logical side of our brains. The next few steps can only happen if the person or child is ready to talk about facts. This can only happen if you have calmed them down and they feel safe. It doesn't matter if it is about getting in a car seat or talking about sex. You earn the right to move to these steps by building trust in the first three. This also might happen hours or even days later, so try to be patient.

4. *Speak truth* - after doing the first three steps, you will have built a bridge between you and your child. They will be more regulated and able to listen and learn the lesson you are trying to teach. They will be able to push away the fear and shame they are wrestling with and hear the truth that you are speaking to them. You might say things like, "I love you very much in spite of your mistakes" or "You are an amazing person because of these things." Bring them back to reality and life by showing them success stories and people that love them for who they are, not what they do or have done.

5. *Offer support* - this is now the time to offer suggestions and guidance for how you can move forward. Ask them what they need and how you can serve them based on

their personality, coping abilities, and resources.
Sometimes that support is just sitting beside them. Shared
tears can be the medicine to a lot of pain.

6. *Make a plan* - now that the brain is calm, truth has been
   spoken, and options have been suggested, it is now time
   to make a decision and plan out action steps. This is the
   time to give them 2-3 choices about how to move forward.
   Have them commit to one and review the support you will
   give them.

These steps will hopefully remind you that you only get to teach, offer
support, and put a plan in place when you have established trust and
when the other human you are communicating with feels loved and safe.
Remember, you always have the opportunity to teach, but if you violate
trust by plowing forward, it can take years to come back from that type of
damage. Be patient, take it slow, and value transformation over
information exchange or instant behavior modification. No one has ever
learned a lesson while in an emotional crisis. Literally, hand on the Bible,
as I am writing this I have gotten up 4 times to soothe my 5 year old,
because he is starving and having a meltdown at our counter. There is
food right in front of him. My logical instinct is to scream, "Just eat your
food and you will feel better!" However, getting up and rubbing his back
and saying, "it seems like you are frustrated and hungry. Daddy is right
here and I am sorry your upset", will lead to him finally putting the dang
pancake in his mouth. Then in about 5 mins all will be right with the
world. Sometimes all you can do is be quiet and give them food. This
applies to my wife as well. Love you, sweetheart.
Now hear me out. This strategy is the ideal. I know you cannot always do
these steps and sometimes you will have to skip them, but for the most
part, if the situation isn't a crisis of life or death, then using this outline
can really help with walking through tough situations or conversations
with kids or adults. Sometimes the steps are done over time to build or
repair trust, and sometimes they are done all at once. Regardless of
whether it is a toddler who doesn't want to go to sleep, eat the pancake,
or wants only the *purple* cup. Or if it is a teen who wants to go to a party
or start using social media, I hope these steps will truly help you!

Building Better Bridges

In the following chapter, we are going to discuss trauma and the ways it can happen in our families, how to know the signs, and how to prepare our children to avoid traumatic situations and help them heal if they do face these things. The information about the brain in this chapter and the steps we have just discussed will be *vital* if your child or peer experiences sexual, physical, or emotional trauma or you catch them doing something dangerous or harmful. If that is the case for you, I hope you will flip back to these steps and feel hope that you have tools under your belt to help yourself and your children.

Reflection & Discussion

1. How much of this brain info is new to you? What parts do you find most interesting or helpful?

2. Do you feel comfortable and confident sharing this info with your children using the hand model or other tactics?

3. Do you see any correlation between the facts given here and your own brain's tendencies? What about the tendencies and behavior of your kids?

4. Are there any changes you might make with any new knowledge you learned?

5. Epigenetics, ACE Scores, and Generational Trauma

Trauma isn't just an event that took place sometime in the past; it's also the imprint left by that experience on mind, brain, and body.
- Bessel van der Kolk, *The Body Keeps the Score*

One of the most important things that I can communicate in this chapter is how much a child's early experience affects their success in the future. Over the past few decades, researchers have begun to observe how our

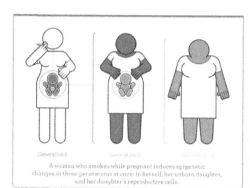

A woman who smokes while pregnant induces epigenetic changes in three generations at once: in herself, her unborn daughter, and her daughter's reproductive cells.

past and our family histories affect our ability to function in society. In church, we call this phenomenon "generational sin."[33] God is not up there, like Zeus with a lightning bolt, harming everyone for their mistakes and punishing their children. It is just the natural order of things. This also doesn't mean that you're to blame for all the brokenness, just that we live in a broken world with consequences. This is not just theology but how science works. In science and psychology, it's called *epigenetics*. Epigenetics is the study of how your behaviors and environment can cause changes that influence the way your genes work. "Unlike changes to genetic code, epigenetic changes are reversible and do not change your DNA sequence, but they can change how your body reads a DNA sequence."[34]

---

[33] Numbers 14:18
[34] CDC, "What is Epigenetics," 2022. https://www.cdc.gov/genomics/disease/epigenetics.htm

This means that what our grandparents ate, drank, and were emotionally and physically exposed to can be passed down from generation to generation. Their past actions impact our biology and our predispositions. Your epigenetics are in a constant state of flux and can be altered based on your exposure to a whole host of things: foods, social situations, violence, alternative medicines, microbiomes, seasonal correlations, and much more. Check out these images to see a couple of visual examples of how epigenetics manifest.

In the visual above[35], a grandparent who smokes can pass down epigenetic changes to her grandchild. What we do can and will affect future generations in a positive or negative way.

This second illustration[36] shows the importance of paying attention to our environment and expresses the idea that what we expose ourselves to impacts our own health. Seems obvious. But looking back at Figure 1, we must face the truth that our habits, for better or worse, will impact the health of our children, and even further generations down the road. Epigenetics is not a destiny set in stone, but it is an indicator of what will happen for our children if we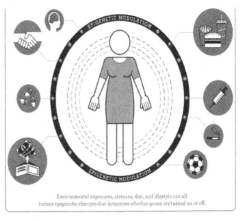

Environmental exposures, stresses, diet, and lifestyle can all induce epigenetic changes that determine whether genes are turned on or off.

do not parent them in a healthy way and practice healthy habits in our own lives. Which, I hate to break it to all of us...starts with us. The good choices of our kids must begin with us making those types of healthy choices for ourselves.

Trauma and ACE Scores

---

[35] Image sourced from Jonathan Shaw's wonderful article "Is Epigenetics Inherited?" from *Harvard Magazine* (illustrated by Jude Buffum)
[36] Ibid.

Building Better Bridges

So, what actually is trauma, and how does it impact our lives? Let's get technical again for just a minute.

Trauma, especially in childhood, can have a significant impact on a person's life, affecting their emotional, cognitive, and physical development. Trauma is any experience that is deeply distressing or disturbing, and it can be caused by a range of events, including physical, sexual, or emotional abuse against one's own body and mind, but also things like neglect or witnessing violence or other traumatic events.

The brain's response to trauma is complex and involves multiple parts of the brain and nervous system. When an individual experiences a traumatic event, the brain's stress response system is activated, triggering the release of stress hormones such as adrenaline and cortisol.

In response to this heightened stress response, the amygdala is activated, leading to feelings of fear, anxiety, and hypervigilance as we discussed in our brain conversation. The hippocampus, which is responsible for memory processing, is also impacted, making it difficult for the individual to form clear memories of the traumatic event, thus changing how they remember the event far into the future. The prefrontal cortex may also be impacted, leading to difficulties with impulse control and emotional regulation. Since this is the part of us that helps with decision-making and processing, trauma can really take a toll on how we operate at very basic levels.

Over time, the repeated activation of the stress response system can lead to changes in the brain's overall structure and function, impacting the way that the brain processes information and the way neural connections and networks are made.

These changes in the brain due to trauma can lead to a range of symptoms and behaviors, including anxiety, depression, hypervigilance, flashbacks, and avoidance behaviors. Understanding the brain's response to trauma can help individuals and healthcare providers develop effective treatment strategies that address the underlying neurological changes associated with trauma. Therapy and other interventions that focus on regulating the stress response system, strengthening emotional regulation skills, and promoting healing and resilience can help individuals to recover from the impact of trauma on their brain and overall well-being. Most of us have experienced trauma in our lives, but many of us walk around everyday either rejecting the fact that we've experienced trauma or ignoring its effects.

If you're like many people I meet, your definition of trauma might be very severe. You might think of trauma as losing a loved one, getting sexually abused, or facing a massive natural disaster. I define trauma as anything that is *not* nurturing. A child is supposed to receive love, security, and stability from their parents. Their young brains should be wired for connection and reasonable risk-taking, not for overprotection or extreme suffering. They are supposed to live in an environment that is safe but that provides room for them to grow and learn and become a healthy adult. When these things do not happen, our brains, bodies, and souls end up changing the way we think, feel, and see the world, ourselves, and others. Even our view of God or a higher power is affected. My friends Terry and Sharon Hargrave developed something called the Restoration Therapy model as well as the Relate Strong Church training. These models point to two foundational beliefs that children should form early on. They say we all need to have a strong foundational belief about *love* and *trust* in ourselves and our children to avoid long term trauma. We also need to believe we are loved and safe in order to be resilient human beings. Another definition of trauma is a violation of love and trust, placed on someone by a person, an experience, or an environmental factor.

What, then, does having a solid foundation of love and trust look like? Two simple definitions, really. Simple, not easy.

1. *Love* is believing that you are worthy, valuable, good enough, accepted, seen, understood, validated, etc.
2. *Trust* means you believe relationships are safe and secure, relationships are consistent/ predictable, and your environment is physically, emotionally, and sexually safe.

Building Better Bridges

If violations of love and trust happen to children early on, this causes deep pain. This pain changes the way we cope with the world around us and the lens in which we see the world, people, and ourselves. Trauma is just this. It is something or someone causing such acute pain in our lives that our entire being responds and prepares never to experience this again. This is the catalyst for most of the unhealthy and toxic coping mechanisms we employ.

I want you to understand that if you want to create real behavioral change in yourself or your children, then you will have to address the underlying traumas that have happened to you and rewire your brain towards health and resiliency. If we have foundational beliefs that say we are not loved or we are not safe, then our thoughts and feelings will follow in that negative line, and our behavior patterns will surely follow. We must learn to rewrite these narratives and replace these lies. If we don't, we will avoid or respond poorly to many of the situations we find ourselves in when it comes to marriage, parenting, and life as a whole. Healing starts by admitting and addressing our own childhood wounds. This may be difficult, but until we acknowledge that we might have been or were victims of trauma in our own lives, we can never understand the impact it has on how we live and interact. We must ask ourselves what have we come to believe about God, ourselves, and other people. If we can understand these root drivers, then we can start to address our real issues. It is scary to walk into the unknown and address pain that has been long ignored. But if we do, we can turn our *pain* into *peace*. The problem is we are living in fear, and we must face our dragons.

Dr. Carl Jung said, "My friends, it is wise to nourish the soul, otherwise you will breed dragons and devils in your heart."[37] Trauma recovery is all about facing your dragons and nourishing your mind, body, and soul. In a video of his, Dr. Jordan Peterson summarizes three options to face our dragons:

> 1.We can avoid them and run away, only to have to face them caught by surprise.

---

[37] Carl Jung's *The Red Book* (p. 280)

2. We can go into their cave and kill them where they live, so they don't make a bunch of dragon babies.

3. We can wait until they come flying out breathing fire and attacking us, our family and our village.[38]

Maybe it's just me, but it would be best if we chose option number 2. We are all victims to our own dragons and deal with their scars, but we also have the strength to defeat them if we choose to face them where they live.

In our world today, *victim* has turned into a polarizing, dirty word. When I use that word, I do not mean *playing* the victim or wallowing in your situation. I mean working through the painful things that have happened to us, so that we can move out of the victim seat and into the seat of empowerment and love. This is a process and not a one-time event. Having a therapist that truly has an understanding of trauma and attachment is something I highly suggest everyone looking into. Making sure our families, schools, and places of worship also understand trauma-informed care is vital for moving forward in this new world.

Trauma affects the whole being of a person. The impact of childhood trauma can be particularly long-lasting and can lead to a range of mental health issues and other problems later in life.

Emotional and Behavioral Problems

Some of the most common effects of childhood trauma are emotional and behavioral issues. Children who experience trauma are more likely to have difficulty regulating their emotions, which can lead to mood swings, anxiety, and depression. They may also exhibit behavioral problems, such as aggression, impulsivity, and hyperactivity. These emotional and behavioral problems can persist into adulthood, impacting the individual's ability to form healthy relationships or maintain stable employment.

---

[38] "You Have to Slay the Dragon" - Jordan Peterson on The Outcome Channel on YouTube

Physical Health Problems

Childhood trauma can also impact physical health. Trauma can lead to chronic stress, which can increase the risk of developing health problems such as heart disease, diabetes, and obesity. Trauma can also lead to sleep problems, such as nightmares and insomnia, which can further exacerbate physical health problems.

Mental Health Issues

Childhood trauma is a significant risk factor for developing mental health issues, including but not limited to post-traumatic stress disorder (PTSD), anxiety disorders, and depression. These mental health issues can impact the individual's ability to function in daily life and can lead to problems with relationships, work, and school. Trauma can also lead to substance abuse and addiction, as individuals may turn to drugs or alcohol to cope with their unresolved emotional pain. If this emotional pain goes untreated too long then it can lead to suicidal ideation or self-destructive behaviors.

Social Problems

Childhood trauma can also lead to social problems, such as difficulty forming and maintaining healthy relationships. Trauma can make it difficult for individuals to trust others, which can make it challenging to form close bonds with others. Trauma can also impact an individual's ability to communicate effectively, which can lead to conflicts and misunderstandings in relationships.

Childhood trauma can have a profound and lasting impact on an individual's life in a range of different ways. The effects of trauma can be far-reaching, impacting emotional, cognitive, physical, and social development. While the impact of trauma can be challenging to overcome, there is absolutely hope for recovery. Seeking professional help, such as therapy and support groups, can be an essential step in healing from childhood trauma and improving overall well-being.

Clint Davis

You might be thinking to yourself "Clint, I don't have any trauma. I was not raped or beaten. I was not abandoned. I haven't lost anyone in my life."
I would challenge you to stop measuring trauma in the wrong direction. When we measure our experience against the worst possible things in the world, then of course our situations look small. You are right that it can always be worse, but this perspective is a survival mechanism that allows us merely to survive the pain of our past. The healthier way to face your dragon is to acknowledge that it exists.[39]

For example: As a veteran, I tended to minimize my trauma all the time. I would say things like "I have not killed a bunch of people," "I didn't get deployed 7 times like some people," or "It's not like I was in the special forces." I did not feel like I deserved to have PTSD. I felt ashamed and insecure to claim that label. Partly I did not want to admit my experience and in part because I didn't know how to acknowledge my own suffering. You see, when I measure my own life against experiences far worse than mine, then I can minimize my own pain and difficulty. I did this because I didn't want to act like a victim. However, when I measure the other way, against someone who has never been deployed to war at all, that gap is very large.

We have to measure our experiences against what God intended for us to receive. We have to measure our experiences against the love and security we were *supposed* to get as children. To go even further, as Christ followers, we have to measure our experiences against Eden. God intended for us to feel completely loved and safe 100% of the time. He created us to be in harmony with Him, ourselves, and all of creation. So, if we experience things like abuse, death, suffering, or anything less than God's original intentions, it causes not small problems, but major ones. Anything less than this original design, anything apart from *shalom*[40]

---

[39] Jack Kent's *There's No Such Thing as a Dragon* is a fantastic book that provides an easy way to explain to adults and children why dealing with the problem makes it smaller and avoiding the problem only makes it grow larger and more unmanageable.
[40] In the Bible, *shalom* means universal flourishing, wholeness, and delight – a rich state of affairs in which natural needs are satisfied and natural gifts fruitfully employed, a state of affairs that inspires joyful wonder as its Creator and Savior opens doors and welcomes the creatures in whom he delights.

affects our minds, bodies, and spirits for a lifetime. This does not mean that we are defined by our trauma. My point is that it is vitally important to acknowledge the how, why, and what of trauma's effects and have a good guide to measure those by.

Like I said, we all have trauma big and small, trauma we should not ignore. The question is are we willing to acknowledge it and deal with it? Are we willing to stop passing it down to our children, generation after generation? I know you have heard it said that "hurt people hurt people." Let's take a look at how this trauma plays out and how to stop it.

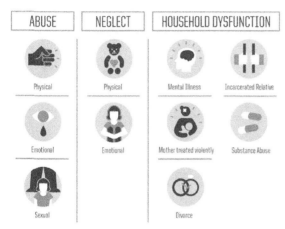

There is an amazing and helpful piece of clinical research called the ACE study. This stands for *Adverse Childhood Experiences*. The foundational ACE study was conducted by the Centers for Disease Control and Kaiser Permanente in the mid-1990s, with a group of patients insured through Kaiser Permanente.[41] The initial study focused on how traumatic childhood events may negatively affect adult health. The 17,000 participants surveyed were asked about their experiences with childhood maltreatment, family dysfunction, and current health status and behaviors.

Through this chart, the ACE study illustrates 10 traumas that can happen to a child that will affect them for the rest of their life. In the study, when a child experiences an adverse experience, they get a number. Every experience we have had or a kid has during childhood increases that number from 1-10. The higher a person's ACE score, the more likely they are to suffer in the future – behaviorally, physically, or emotionally. For

---

[41] National Center for Injury Prevention and Control, Division of Violence Prevention (https://www.cdc.gov/violenceprevention/aces/about.html)

my part, I would add that their spiritual life is also negatively impacted due to the beliefs that they build about God, others, and themselves based on their various ACEs.[42]

A second illustration[43] also gives examples of consequences that a person might suffer from a higher ACE score. *What happens to us in childhood and how we are parented has a significant impact on our success in life in almost all areas.*

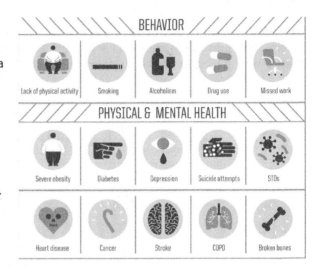

This means that many of the issues in our society listed as the top causes of death (heart disease, addiction, obesity) are not just behaviors to be modified, but have causes rooted in the emotional impact of relationships and environments our parents and grandparents were exposed to decades back in time.[44] Perhaps scarier still, this means that a lot of the unhealthy habits we have adopted evolved from coping mechanisms which allowed us to survive the various difficulties we went through as kids. Now, though, as parents and helpers ourselves, we can start asking children not only what happened in their past, but who was there, when did it happen, and who has helped them through it since. The power for

[42] Images also come from National Center for Injury Prevention and Control, Division of Violence Prevention (https://www.cdc.gov/violenceprevention/aces/about.html)
[43] Ibid.
[44] Bhushan, Devika et. al. "The Roadmap for Resilience: The California Surgeon General's Report on Adverse Childhood Experiences, Toxic Stress, and Health," *Roadmap for Resilience,* 2020.

change as we look ahead lies in safe connection for anyone who has abuse in their past, allowing them to be seen and heard. By anyone, I mean *everyone*. We all have the power to change our future!

I have spent this brief chapter on the ramifications of childhood trauma and what the ACE study is. The truth is, whole texts have been written on this one thing, and one of the best is *The Body Keeps the Score,* by Bessel van der Kolk. Whether you prefer books, podcasts, articles, etc., there are many resources out there for you on the brain/body connection and how crucial it is for dealing with trauma.

I include this chapter and the chapter before it for two reasons. First, because I think some of the jargon, studies, and tools used by clinical psychologists should be more widely placed in the hands of the people who need it. Awareness and relevant information are just the first line of defense we have in tackling some of these deep-seated issues. Most parents don't want to listen to 85 hours about neuroplasticity and synapses, but some knowledge of the brain - yours and those around you - is vital and can change the way you teach and interact forever.

Secondly, and to wrap up the technical bit, ***I write this to let you know that we can pass down addiction, depression, anxiety and all sorts of unhealthy problems, but we can also pass down recovery.*** If we change our patterns and behaviors and do the work to heal our own hearts and bodies, then we as parents can start to bring hope and healing to untold generations of children. You can start right now making an impact! How, you ask? When we live out of a place of truth and confidence that we are loved and safe in God's care and in our own bodies, then we can be walking, talking models of God's love to the world and to our own spheres of influence. People need to experience love and safety not just be told about it. We can write books and create catchy videos about inclusion, acceptance, and healing, but the most sure fire way to change your family and our world is to be an example. If you can learn to recover from the trauma you have experienced, that means you have changed what you believe about yourself. Trauma recovery is not about changing just your behaviors, but changing what you believe deeply about your worth and ability. This whole body change will let all of the struggles and troubles of life be far easier to face. This change will allow you to deal with conflict, failure, success, and all sorts of external factors with a firm foundation. Then and only then will you be able to change EVERYTHING for your kids and grandkids. Are you pumped yet? I know I am!

This concept is especially true if you are a believer. This should be one of the strongest callings you have in your life. We are called to be the hands and feet of Jesus. This is the work of helping people with trauma or abuse that has broken their hearts and that, unresolved, is damaging their daily lives. We have a mission field right in front of our faces. Our churches, homes, schools, neighborhoods, and communities are filled with children and adults who have painfully high ACE scores and parents who have a lack of resources and are blind to the effects of their unhealth and lack of support. I challenge us all to learn more in this area and spread the word that help is available, and we can make it easier and more accessible for people to recover from the pain of their past. Then and only then can we all start changing our present and future! Hurt people do hurt people, but the good news is that science and scripture tell us that healed people can heal people!

Speaking of practicing healing...there are two phrases that I would *love* to stop hearing people say in our society. These two phrases tend to ostracize people, condemn them, and place them in the "other" position. They are a sign that a person does not understand the complexity of the human experience or that a person is calloused to the struggles of life. The first one is said when something happens that we feel is awful or unhealthy. The phrase is *"How could they!"*

I usually hear this spoken when there is a school shooting on the news, or someone finds out that someone stole something from a neighbor, or worst of all, a child was harmed, neglected, or abused. All of us have this reaction to the brokenness of the world sometimes. I get it, and I have said these phrases in the past myself. There are horrors in the world worthy of disdain, rebuke, and disgust. I will not try to minimize that. The thing is, the more we learn about trauma and the more we understand how past abuses and events can shape our body, minds, and souls, the less often we have to ask "How could they," and the more we can start saying, "I wonder what happened to them that made them think that was a good choice or that it was their only choice." Such a perspective doesn't excuse toxic behavior or minimize the trauma for the victim. Abusers and the evil people in our world need accountability. The point is that understanding and empathy can help us to realize that we actually *do* know why people do awful things, and it's usually because awful things happened to them and healing never took place. Understanding also gives us the ability to find peace and forgiveness in our own hearts even if reconciliation never happens. This can go for smaller situations like children throwing fits in public, talking back to adults in school, cheating or stealing from the store, having sex or watching porn. Things do not happen in a vacuum; behaviors are symptoms of a problem. If we have more understanding and wisdom, we can then have more grace for people and true healing can happen in our families and our communities. Better yet, we can prevent them in future generations or today in our sphere of influence.

The second phrase I hear when bad things are mentioned is, *"I would never do that"* or *"That would never be my child/spouse."* If we think we are morally superior to other people and that we are somehow incapable of doing awful things, I want you to know that 1) we are all capable of horrible things and big mistakes given the wrong circumstances and lack of strong supports, and 2) it is only because you didn't go through what they went through. You are not them and do not have their story. The truth is that if you had their negative experiences, you might have done the same things or turned out the same way. Had you grown up with their parents, their gender, their ethnicity, their culture, or their traumas, anything would be possible. The question to ask is why did I not turn out like them? What kept me from letting similar experiences or traumas lead me down a path of destruction? When you hear someone had an affair, got caught in addiction, or compromised their business, instead of gossiping, slandering, or looking down off a high horse, it is best to just take a moment to be thankful that you didn't take the wrong steps that could of led to the same sad outcome. Or better still, look back on your own life and realize that you might have been one step away from doing worse. One of the most important things we can figure out as a society is what are the positive things in life that shape us towards healing and health, instead of disaster and destruction.

If we can honestly say we haven't done *anything* we are ashamed of or deeply regret, then maybe we should be thankful for the grace of God that kept us from experiencing the things that they experienced that drove them to such awful behaviors. Maybe by understanding trauma, epigenetics, and the ACE study, you will move through the rest of this book, and the rest of this life, with a lot more forgiveness for yourself and a lot more forgiveness for others. I know we could all use a lot more of that as we live on this spinning rock together.

Reflection & Discussion

1. Had you ever heard of the ACE study before? If no, how are you feeling after learning about it? Did you experience any of things on the study?

2. What are ways your early experiences have shaped how you parent your own children?

3. When you face your "dragons," what is your tendency? Fight, flight, or freeze? How would you change your response if you could?

4. If you have some of the traumas associated with the ACE study, have you addressed them? Are you willing to?

Important Intermission

For those of you who read all the way up to this point, I am tremendously grateful for your patience in getting here. For those who skimmed or skipped the first part entirely, you are still welcome here, and I am grateful to you too. I know that many of you are reading this to find resources and help, and that is admirable all on its own.

However, I felt obligated to build some foundation before getting here, and I really recommend giving those first chapters a read. I do not like just giving advice to people or providing direction on a particular issue without first explaining the root causes and the whys. Implementing the tools well can only happen after understanding how to use them and what job they ought to be used for. You don't want to use a hammer to chop down a tree. Well, I suppose you could, but that's not the tool I'm choosing, and it won't be very effective anytime soon.

In my experience, understanding precedes action. Basically – when we do not know *why* we are doing something, we will inevitably go back to our default reactions in moments of panic, even if those strategies don't work or are unhealthy. ***Understanding the basis for our struggles creates space for us to respond instead of react***. I truly believe understanding the history and roots of the topics here – trauma, body chemistry, parenting, cultural toxicity, etc. – will motivate you to follow through on the steps that are coming.

Quick personal example of this:
I spent ages reading articles about sleep training in an effort to get some sleep for my young son and for me and my wife. I didn't care about the "whys". We just wanted to sleep. This did not go well. The advice went something like this…"put the baby in the bed, don't put the baby in the bed, put the baby in a crib, don't ever use a crib, swaddle the baby, never swaddle the baby, swaddle the baby in the crib, and put the crib in the

bed." It was maddening, exhausting, and I lost it multiple times. Tears, yelling, and heartache followed.

I followed the contradictory advice of dozens of different dads, moms, doctors, sleep coaches, and psychologists. None of that helped, and I likely made my oldest even more upset than before.
Well. As it happened, he had allergies and also struggled with sensory issues that were making it impossible for him to fall asleep or get good rest. If I had been able to take the time to understand the *why* of his crying and pain, I would not have wasted my time on so many useless resources and tools. Sure they worked for "everyone else," but we were not raising everyone else's kid. Nor would I have wasted my son's time and precious sleep. We will always do better when we know the why behind our actions.

I hate to assume anything about your life, but I have a feeling you have been in a similar boat. Consuming dizzying information only to realize you missed the root issue all along or settling for life being "not awful."
So if you haven't already, I hope you will flip back to the beginning and then meet me back here.
Okay, cool. See ya soon!

Moving forward, I pray this book proves to be the moment you stop being dazed and confused. I cannot promise to have all the answers, but I hope to clear up a lot of subjects and topics that we rarely talk about. Topics that are critical to our lives and the lives of our children, yet that our society seems to have very few resources to address. I also hope to give you a few direct solutions to these very scary and overwhelming issues. I want to remind you that we are the *first generation* of parents to deal with some of these issues, so don't feel like you have failed. Many others, myself included, are figuring out how to navigate this storm of technology, social media, and internet exposure right along with you.

On the other hand, there are some issues that parents have faced for generations: things like childhood sexual development, having "the talk," and a lack of education on childhood developmental stages or body safety. I want to help us stop repeating toxic cycles and start a new way forward where our society, our families and our children thrive! With that, let us jump into the deep end.

Clint Davis

Part II:
What to Do Now

6. What is Childhood Sexual Neglect?
(and why you've never heard of it)

Neglect is a form of abuse that is often invisible, but can have lifelong consequences.
- Andrea Brandt

I have talked to you about parenting, hormones, development, the brain, and what trauma means. Now I will be focusing on what we can do about some of the deepest issues we are facing today. In fact, talking is honestly one of the main solutions because it is one of the main problems. We either talk too much about the wrong things, or we avoid talking about the most important things. Which is what brought me to write this book in the first place.

One of the main things that I have dedicated my life to is shedding light on areas of suffering that are not commonly talked or thought about. Things that have been swept under the rug by our families, our friends, and society as a whole, simply because they are difficult or uncomfortable to talk about. I have been blessed to speak at schools, colleges, graduate schools, churches, businesses, and all over the world about this topic. I am excited to share what I have found and God has revealed.

One of these things is the term *Childhood Sexual Neglect*. This is a term that I am defining and that I am trying to make commonplace in the ethics and practice of psychology and theology. I am not the only person talking about this concept, but I am trying to give the first holistic view and understanding I have seen between the pages of this book. I am trying to give this enemy a name. I am also trying to create a term that encapsulates the process of allowing children to go unsupported and traumatized from birth to adulthood in specific areas. As I stated earlier, I have met with hundreds, if not thousands of people who have expressed that they were neglected, but did not know it. Many people do not know they have been neglected, because there is not a large body of literature around this topic, and there are no specific terms to describe it or flesh it out.

Let me break it down further. If you look back at the ACE study image in Chapter 5, physical and emotional neglect are listed, but there is no spot for childhood sexual neglect. The study also covers three types of abuse: physical, emotional, and sexual abuse, along with other negative environmental circumstances that can lead to trauma. But again, no mention of childhood sexual neglect.

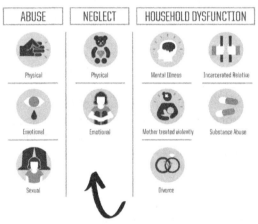

Now, when you hear the term "sexual neglect," you may think I mean a person not getting enough sexual exposure, engagement, or fulfillment. In fact, in clinical settings or in the context of marriage therapy, you might hear that a partner is being sexually neglected, meaning their spouse withholds sex as a punishment, a tool for manipulation, or for some other reason. This, of course, is not what I mean when it comes to children. I mean the exact opposite. We should limit our children's exposure to adult sexual content, while preparing them for their own biological development and make them aware of various dangers as they grow. A child does not need erotic content or experiences at an age where they are easily confused, manipulated and vulnerable. They need to be protected at all costs. What they do need when it comes to sexuality is support, resources, and a healthy understanding of their own bodies and the bodies of others. They do not need to be placed in a bubble, but they need to be equipped over time to live outside of that bubble in the world that exists.

Building Better Bridges

Here is my definition for childhood sexual neglect:
"A child growing up from birth to adulthood without healthy and age-appropriate conversations about sexual development, proper terms for private parts, consent, or body safety rules."

If we do not feed our child we would be neglecting them physically. If we do not hug our child or tell them we love them, we would be neglecting them emotionally. If we do not protect our child from erotic content, educate them on what is healthy and normal about their bodies, and attempt to prevent sexual trauma from happening to them, online or in person, we are neglecting their sexual development and future success.

I know neglect is a strong word. There are legal ramifications for neglecting children. The updated research and my clinical experiences show that if we are not protecting and preparing our children in this area it is extremely harmful and detrimental to their whole person. I hope that laws, resources and support can change the course of our future and society. Even as I write this, the surgeon general put out a statement about social media and its effects on children's mental health.[45] This is fantastic, but it is still only treating a symptom. Sexual neglect is at the root of many issues.

For many people that I have spoken to, counseled, or met at events, childhood sexual neglect runs rampant. When surveyed, very few adults can tell me that they have had these conversations with their own parents or caregivers when they were growing up. At nearly all my talks, I ask people to raise their hand if they had candid conversations about sex with their parents. Whether it's a crowd of 30 or of 3,000, the hands raised rarely number more than a few. This could be because they are too scared or nervous to raise their hands. However, after having thousands of conversations privately and publicly, I am led to believe that the mass majority of people in our society (and dare I say the world), have been neglected in this area.

---

[45] "Surgeon General Issues New Advisory About Effects Social Media Use Has on Youth Mental Health," U.S. Department of Health and Human Services, https://www.hhs.gov/about/news/2023/05/23/surgeon-general-issues-new-advisory-about-effects-social-media-use-has-youth-mental-health.html, 23 May 2023.

Maybe it seems insane to you that I am this worked up over a few conversations we didn't have. Or it could seem like I am overreacting to what it means to be sexually neglected as a child. I get that. I spoke with my editor about this, a woman who, like many of us, didn't really get an education on body parts, menstruation, or healthy views of sexual development. This led to years of confusion and fear on her part, including crushed self-esteem and a lot of learning that she had to do on her own in a world with very twisted views on the subject of sex and the human body. She told me recently that the stuff in this book will change her life.[46] I hope you see the importance of this the way Sarah does. This will be some of the simplest advice you might ever get, but it is more crucial than we even realize.

I fear the reasons for a great deal of childhood sexual neglect are that a) our parents didn't model these tools for us, and now we don't know how to do it, b) we are simply afraid or unwilling to be uncomfortable, or c) We don't even know it is an option. Is any one of these things true of you? I hope you won't punish yourself or be dismayed. This is about recognizing where we have fallen short and being brave enough to make changes that will save our family! Imagine letting something like fear stand in the way of creating the best possible life for yourself and your kiddos. I know we can all do better.

Because here is the truth: when a child grows up without being educated and protected, there are major consequences. Sexually neglected children often experience actual trauma.

Let's look at just a few of the main consequences for sexually neglected children:
>   1. They form an unhealthy or confused view of their own sexuality, sexual development, and/or the sexuality and sexual development of others.
>   2. They are unprepared and unable to protect themselves from abuse or trauma in person or online.

---

[46] Hey, guys. Sarah here. Just an FYI...he's not lying. I felt like this book gave me a breakthrough. And I don't even have children yet!

3. They are unlikely to report to a parent or caregiver if someone has harmed them, attempted to, or if they have been exposed to adult content.

Let me put it this way. Remember when you taught your child how to cross the street or when they first learned how to walk? We tell our child to hold our hands, look both ways, watch out for cars, and to stay on the sidewalk. We tell them these things to give them boundaries that keep them safe and to know what is expected. We would never just let our toddler run out on the sidewalk or into the street into danger. When it comes to sexual development or healthy sexuality, it is like our society is allowing children to walk out in the street and be hit by cars that they don't even know exist.

Our first experience with masturbation, menstruation, or any other normal developmental stage should not be filled with surprise, fear, or shame. This can lead children to a life full of addiction, mental health problems, and an unhealthy view of themselves and others. That being said, we as parents have to know *how* and *when* to talk to our children about these topics before they experience them for the first time alone and with no guidance. Much of the rest of this book will be spent discussing how we can avoid this, when we should have these tough conversations, and how to have them in ways that our kids will receive.

We must educate our children on our families values around sexual development or they will learn it from a friend or online, and those lessons will come at a great cost. Neglect leads to trauma, and trauma seems to be running rampant these days.

Research from Alice's Place, an organization dedicated to helping victims of domestic or sexual abuse, shows us that sexual trauma is affecting us all. It is a cross-cultural and worldwide issue.

- 1 in 3 girls and 1 in 5 boys experience sexual trauma before 18. 50% of their abusers commit their first offense before 18. Which means that half of the sexual trauma that we experience is inappropriate child on child interactions due to sexual neglect.

- 82% of sexual abuse happens by a family member, teacher, or friend. Educating our children on body safety and proper terms for private parts is a must.[47]

As many cultures are being immersed in technology, digital devices, and social media earlier and earlier, sexual trauma is not just happening in person, but online as well. Here is just a little of what they are facing:

- Some adults and teens are creating worlds of sexual exploitation and exposing children to adult content all while watching YouTube Kids, playing Call of Duty, Minecraft, or Roblox. Yes, even YouTube Kids is unsafe, without monitoring and filters.
- Today, the average age that a child is exposed to violent porn is around 8-11 years old, not because they are all looking for it, but because less than 15% of parents know how to monitor or protect kids from online exposure. (due to algorithms and A.I. the inappropriate material is looking for them)
- Middle Schoolers and even younger children are sending nude pictures of themselves to friends, air dropping pics to strangers, and even posting sexual content on social media and adult websites.

In the Internet age, offline sex abuse is fueled by pedophiles' unprecedented access to child pornography and exacerbated as perpetrators post pictures online of their exploits:
In 2018, tech companies reported over 45 million online photos and videos of children being sexually abused — more than double what they found the previous year.

- In 1998, there were over 3,000 reports of child sexual abuse imagery.
- Just over a decade later, yearly reports soared past 100,000.

---

[47] https://alicesplace.org/sexual-violence/

Building Better Bridges

- In 2014, that number surpassed 1 million for the first time.
- In 2018, there were 18.4 million, more than one-third of the total ever reported.[48]

The world is changing, and we must be equipped in this new digital age. With all the changes the world has undergone in the last 30 years, sexual trauma is directly connected to our digital lives.

This means that educating our children and giving them awareness, resources, and tools is more important than ever in order to avoid sexual trauma online and in person. While the devices have dramatically changed things, I truly believe that sexual neglect and unresolved sexual trauma is the root cause of many mental health struggles in our society. I also believe the information in this book can help us change directions and limit sexual trauma for generations to come and maybe, just maybe start to heal our own.

Throughout the next few chapters, you will see how sexual neglect manifests itself, how some of these consequences arise, and how to avoid them. If I wrote down everything I wanted to say about these topics, this book would be very long, and no one would read it. I promise to be as concise as possible while still addressing the major points and giving a few real-life scenarios that taught me a lot on my own journey with my two sons and countless clients.

Like I said, a lot of this book is about having conversations. Conversations, plural. These conversations build better bridges that can hold heavier and heavier subjects and topics. If the bridge between you and your child is made of straw it will not be able to handle the weight of a talk about porn or masturbation. If it is made out of steel and has lots of support beams, then it will be able to handle the weight. There is not one talk and you're done, and there is not one perfect way to do it. Every child and family is different and has different struggles or barriers. It is important to find support from a professional, a spiritual mentor, or another family who is achieving the things you look up to. Many of us have no clue how this is supposed to work because it has not been

[48] This information comes from a thought-provoking article, "Predators 101," put out by the Enough is Enough non-profit.

100

modeled for us, but we are going to try to fix that, along with attempting to dispel the discomfort many of us feel in discussing such things. I wholeheartedly believe with just a few tools and a little bit of courage, we can prevent childhood sexual neglect in our homes and communities.

I felt it essential to define and discuss this new term before we keep going, because I want you to understand that childhood sexual neglect is a foundational developmental issue that looks to be the root cause of so much of how we perceive and express sexuality and our identities in general. This is a driver to many of the mental health issues of today.

If 90% of adults have possibly been sexually neglected as they grew up, then it should come as no shock that we are seeing dramatically high abuse rates and trauma rates.[49] No wonder children are being exposed and addicted to porn like never before. No wonder mental health issues and negative body image are so prevalent through our children and teens. No wonder so many people are confused about their sex, gender or sexual identity. No wonder we feel more isolated and lost like never before.

Now, to be clear, I am not here to argue about LGBTQ or sexual identity issues. Everyone's situation is different, and it is not for me to make any sweeping assumptions or claims. I am only stating that many people in our society have clearly suffered from childhood sexual neglect, and the effects of such neglect are far-reaching. Despite the pain I see in so many kids, I see very little research on the topic and certainly no widespread change for the better. All I see is more chaos and confusion in children and their parents. Rather than discussing these things, I see a complete lack of conversation on these hard topics, sometimes even suppression of them. Topics such as the overexposure and oversexualization of our kids in a culture too blind or too hurt to see what is going on. In the last year or so, some of these topics have been brought to light. With drag queen readings at libraries to small children and hyper sexualized books being available at public elementary schools, I do see people paying more attention and raising their eyebrows. However, there is still so much work,

---

[49] Check out this infographic on abuse if you are interested - https://laurenskids.org/national-statistics/

discussion, and healing to be done. This culture is hurting so badly. We are arguing politics, selfish perspectives, and positions while our children are suffering to the point of suicide and death. We are confusing them more and more, due to our own confusion and painful pasts. We are projecting our own childhood traumas and agendas onto young kids while they collapse into confusion, mental health problems, and addiction. The pendulum swings from one extreme side to the other. We must find some balance.

Whatever your beliefs might be on the subject of sexuality, the point is that the science and research on such things is miles away. We have thrust our children into untested waters, and to me, it seems like we have done so merely to prove a point that kids can be whatever they want to be at an age where their brains aren't even fully formed.[50] We need to tackle the neglect our kids are facing regarding their identity and the foundations of sexuality and physical development. The thing we should be focused on is helping our children learn safely about their bodies and avoid the sexual content and trauma that causes so much pain and confusion as they grow.

Childhood sexual neglect leads to a future of shame and fear, and also unnecessarily disorients a child to what should be common and normal stages of life and development. The research and studies are all so new. Who knows how many issues and how much confusion is caused by a simple lack of safe discussion and education? My attempt here is to start a conversation in our homes and in our society about what it would look like if our children *were not* neglected and did not live in shame and fear of their own sexuality throughout childhood and adolescence. What if they felt comfortable and knew how to protect themselves online and in person? What if we would have known? How different would life be?

I mentioned it in the first few pages of my introduction, but this would be a really good place to pause and check out my TedTalk for some more context on this topic before continuing. Whether you watch or not, here is the most basic rundown of what I say:

---

[50] This goes back to our conversation on brain structure and formation in chapter 5.

Clint Davis

- I am a counselor, Trauma and Sex-Addiction Therapist, and a sexual trauma survivor myself
- My son's "Penis Rules": who can touch them, who can see them naked, and when and where this is appropriate
- Defining "sexual neglect": a child that grows up without age-appropriate and healthy conversations about sexual development, private parts, consent, and body safety
- We teach our kids safety and boundaries in many other aspects of our child's life, why not development?
- A sexually neglected child has long-term issues with their bodies, are unlikely to report abuse, and have trouble protecting themselves
- Children face dangers on the internet, streaming platforms, and video games even for content marketed to children - a child has likely seen pornographic content by 11 years old
- Digital Converts vs. Digital Natives - we need resources to reach and protect our children
- Bring awareness to these issues by having tough conversations and helping generations to avoid sexual trauma and abuse
- I use my story of shame to prevent shame in the future surrounding sex, sexual development, and our online lives
- Did your parents have these tough conversations with you? Are you having them with your children? Are you willing to be brave and stop this cycle of neglect?

Talking is simple, but it's not easy. The conversations we need to have the most are often the ones we are quickest to avoid or stumble over. Talking sounds easy until your child walks up to you and asks what masturbation means (they will probably use a term you might have to look up in Urban Dictionary) or your daughter questions what the point of menstruation is. It has truly helped me to realize my avoidance of tough conversations actually constitutes a form of neglect towards my boys.
We talk all the time as humans, but I want to apply my clinical knowledge and personal experiences to help us all hone in on the things we should be talking about with our children or kids in our care.

Reflection & Discussion

1. Based on this definition of "sexual neglect," do you think you experienced this in your own childhood?

2. As a parent, do you see any ways you might be sexually neglecting your own children? If so, how might you re-correct and start fresh?

3. What do you know about your child's digital life? How aware are you of the dangers in videos, apps, or video games?

4. Take a moment to reflect on your own fears regarding your past and present. How might you do things differently in your home than you experienced in your childhood household?

7. Little Kids, Big Conversations

When you talk to your children about tough things, you give them the tools they need to navigate life's challenges.
- Mr. Rogers

Now that you understand what childhood sexual neglect is, I want to cover some of the conversations we have to have to build better bridges between our children and ourselves.
Here is the simple but profound truth: without healthy and age-appropriate conversations, children grow up with no knowledge that things like masturbation, menstruation, or erections are things that *will* happen to their body. As a result, their first experience with these normal and healthy developmental milestones is met with shame, fear, and surprise, which is quite possibly what you experienced with these biological occurrences in your own childhood. If so, then you experienced childhood sexual neglect. Maybe that has affected you into adulthood, or maybe it hasn't. Either way, there is a different path we can take with more resources and greater understanding of a child's brain, and this new path can help us raise kids that are informed, equipped, and who trust us to give them honest guidance.

Experiencing biological changes alone or without proper information or support, can lead a child to anxiety, depression, and even addiction in their present and future. As parents, it is vitally important for us to have talked with our children about these things *before* they happen, before they are left alone with other children or adults, and certainly before they are allowed on devices. This section is not written in stone, and it is not meant to be a one-size-fits-all script. Children develop at different rates, and life sometimes forces our hands sooner or later than we would like. The goal is to try to time these conversations right before the next stage of development. This allows the parent and child to build trust between each other so that throughout the process of growing up, discussing difficult topics becomes easier and more common.

One more thing on this before we get into specifics. Being up front and honest with your children, especially when the topics are tough or awkward, will build trust in them when the really difficult questions come their way. They will know you are telling them the whole truth, which is a priceless gift as they grow older. Remember, authenticity is one of the keys to raising a successful and healthy child. Alright, let's get into some of these conversations.

Menstruation

One of the most common examples of a conversation we don't have is menstruation. So many women did not have a discussion about their first period until it actively happened to them. I have heard many painful stories about girls who did not know this was going to happen, and when it did, they had a horrible experience that caused them terrible fear. They thought something was wrong or even that they might be dying. This negative and completely avoidable experience can cause them to associate their private parts and their normal female development to shame and fear.

For example: A youth pastor told me of a time when he was on a retreat with middle schoolers. One of the children started her period in the shower. She started crying and thought something was wrong. The other girls, some of which had already started and knew what was happening, started laughing and making fun of her. They threw pads, liners, and tampons at her as she lay in the fetal position crying for help. Once the adults were told, the damage was done. This little girl left camp and went home traumatized, never to come back to that church again. This is a totally avoidable trauma. If we can have these conversations, we can prevent anyone going through something like this ever again!

How many adult or teenage females reading this still view their period and menstrual cycle as "gross"? This very *wrong* belief starts from childhood and as I stated, is extremely preventable. Avoiding the vagina and menstruation topic with our daughters can lead to negative body image and stunt their sexual development for years into the future.

Since this conversation often isn't held in a safe environment or in private, it instead occurs in group settings...a classroom, pool parties or sleepovers where girls and children aren't always so kind. This is a nightmare for a young girl. Due to a lack of parental involvement or preparation, other adults have to intervene and help these girls process and address what should be a normal and healthy bridge into womanhood. **If we know better, we can do better.** As parents, we must do better and get educated on how to have these talks with our daughters, both mothers and fathers. We must get past our own shame and misunderstanding in order to help our children attain a healthy view of themselves and their bodies from the start. This type of experience for little girls is just one example of childhood sexual neglect, and I am here to say that this does not have to be the case for your child. Be bold, and address periods and menstruation with your little girls ahead of time. Walk them gently through the process, what it means, how it shows we are developing in a healthy way as women! If you are a female, you are the expert on this! Help guide them with all that you have learned, perhaps knowledge you weren't given when you were a young woman.[51]

For those that did grow up without such discussions and experienced fear and perhaps still suffer from wrong assumptions about yourself, I hope that you will seek counseling to repair the damage done. You are not gross whatsoever, and you should have never had to experience that shame.

On a positive note, I am happy to report this is an area of recent growth in our culture. I have seen women have "period parties" where they educate girls on the healthy ways to handle and address this normal developmental experience. More communal support and education can minimize the shame and negativity surrounding these experiences for little girls. Making periods common and acceptable to talk about is a first huge step in the right direction.

---

[51] If you need more specific guidance on this topic and how to address it with your daughter, here is a wonderful link for just that! -
https://mytruegirl.com/blog/how-do-i-talk-to-my-daughter-about-her-period/

Building Better Bridges

Let me be very clear about something, though. As important as our communities are in raising our children and helping to educate them – on this issue and many others – these dialogues *must* begin in the home, with a trusted relative, friend, or guardian. None of us should rely solely on social institutions to guide our kids' most crucial conversations.

Consider the specifics of a conversation surrounding periods with your daughter or son. I include sons here because they too need to understand how amazing the menstruation process is, for the sake of their sister, their mom, and their future wife. Boys need to see it in a positive light and appreciate the difficulty and value a period brings.

In such a conversation you can use flowers or other animals to show the differences in male and females. You can show that they bloom and produce different materials like blood, pollen or babies. God has designed boys and girls to be different, but good. As a girl reaches the age of 8-10, she will start to bloom herself. The first sign is the development of breasts. This is typically a couple of years before her first cycle happens. Take her aside and talk to her about the beauty of God's design for her. How she is made special and amazing. Tell her there is nothing to be ashamed of, but that she has a right to protect herself and be protected by others. Refer back to "talking to the right brain" chapter. It is helpful to validate her feelings of disgust or fear because, in truth, anything new is quite frightening. But be sure to help redirect those over time. Watch for the developmental signs like pubic hair and growth spurts. Then you can begin to talk to her about where babies come from and how her body will be given a great gift. Her first period is a gift and sign of her ability to be a mother one day, if she so chooses. Tell her about how special this is and how amazing her body is that it can create and carry another human being. Make the focus on hope, life, and positivity. Also normalize that in most cases bleeding and blood can be scary, but in this one is a sign of the possibility of life. It also makes it possible for us to follow God's desire for us to be fruitful and multiply. In a blog by True Girl, they give a wonderful idea to give your daughter a gift basket full of goodies like a "new bra, mini-pads, regular pads, teen-formula pain pills, body spray, books, chocolate, heat wraps, and a letter welcoming her to womanhood. Also, consider including a small zippered canvas or fabric bag that's filled with the basics so she can discreetly take it to school." You can put sticky notes with simple instructions for each one, but also understand this might be overwhelming at the beginning. Walk her through the steps and uses of different products. As a mom, you are a period expert and should pass down guidance to your daughter! As a dad you can be encouraging and positive!

Erections

How about the discussions we have with our sons about getting their first erection or nocturnal emission? Is it something we are talking about with our young boys? If you have sons, you know that erections can start from when they are toddlers and they are constantly touching and pulling their penis. For the most part, this is a typical part of development. We must educate and redirect them without shaming them. Problems come into play when we start to project our own fears and trauma into the situation or when we do not know what is healthy behavior.

Let me give you another example of a common situation and how I addressed it. When my oldest son was 4 or 5 years old, he would swim in the bathtub and rub his penis on the bottom. One day he got an erection and stood up crying that it hurt. We had a conversation about blood flow and how his penis is for using the bathroom. I told him that if he continued to rub it with his hand or on an object, it would fill up with blood and hurt. "This is called an erection, buddy." This was a simple conversation we have had 3 or 4 times over the course of the last 5 years. Not always easy, and yes, sometimes awkward, but I would rather feel a small amount of discomfort now than have my son face shame and confusion later. He didn't make a fuss about it or ask too many questions. I let him know that I understood what was going on, that it was totally normal, and that he didn't have to feel weird talking to me about it.

On another occasion, he was rubbing his penis under his blanket while we were reading. I gently asked him to put his hands on the top of the sheets and explained that it is normal to touch his private parts, but we don't want to get in the habit of doing it mindlessly or when someone else is right beside him. My oldest is 8 years old now, and he has no negative memories or feelings about these conversations. As his parent, I have taught him about what is appropriate and what is not in an age sensitive way. Obviously, more in-depth and mature conversations will happen as he gets older when those topics become appropriate for him. When he was little, though, such conversations took place so my child would know what was happening and wouldn't be forced to build his own narrative, alone and without guidance.

This did not happen for many of us. You may have experienced normal sexual development or play without preparation or confidence. If this has never been addressed it is very likely to be affecting you and your children.

I want to quickly explain what I mean by age-appropriate. I want to address topics with my own children as they arise or before, but I also don't think we should be talking to our three-year-olds about masturbation. I am, however, advising parents to take full advantage of conversational opportunities that will lead into older and more mature discussions as your child grows up. Imagine I never said anything to my sons in their early years, and when they get into their teens, neither of them have any foundation to address masturbation or sexual desire in a healthy way. Imagine then that they are alone and ashamed to talk to me, because by not talking to them, I have already communicated "we don't talk about those things."

The erection conversation will eventually lead into the conversation about where babies come from, what sex is, and a host of other questions. For toddlers and little kids who ask all manner of these questions, a short and simple explanation is appropriate, and they will usually move on. When we respond to these difficult questions with a lie about how the stork brought them or some other make-believe tale, we are expressing our own insecurities, embarrassment, or lack of confidence. "White lies" like this don't protect our children and will not prepare them for a healthy conversation down the road. What it does teach them is that Mommy and Daddy feel weird about these subjects and that something about these things is weird, strange, or taboo. Telling the simple truth is always better than a complex lie that we will have to explain later anyway.

Clint Davis

Nocturnal Emission

If you don't know what nocturnal emission is or have never heard the term, it is also known as a wet dream.[52] In REM sleep, or during a stressful dream, a child going through puberty can have an orgasm while sleeping. You might expect nocturnal emissions to begin around the same time as puberty or possibly later, however, not everyone experiences them. Regardless of if your child deals with this or not, it is helpful for a child to know it's a possibility in order to avoid fear, disgust, or shame if it does happen. We must understand and teach our children that nocturnal emissions are involuntary, incredibly common, and signal nothing bad about them whatsoever.

Many people have told me horror stories of their first experience with this normal developmental milestone. 90% of the people I have talked to did not know it was going to happen and felt gross, scared, and ashamed when it did. They did not know who to talk to about this and if it was right or wrong. For many Christians especially, the conversation about nocturnal emission – let alone masturbation – has never taken place, and so children going through it feel like they are sinning or have done something wrong. This is especially true for children from religious families. This also very likely prevents children from seeking out their parents when big and scary things come up like a period, an orgasm, and so much more. In reality, none of our biological changes have to be met with shock and disgust.

Talking about these things in a normal and healthy way is so fundamental to raising healthy and prepared children. If well over 90% of people haven't had such conversations then this may contribute to the major identity and sexuality problems in every age group. Look around you, and I feel confident you will see it too. Once we are aware, it is almost impossible not to see a lack of discussion all around us! Once we are aware of the things we aren't saying, it will become more and more

---

[52] For more information on this very normal phenomenon, here is a link for you - https://www.sciencedirect.com/topics/psychology/nocturnal-emission

111

obvious the ways that we missed out on some massively important conversations in our own childhoods.

So, I saved discussing the "sex talk" for the last in this chapter, but most experts say the sex conversation needs to happen a bit sooner than discussions about nocturnal emission and masturbation. However, if exposure to these events happens sooner than expected, try not to panic. Just change the timeline up a bit and address anything that comes up as it occurs with gentleness and love.

If a child has been abused, had child-on-child sexual play, or seen pornography or sexual content before puberty, then they will likely be more aroused and stimulated which can quickly move up the timeline. We will cover this later, but as a reminder: if or when trauma or exposure happens, having a relationship where conversations are normal and safe can lead to quicker recovery and limit the lies that these events can cause. These lies and shameful thoughts are what lead to all types of negative behaviors in the future.

Sex/Intercourse

As I mention the words "sex talk," I can feel you cringing through the pages. You are probably thinking of the countless movies, books, and TV shows that make fun of the sex talk, or perhaps even remembering the awkwardness of your own sex talk experience from years ago. You might have already tried and it did not go well. I hope this will help you try again with better tools and understanding.

You can briefly breathe a sigh of relief because this topic requires more than a few paragraphs. In a few pages, there is a full chapter that covers having the sex talk with your kids, whether they are younger or if you have put off the conversation for fear of what to say or how to say it. That chapter will go deeper into how-to's, more specific suggestions, and a timeline of when to talk about what topics. When we get there, feel free to bookmark that chapter to reference later!

I will just give a few overall words of advice here. We often use the same tactics with discussing sex with our children as we do pregnancy. Calling sex "the birds and the bees" or saying babies come from a stork simply won't cut it. We make things unnecessarily childish and weird, while increasing the awkwardness for everyone involved. It is also just a pattern of lying for no good reason. Not to mention, we deprive our kids of any real and helpful information, communicating to them they aren't mature enough for the truth or even worse that we as parents are not confident in our knowledge.

The point I am making is that due to generations of childhood sexual neglect, these conversations have become taboo and uncomfortable. They are only uncomfortable because we do not talk to our kids about anything related to these subjects and developmental events until they are older. If they grow up having conversations all along the way and we normalize Mom and Dad as being the primary voice in these conversations, then these topics don't have to be very awkward at all. Most of the time when I hear that these conversations go badly, it is because it was the first one of its kind well into a child's teen years.

Obviously, there is more to be said on this, so we will talk about this again in Chapters 13 and 14. See you there in a bit.

I am not trying to give you a false sense of security here. Each conversation mentioned, and a myriad of others, are difficult. Trust me, I know. The thing is, though, that we are making them even more difficult than we realize, but we can change that.

The problem is that as our kiddos grow, we aren't building bridges between ourselves and our child to sustain the weight of these heavy conversations. If we can start discussing body parts and sexual development early and in small daily ways, our child will become more comfortable talking with us about those things, will be willing to come to us for answers and advice, and can trust us if something bad happens. Sex talks with our kids don't have to be scary or uncomfortable, nor do they have to take place once in their entirety. They can be just like the hundreds of other conversations we have already had with them in day-to-day family life.

Building Better Bridges

Let me say again that there is no perfect way to talk about these things, but I believe that if we don't, we might be sentencing them to what so many of us dealt with as we grew up: fear, shame, and uncertainty with ourselves and others. Think of how you introduce your kids to the ABCs. Do you wait until they are able to talk, read, and comprehend language? Or, do you start slowly, mimicking alphabet sounds and pointing at the written letter, singing them the ABC song long before they utter a word?

We give kids context and time, and before we know it, our child is saying the alphabet and is comfortable and confident doing so. They learn from us, watching and copying us from day one. In education, this is called building a scaffolding: a temporary support that adults or other competent peers offer when a person is learning a new skill or trying to accomplish a task. We help a child to complete a task or move through a stage of life that they could not or should not do on their own by being beside them and guiding them through it. If we do this with language, tying shoes, using a fork and spoon, on and on, why should we not employ the same tools for something as critical as a child's sexual development?

Of course, we can eventually move past strictly talking and allow our teens to have experiences on their own, without having to guide them through each and every step of their lives. By establishing trust and support early and often, they will know how to respond and who to come to when they have a negative or confusing experience – even into adulthood! (Thank goodness for that.)

Point being: when we have prepared our kids their entire childhoods for conversations about their bodies and sexual development, then the conversations are not forced or uncomfortable later. Also, remember that order is important. Just like the ABCs, we want to have these conversations earlier rather than later. Before a) someone else tells them, b) before they hear about it secondhand through media or the internet, or c) before something physically or emotionally traumatic happens to them. We have tools to offer them before they are exposed to anything dangerous. We absolutely must use those tools.

Similarly, on the topic of order, we don't want to try to have a conversation about masturbation before we have a conversation about sex. This can confuse the function of both and the way we are wired to develop. Fear not, we'll cover more on this in a little bit.

For now, I would just stress that having these conversations regularly, gently, and at the right time is of utmost importance. We have only talked about a few of the main questions our kids will have as they grow, but for my folks who love a good list, here is one that encompasses more of the foundational topics we should be addressing in age-appropriate ways. In no particular order:

Values & Beliefs | Erections | Masturbation | Menstruation | Sexuality | Safe Sex | Safe and Unsafe Touch | Sexual Boundaries | Consent | Private Parts | Nocturnal Emissions | Pubic Hair | Body Odor | Hygiene

You'll notice I included the topic of Values and Beliefs. I know every home is different, with varying spiritual, cultural, and moral beliefs in place. Whatever your foundational beliefs may be, conversations about belief structures and core values are crucial to have alongside all these other sensitive subjects. Our various beliefs will guide us in how we address these things, but whatever the beliefs in your house, you must offer your children those perspectives as well. As with anything, kids will find endless information out in the world, and we should arm them with as much knowledge and understanding as we can before the world makes those decisions for us.

Regarding all of these subjects, as well as many of the ones to come, one of the biggest issues with the human body today is shame. Sadly, I'm sure you know what I mean. You might feel the truth of it yourself. Our identity has become rooted in how our bodies look or perform. This is not the truth. Our worth and identity doesn't lie within our bodies – not their size or shape, and definitely not what our bodies have been through, at the hands of someone else or ourselves. One of our best friends, Ashley, is a dietitian with our practice, and she has taught us so much about the damage done to children and adults.[53] As believers, we need to teach our

---

[53] I highly recommend looking Ashley up at www.fulfillednutritiontherapy.com!

children that our worth and value is found in the creator of the universe. For me, my identity comes from who Jesus says I am, and nothing more or less than that. I lean on what scripture says I am. Beautifully and wonderfully made. Worth dying for. Fully known and fully loved. God says these things about you, too. Really. The Bible teaches that nothing can separate us from the love of God.[54] No sexual abuse. No porn or addiction. No adultery. No lust or assault. *Nothing*. Not even neglecting our children.

Our bodies are not perfect, but He uses us anyway. I don't know if you teach the scriptures in your home, but either way, *please* do not live in your own fear or shame. Don't let a painful past stop you from carving a new path for yourself and your family. You are still loved and worthy, and you can be an active participant in the development and safety of your own child and their friends and families. You can help create a future for them that is free of shame.

As we arrive at the end of this section, you might be feeling many things. Discomfort over the subject matter, frustration that your parents didn't talk to you about these things in a healthy way, fear that you might influence your child in a negative way or say the wrong thing, shame that you missed these conversations with your own kids, or possibly all of the above.

First and foremost, take a deep breath. I truly recommend speaking with a trusted friend, spiritual advisor, or professional counselor about your feelings, because those feelings are valid. But being in your shoes myself, I have a few things to say to you. As you need, feel free to grab some water, take some deep breaths, and give yourself a break.

---

[54] "For I am sure that neither death nor life, nor angels nor rulers, nor things present nor things to come, nor powers, nor height nor depth will be able to separate us from the love of God through Christ Jesus our Lord." -Romans 8:38-39 (ESV)

Reflection & Discussion

1. Did your parents have any of these conversations with you? How did those go, and do you want to do something similar or different?

2. Have you started having any of these conversations with your own kids?

3. If you haven't had any of these conversations because there is fear for you, where do you think those fears might come from? Are there ways you can push past your discomfort?

4. How are you feeling after reading this chapter? Does it cause negative emotions for you to think of avoiding these topics as neglectful?

8. Overcoming Your Own Barriers

When people don't feel safe, they don't share. Fear is the biggest barrier to conversation.
- Glennon Doyle

Hey. For the folks reading this that are already uncomfortable, or for those of you that get anxious, uncomfortable, and fearful merely thinking of talking to your kids about these things...*you are not alone.* Understand that we have barriers to conducting the conversations discussed above, as well as barriers to the conversations that are yet to come, but also know that barriers are there to be climbed and overcome.

I want you to understand that one of the main reasons we feel this discomfort is simply because we are adults. We have our own histories with sexuality, neglect or abuse, or just our own private parts and sexual desires. We have grown into eroticism and adult sexuality, whether in a healthy way or not, and it can make us avoid those subjects with our young children.

I want to ease your worries, at least a little. Your child does not think about these things in the same way you do. Hopefully, and in most cases, a child is a blank slate when it comes to the areas of sexuality and private parts. When *you* say the word penis, vagina, or masturbation, you are flooded with your sexual thoughts, memories, and experiences. Good and bad. When we teach our *children* about these things, they, hopefully, do not have the past that we do, and they don't get overcome with those same sexual thoughts and feelings. If they do have negative experiences, then it is even more important for you to find professional guidance to help your child through the necessary conversations in order to make sure they are learning the lessons you are trying to teach and not learning lies about themselves due to their own trauma. This is especially true for foster parents and parents who have adopted children.

Unless they have been exposed to adult content, abused, or taught differently, a kid will (for the most part) think of their penis or vagina like they think of an arm or a leg. They will only feel uncomfortable when we frame it that way. They may act silly or bashful because they know it is an area to be protected, but they will hopefully not lean towards confusion and fear of those areas. When we normalize these dialogues and make them commonplace in our homes, then our children learn to feel comfortable and confident. This is why it is so important to start early with these talks so that they build on themselves over time. What's more, as we gain the courage to talk candidly, we become more comfortable and confident as well, perhaps even contributing to healing of our own.

If you are reading along and realizing the sexual neglect in your own childhood, I hope you realize you aren't the only one, and you are not to blame. So many adults today have experienced some form of this neglect, myself included. You might be wondering why these things happened to you and why your parents did not know to have these conversations or why they had them poorly. I understand, but the point of this book is not to trigger people into being mad at their parents. It is not to blame our parents for everything in our lives. The point is, however, to bring awareness to things we may need to work on and be freed from, so that we can have these conversations with our own children.

To have certain discussions in our family while we are living in shame and bondage from our own past would be incredibly difficult, impossible even. The thing is, we must have a healthy view of these things ourselves so that we protect our children from the same struggles we faced. To get to a place of health will look different for every single person and family: forgiveness for yourself and your parents, painful confrontation, setting new boundaries, and so many more roads that lead the way to healing. Whatever those steps are for you, I hope you take them. For yourself and for your present or future children. You and your family deserve it.

If we don't recover, we can look around and see the overwhelming consequences for individuals, families, and our society as a whole. Postponing our healing and avoiding the hard conversations will just ensure the cycle goes on turning. If the mere existence of this book is any indication, I can confidently say it's not too late for us to turn things around and learn a better way forward. There is cause for hope.

In an effort to dispel any anger you might have toward your parents for avoiding hard conversations, and as a way to demystify some of your own fears, I am going to give you a list of reasons sexual neglect might have occurred in your life. This is relevant if you are a parent who is trying to avoid these pitfalls in your parenting, but this is also a guide for those who experienced neglect as children and want an explanation of why. I hope this will soften your heart and possibly give you some conversation topics as you journey towards healing.

>*Ignorance:* Lack of awareness of certain tools and no understanding of the importance of having certain conversations with our children. Many well-intentioned people just do not even know what should be addressed or done before it is too late

>*Fear:* Fear of doing or saying the wrong thing or causing more problems. We choose avoiding tough topics and put them off until the situation or issue causes conflict

>*Shame:* Issues exist internally that need healing, and we shut down or overreact because of personal shame or embarrassment. We might have our own insecurity and history with certain topics that sends us into fight, flight or freeze

>*Avoidance:* Daunted by fear and awkwardness, we continually postpone the conversations hoping they will just go away or someone else will have them. We minimize the seriousness of the situations or over normalize them so that we can avoid addressing them

>*Generational brokenness*: Multiple generations avoided tough conversations, and now we have no frame of reference for healthy discussions and don't even know they're an option. Society continues to change quickly and the ways that these

conversations need to happen seem to be changing faster than we can keep up

Absence of a healthy model: Most commonly, we don't have an example where biological and sexual discussions were conducted, especially not in a healthy or uplifting way. Many people view sexuality as bad or dirty or act as if sexuality doesn't affect anyone and an all out free for all is acceptable

Lack of community support: Due to many things including radical individualism, the increased divorce rate, death, or illness, many people are parenting alone and having to fulfill both parental roles with no support and encouragement from a healthy community. Nor can institutions be solely relied upon to disseminate good information on particularly sensitive topics

Changes in culture: In a culture that swings to the extremes and is reactive to old ways, we have been so neglected, traumatized, and even politicized that having these conversations causes ostracism and severe judgment, even without saying anything harmful or unhealthy. Few people can have a dialogue about this topic without being reactive and aggressive

Advances in technology: With the rapid evolution of the internet and the smartphone, many of these conversations are having to be had earlier and more intensely. This generation's children are so overly exposed and manipulated that we must have conversations with our children earlier because someone at school or on their favorite show is going to be talking about it or alluding to it

A lack of resources, research, or materials: Previous generations of parents and leaders didn't have a therapist or a professional to turn to in these areas. There were literally no trauma therapists or parenting books. Without all the books, podcasts, or resources to teach them how to navigate certain issues, they simply had to work with what they had. Even with the increase of resources in recent years, we are still way behind when it comes to acting on the information

This list is by no means exhaustive, rather it is a place to start conversations over coffee, or dinner with friends and family, in an effort to establish a foundation and culture that is willing to educate on sex, body parts, and sexual development in a healthy and productive way. If such discussions also help you recover from your own childhood and cultivate empathy and perspective for your parents, then I sincerely hope that you can courageously bring these topics into therapy or your pastor's office and find the freedom you deserve. Freedom that you can pass on for generations to come. If you are a parent or grandparent and your instinct is to get defensive or shame yourself, I pray that this list allows you to see that we know it was not all your fault and that you may have been doing the best you could with what you had. Of course, as many of us know, in some cases parents were not doing the best they could and were just being intentionally neglectful or abusive. I strongly doubt that those people are reading this book, but perhaps some of you reading had parents like this. If so, I am so sorry. I can't begin to fathom your experience, and I don't know every detail. What I do know is that God doesn't command us to forgive for no reason. We forgive because He first forgave us, but also because carrying that weight will only stand to hurt ourselves. Forgiveness does not mean full reconciliation or even being in a relationship. It means understanding and letting go. Reconciling can only happen when the person who harmed you takes responsibility, makes amends, and changes their behaviors. Check out *Families and Forgiveness* by Nicole E. Zasowski and Terry Hargrave for further discussion on this topic.[55] I hope this information gives you tools and encouragement to create a different life for yourself and your children.

The next set of conversations we will talk about deal more directly with avoiding abuse through education and preparation. Know that I don't talk about any of these things lightly, nor do I mention things just to be provocative. I honestly think the best way to inspire us to action is to know the facts, however difficult or scary they may be.

---

[55] Zasowski, Nicole and Hargrave, Terry. *Families and Forgiveness,* Routledge, 2017.

Reflection & Discussion

1. Do you feel any frustration or disappointment in your parents for the way they approached (or didn't approach) these topics with you?

2. What are the ways you can learn from your own childhood experiences?

3. What do you think the barriers are in your own heart to openly discussing sensitive subjects with your spouse or children? What would it take to boost your confidence?

4. Who are the peers and trusted friends in your life that would be willing to walk a hard path with you?

5. What changes would you be willing to make in your home? What changes go too far?

9. Sexual Abuse and the Talks That Prevent It

Preventing sexual abuse requires education, awareness, and action.
- Kristen Houser

Earlier, we discussed why age-appropriate biological/developmental conversations are integral to preventing our children from having unhealthy views of themselves, their sexuality, or their sexual development. Here, I will talk about why abuse is most common in sexually neglected children and why those children are less likely to report to us when such abuse, exposure, or trauma happens.

Beyond what we have already discussed, there are three more topics we often don't cover with our children. A lack of instruction regarding body safety, proper terms for private parts, and consent considerably increases the risk our child will be abused, whether in person or online. If we want to lower this risk in our own children and see positive changes in the abuse statistics in our society, then talking about these three topics is vitally important.

Before we approach how to talk about those three things, though, let's address a few truths about sexual abuse, some of the statistics, and their ramifications.

As a clinician, I have worked with hundreds of men and women who have experienced sexual neglect and abuse. Given the statistics, there is a great chance that someone reading this book has unresolved trauma or an abuse experience in their life.

First and foremost, if you have experienced abuse of any kind, whatever the circumstances may have been, I want to tell you right now how sorry I am. I want to tell you it was not your fault. Most of all, I want you to know there is hope for you to find healing, and there are tools for you to prevent the same trauma from affecting your children, both now or in the future. I pray and hope that you won't define your life with shame or with what happened to you and that you will get the help you need to recover from your trauma and abuse.

Because many of these topics can be heavy and triggering, please take your time, and use your supports. I'm afraid I can't make this subject less painful, but I can tell you that you are not alone. You are not uniquely broken. God sees you as beautifully and wonderfully made.[56]

Brace yourself for a sad truth.
Sexual abuse is not rare. Research shows that 1 out of 3 girls and 1 out of 5 boys experiences sexual abuse by 18 years old. Research also reveals that 50% of abusers commit their first offense before 18.[57] This means that they were only kids themselves when the abusive behavior began. Hurt people hurt people, remember? This is partly why the topic of sexual neglect is so important and why it's imperative that we avoid it early. Most of the traumas we experience as children are negative child-on-child interactions due to childhood sexual neglect. These are usually the experiences that we never tell anyone else about and which many people carry to their grave. Unfortunately, these harmful experiences color the way we see ourselves and the world from a very young age, and this negative perspective is crippling our entire society.

Additionally, abuse doesn't often occur at the hands of strangers. I have worked in human trafficking for almost a decade, and although they are horrible crimes that do happen, the abduction and kidnapping of children are both incredibly rare. Yet, when my child walks around the aisles at Target or wants to ride his bike to the store, overwhelming terror fills my heart in an instant. I am afraid of the wrong things. We all are. See this segment of an article by Paula Fass:

> "Our fears about the sexual abuse of children—both real and perceived—grew sharply in the turbulent context of the more liberated sexual behaviors following the 1960s, among other

---

[56] I praise you, for I am fearfully and wonderfully made. Wonderful are your works; my soul knows it very well. -Psalm 139:14

[57] https://laurenskids.org/national-statistics/

factors like the boom of employment for married women in the 70s and our culture's increased focus on homosexuality in the 80s.

By then, we were exposed to the publicity surrounding the kidnappings of Adam Walsh, Etan Patz, Kevin White, and Jacob Wetterling – children who lived in all parts of the country, in communities large and small. We began to register how deep our fears ran with respect to child abductions as sexual crimes. The worst crime we could imagine. Parents of victims during this period led the charge for the creation of the National Center for Missing and Exploited Children. This was the movement that brought us faces on the back of milk cartons and posters at the local grocery store."[58]

Despite the media coverage and the fear it instilled in us, child abduction, especially by a stranger, is extremely rare in comparison to childhood abuse. I write all this not to diminish the tragedy of childhood kidnappings, but to help us discern between a perceived fear and the greater risk of sexual abuse happening right in our own backyards. For those who have experienced a missing or kidnapped child, I can't imagine the pain and fear associated with such an event. I am incredibly grateful for the focus on childhood abduction and the ways that attention has improved the statistics in that area. For tips on preventing abduction look at the notes at the end of this chapter. We do have a major problem with human trafficking in our world. I do not take that for granted. I have been personally fighting this battle with *The Hub:Urban Ministry* for a decade[59]. I have also had the privilege of speaking at the *South Central U.S. Human Trafficking Conference* for the last 4 years on stopping the demand side of this equation. For more information check out the resources we have in the footnotes.[60]

---

[58] Fass, Paula. "Child Kidnapping in America," *Origins: Current Events in Historical Perspective*, OSU, 2019.
[59] The is an amazing outreach program that does incredible work. - https://thehubministry.org/
[60] https://www.justice.gov/humantrafficking/resources

The goal of our conversation here, though, is to point to what is *more* likely to happen to our children and what we can do about it. If we are going to be afraid, we must be afraid of the right things. We are missing the sexual abuse happening right under our noses. Alarmingly, the YWCA tells us that upwards of 90% of sexual abuse is committed by someone the child and family know. A neighbor down the street, a friend at a sleepover, a teacher or leader at a summer camp. We know that adults abuse children, but much of this abuse is happening child-to-child due to a lack of education and understanding on crucial topics. Childhood sexual neglect at play, yet again.

Unfortunately, once a child experiences sexual abuse, if they don't get help or guidance, they can be more likely to go on to abuse other children. If we do not help them recover from their trauma and build new patterns of thinking, victims of childhood sexual assault may go on to be the offenders.

It shatters my heart when I hear about a 13-year-old being labeled as a predator or a molester. Yes, abusers are wrong for their actions no matter their age, but statistics show that it is highly likely they were victimized, playing out what has been done to them, and in great need of help. This especially true if a child is actively being abused, exposed to adult content and left to their own devices. Of course they have a high likelihood of acting those some things out on another child. Hurt people hurt people might just be the mantra of this chapter.

We have seen this cycle of hurt play out time and time again, but now we know better. We know that with counseling and support children can heal from their trauma, lower the likelihood of them acting those things out on others, and we can see an end to a painful cycle of abuse. With our help, children can change their arousal templates, learn better coping skills, and eliminate the shame and anger they feel because of their experiences. They will not have that opportunity, however, if we don't inform ourselves, gain the courage to discuss these difficult topics, and ask better questions. If we are not having conversations in a healthy and age appropriate way, then how are we going to have a healthy conversation when our worst nightmares happen? If we do not understand the basics of human sexual biology, how will we know what is not healthy or when things have gone off course? Caregivers do not have to be doctors, psychologists, therapists, or scientists to have a basic understanding of these things, we just need someone to tell us!

In my training as a certified sex addiction therapist, one of the most mind blowing things I learned about was the human arousal template. In all my work in undergrad, seminary, and graduate school I had never heard of one. This is a basic biological and genetic experience every human has and I had no clue. It made many of the struggles my clients had make so much sense. Hopefully it will do the same for you and your child. The goal is to bring awareness and understanding to you as a parent and an adult so that we can take a moment to assess how the past may or may not be affecting the present. So, let me quickly explain what an arousal template is and how it affects you and your child. In the context of psychology and human sexuality, an arousal template refers to an individual's unique pattern or template of stimuli that elicit sexual arousal and desire in them. It encompasses the specific characteristics, scenarios, or experiences that a person finds sexually stimulating.

The development of an arousal template is influenced by various factors, including personal experiences, cultural background, upbringing, and individual preferences. It can involve a wide range of stimuli, such as visual, auditory, tactile, or emotional cues. For example, someone may have a particular preference for certain physical attributes, specific activities, or particular fantasies that consistently trigger their sexual arousal.

Arousal templates are highly subjective and can vary significantly from person to person. What arouses one individual obviously will not have the same effect on another. These templates are shaped by both nature and nurture, reflecting a combination of innate predispositions, and learned associations.

Understanding one's own arousal template can be helpful in cultivating a fulfilling and satisfying sexual life. It allows individuals to identify and communicate their desires and preferences to their partners, leading to enhanced intimacy and sexual compatibility. It is important to note that arousal templates can evolve and change over time as individuals explore new experiences, develop new interests, or encounter different stimuli. This is why children's exposure to adult content and erotic material should be carefully monitored and also why we as adults should be mindful of the things we watch and expose ourselves to.

With that context in mind, imagine a child experiences erotic material, erotic touch, or any other sexual situation before puberty. This can shape the ways in which they are stimulated for the rest of their life, especially if this trauma or exposure is not addressed or corrected. If a child is supposed to be learning how to emotionally attach, regulate their emotions, and self-soothe in a non-sexual or non-erotic way, but they get abused or exposed to content that disrupts or alters this process, it can cause many problems including addiction and the pursuit of sexual situations they would have otherwise never desired. Due to this trauma and neglect, arousal states form inappropriately. Our culture and research is showing us that this phenomenon of early and inappropriate exposure is shaping generations of human beings to have arousal templates that are unhealthy and unaddressed. Now as far as consenting adults, I have no room to judge or critique your sexual proclivities or desires. You are free to do whatever you choose in private. I do want to educate people to look for root causes and ask yourself are my desires rooted in something healthy? Are these desires or the things that arouse me built on safe relationships or are they built on something from my past that I am desperately trying to avoid or that I am trying to control? If we are not aware, we can be acting out a form of repetitive compulsion. Repetitive compulsion, also sometimes called trauma reenactment, involves repeating physically or emotionally painful situations that happened in the past.

I want you to understand this because this is where shame can live and fester. When an adult or child is aroused by things that should not arouse them or that are toxic, it is important to understand that this is not a choice, but is an actual brain response to past trauma, exposure, or neglect. Yes of course, some unhealthy patterns and the acting on those patterns are a choice and a bad one, but the original wiring of those desires, if brought on from early trauma, exposure, or without consent is where the problem started.

Here are some ways trauma can disrupt an arousal template:

- *Negative associations:* Traumatic experiences can create negative associations with certain stimuli, activities, or contexts that were present during the trauma. These associations may trigger fear, anxiety, or aversion, leading to a decreased or altered response to previously arousing cues. This can be to sexual acts entirely. Many adult clients who complain of unhealthy sex lives fall into addiction, adultery, or divorce because of unresolved past traumas that their spouse has not recovered from. Preventing sexual trauma will increase the likelihood of healthy sexuality and relationships in the future.

- *Hyperarousal or hypervigilance:* Trauma can lead to a state of hyperarousal or hypervigilance, where individuals remain on high alert, anticipating potential threats or danger. This heightened state of arousal can interfere with their ability to relax and experience sexual pleasure. Lots of people who do not like physical touch or who are touch averse have suffered some trauma in their past. When touch is unsafe and consent was never given, it can shape a human being into someone who constantly tries to stay closed off for safety reasons.
- *Flashbacks or intrusive thoughts:* Trauma survivors may experience intrusive thoughts, memories, or flashbacks related to the traumatic event during sexual experiences. These intrusions can disrupt arousal and make it challenging to engage fully in sexual activities. A person may recall trauma from the past or pornographic images during sex with their partner that can disrupt this healthy process and turn it into a disaster.
- *Emotional numbness or dissociation:* Trauma can also result in dissociation, where individuals feel disconnected from their emotions or physical sensations. This disconnection can hinder the experience of pleasure and intimacy during sexual encounters. Not all, but many sex workers and prostitutes have survived by disassociation from their bodies during sex. The same can be said for a child who has experienced sexual content before they were age ready for it.
- *Trust and intimacy issues:* Trauma can erode trust and create difficulties in forming and maintaining intimate relationships. These trust and intimacy issues can manifest as challenges in establishing a safe and secure sexual environment, which is crucial for a healthy arousal response. Your nervous system has to be calm and relaxed in order to be present during healthy sex. Intimacy is not intimacy if one person is emotionally checked out.

Trauma affects individuals differently, and not everyone will experience the same disruptions to their arousal template. Additionally, the impact of trauma can vary in intensity and duration. One thing is clear, though. These disruptions can start from early childhood.

This topic might seem like a sidebar or something on the fringes, but maybe you see the effects of these things in your own marriage or relationships. I know that I have my own experiences in this area, and it is my fervent prayer that my sons won't go through the same things. Additionally, I know it's not just me seeing arousal template turmoil. It is something that has been right under our noses for years, even in pop-culture.

Take the song "Fat-Bottom Girls" by Queen.

When I was learning about how trauma affects arousal and sexual development, these lyrics hit me right in the gut and in the face. Sometimes we do not notice things until we have a better lens through which to see

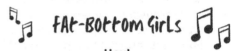

FAt-BoTTom Girls

Hey!
I was just a skinny lad
Never knew no good from bad
But I knew life before I left my nursery
Left alone with big fat Fanny
She was such a naughty nanny
Hey, big woman, you made a bad boy out of me

I've been singing with my band
Across the wire, across the land
I seen every blue eyed floozy on the way,
But their beauty and their style
Went kind of smooth after a while
Take me to them dirty ladies every time

them. "Fat-Bottom Girls" is a popular song that many people have belted out at the bar or a club or in a concert. It is even in the game "Guitar Hero World Tour" for kids to play! This in and of itself shows how numb we are to what we read, listen to, and take in as children and adults. Here are a few of the lyrics:

This is a prime example and description of a distorted arousal template. The boy in the song is sexually abused by his nanny in the nursery. Larger women, or "fat bottom girls", then become a turn on for him.[61] He goes all over the world and finds many beautiful women, but no matter

---

[61] This is NOT me saying liking someone larger is a problem. I am simply saying the lyrics exhibit how arousal templates get distorted from a young age.

how hard he tries, larger women are who get him the most stimulated. We have to wake up and we have to be mindful about how exposure and abuse shapes our desires and our sexual functioning in relationships and in the world. We have to stop ignoring root causes or minimizing these experiences and their effects. Children and adults alike deserve to grow to have a healthy view of themselves and others, in the context of sexual desires and arousal states. Saying things like "Well, this is just who I am, what I like, or what makes me happy," is 1) not a good enough explanation and 2) may be a reflection of what happened to us as children and neurological connections that we were never supposed to occur.

Quick example: I have had many clients with unhealthy sex lives or views of sexuality, tell me about the first time they were caught watching porn, masturbating, or engaging in child on child play. They tell me a common story of their parents yelling at them, shaming them or even spanking them for this behavior. Not all, but some, go on to enjoy pain with sex. They go on to like to dominate others sexually. They can go on to enjoy being shamed or shaming others during sexual interactions. Again, it is important to protect our children so that they can go on to have a full and healthy sexual experience as adults.

Now, disrupted arousal templates are not the case for everyone, but they are way more common than we think. If you find yourself, someone you know, or your child struggling in this area, I want you to know that therapy and recovery can help you rewire your brain and body, to find healthy and helpful sexual desires and functions. I do not want anyone to be ashamed of their sexuality or their choices, but having an understanding of where things come from can help us choose better places to go.

I feel confident that the mental health crisis we are experiencing right now is largely rooted in the sexual abuse and sexual neglect that people have experienced in their childhoods. This is an issue that is slowly being addressed, most often on an individual basis. The answer to making greater progress is for all of us to feel more comfortable having conversations with our kids about sex, body parts, sexual development, and boundaries. If we get equipped to have these discussions, the hope is that we can prevent instances of sexual abuse and exposure to adult content, but we can also respond more quickly if and when something happens.

I want to make one more thing clear. False reports of sexual abuse are *extremely* rare. If a child or an adult says someone abused them, then we should treat them like they are telling the truth. We can still hold the alleged offender in suspense until an official verdict is reached, but we should always support the child in a validating and emotionally healthy way. Same should go for adults. According to some researchers, false reports of abuse in adults is around 2%, and in children are even less.[62] Among types of abusers, one of the most difficult to face is Minor Attracted People (MAPS), or what some would call pedophiles. The science regarding why teens or adults become sexually attracted to children is limited, but we do know that it is linked to childhood sexual trauma and exposure to pornography. Naturally, I believe childhood sexual neglect is partly responsible as well. With the boom in access to the internet for younger and younger children, I feel like this area is one we ought to be especially aware of as we raise kids in the internet era and digital device era.

I want to talk a little about what it looks like for abusers getting counseling or help. If this is a discussion that will upset you, feel free to pass it by.

Despite how horrifying abuse might be, these warped tendencies can be addressed and even healed through trauma therapy and implementation of strict boundaries. Abusers were abused. Everyone was a child at one point and experienced things, good or bad. This means the more prevention and protection we can provide for our children in their early years, the less of them will grow to have unhealthy arousal templates and sexual preferences. The more we talk with our children about healthy perspectives on sex and their bodies, the less likely it will be for another source to feed lies to them or for another child to be harmed. I dream of a world where that is possible, and I hope that by exposing and demystifying such discussions, you will see that hope too. This does not

---

[62] Lonsway, Kimberly, et. al. "False Reports: Moving Beyond the Issue to Successfully Investigate and Prosecute NonStranger Sexual Assault," *The Voice,* The National Center for the Prosecution of Violence Against Women, Volume 3, No. 1.

mean there should not be major consequences and extreme supervision for child abusers, - there absolutely should be - but it also means that we have to realize that many child abusers have a traumatized inner-child living inside of them. For that inner child, redemption or recovery may be possible. Misunderstanding this is why our prison system is filled with people who do not find rehabilitation and end up becoming repeat offenders. Punishment does not change their trauma induced proclivities. We must find a way to give these abused children an off ramp, so they do not go on to either abuse other children or become adults who go on to do so online or in person. I know it turns all our stomachs to talk about this, but talk about it we must if we are to stop child abuse.

We all know I'm a stories guy, so let me give a real scenario to paint a very vivid picture for us.

A little boy gets raised by a single mother who has multiple sexual partners throughout his childhood. One of these men sexually abuses this little boy from the ages of 5-10. During this time, he is also exposed to pornography and sexual play with other children. Some of this behavior is initiated by the abused boy and some by other children who have also experienced similar trauma. As he moves into puberty he finds himself being aroused by younger children. This is confusing, but he doesn't know any better. He might have flashes of his own abuse or exposure or he might have been too young to remember it at all. At several events or sleepovers he acts out sexually with or attempts to play with other children in sexual ways. His parents do not know so they allow him to sleep in the bed with his cousins and friends. They play alone for hours at a time and they have open ended devices with no monitoring. This continues to shape his arousal template and causes him to search the internet for similar things that he experienced. He feels powerful and aroused by being in control of sexual situations, unlike when he was being forced into it by his mom's boyfriend years before. He hides this in his teen years and shoves it way down in his memory. By 17 years old, he finds himself still looking at child pornography online, finding it difficult to know any other way. He tries to white knuckle his abusive tendencies and swears to God he won't do it again.

That's not a fun story to read. I know. But tell me at what point in this narrative could he have gone to someone for help and not be arrested or prosecuted? At what point did this child know he could ask for help and be met with support and understanding? He has heard the friends and family talk about child molesters and how they should be executed or castrated. I can understand the pain and fear that motivates this type of rhetoric surrounding abusers. But this attitude also keeps hurt children isolated and alone in their desire to change or seek help, only prolonging their struggle and morphing it into something worse and worse over time.

Back to our little boy. Imagine that he moves into adulthood. He does not act on his desires or broken arousal template for years and eventually gets married and has a kid or two. One day he realizes that he is having thoughts and desires towards his child's young friends. I ask again - who does he go to for help? Who can he tell his story to in order to be met with understanding, compassion, and empathy? He truly wants to stop having these desires and wants to change. What programs are available to change his desires and heal his trauma? Where can he go? Sadly without a proper avenue for help, what happens is that he eventually abuses these children and becomes the same monster that hurt him. I fear there is no off ramp for these people.

I want to make abundantly clear that adults who molest children need consequences and accountability. They need to suffer punishment to some degree or another. They also should be assessed for if recovery is even possible. If not then they should be kept away from society forever. There are evil people out there without empathy, sympathy or compassion. Typically they were created and not born that way, as we discussed, but sometimes there are those that just do not have the ability to change. I agree we should lock them up and throw away the key. I write this short, but extremely heavy section as a reminder of who a child can turn into if we do not protect and equip them. I also want to point out that people's behaviors do not usually happen in a vacuum. It is not like the story is, life went well and people are protected and then they start cheating, watching porn, or sexually abusing people. They start out as innocent kids who get abused or neglected, without help and support, they turn into very broken adults. These stories are many of the people you know. For anyone, but especially Christ-followers, it is crucial that we remember that God is still in the business of healing, restoration, and resurrection. We are all his children and he wants to save each and every one of us from living broken lives if we will repent and turn to Him.

As our society continues to accept different things as "normal" and we go on pushing the line of what is tolerable, I fear more young people will be exposed to things that cause trauma, and where there is trauma, there is the potential for abuse. As we change language and make exceptions, we do so to our own peril. We cannot just accept that some people are attracted to children. We cannot just accept that some people are "born this way," without having the ability to assess and determine if trauma and abuse has played a role in their development. We must keep the safety and protection of women and children at the forefront of our minds. Every civilization that ever imploded, did so shortly after women and children became less protected and supported. This is not to say that men are not equally worthy of protection, but unfortunately, when powerful people come from abuse, the powerless are the ones that get destroyed. I fully believe that God will one day restore Heaven and Earth and that we will no longer experience abuse, sexual trauma, or exposure, but until that day, our job is to fight and push and give voice to the voiceless. This is a way to bring heaven to earth now! I hope that you clearly hear that in this book and become part of a solution that extends far into the future.

I know as individuals, we can feel powerless against a giant and terrifying phenomenon like abuse. I know that merely talking about it doesn't feel like enough and that simple awareness won't help. But what else is there? Talking, discussing, and communicating with our kids is our first and greatest defense against trauma. Imagine the life-changing impact of just being honest with our children, helping them feel confident in their own development, and sharing with them the very tools that will protect them against abuse online and in person. With the right conversations, we can likely reduce the chances for childhood sexual abuse by 85%, if not more. Abusers are often not born overnight, and we have the power for change in our churches, schools, homes and communities. These big, scary, horrible things we have been talking about are all extremely preventable. If someone told me I had an 85% chance of winning the power ball tonight, I would be at the corner gas station this very minute buying a dozen tickets. Would I let my fear of driving stop me? How about the fact that I feel awkward at the register talking to the clerk? (These aren't my actual fears, per se, but you get the idea.) Only our fears stand between us and changing the statistics.

I hope talking about these things will prove how simple the discussions can be, help dispel your worries, and give you the tools you need to feel confident about the sexual safety of your child out in the world. I know after those scary and intense conversations you are ready for some practical steps. Let's dive in together. I'm a parent too, and I am right here with you.

Having healthy and age-appropriate conversations with our kids might seem overly simple, but it's the way we can change the world. If you have read this far, I am sure you see a theme emerging. You might think I'm being repetitive, which I understand. But what strikes me as odd, is that despite how easy these ideas are, we just don't see them being put into action. So maybe a little repetition isn't such a bad thing. As I said early on, all the talks I give show me that 95% of us did not have adequate discussions about sex, basic biology, and sexual development as we grew up. So, let's change things and start having those conversations. Let's have them gradually, consistently, and openly in order to show our children we aren't scared of things that are normal. **We as parents must build better bridges between ourselves and our children that can hold heavy things.**

What do those bridges consist of? There are countless things. Here, I will mention 3 more topics to examine with your children, and these in particular are crucial for avoiding the abuse that exists in our broken world - proper names for private parts, what it means to establish body safety and boundaries, and how to define consent.

Proper Names for Private Parts

One of the first things we must teach our children is proper terms for private parts. Using the real medical terms for penis, testicles, vagina, and scrotum, we remove the taboo or awkwardness from such body parts. We should be sensitive, no question, but our job is to show confidence and ease, not shame. We teach them that their private parts are the areas of their body beneath their underwear and swimsuits. All these parts of our body are healthy and good, but some are not for strangers and other friends to touch, look at or take pictures of. That is why they are called *Private* parts.

Using proper terminology is not insensitive, it's protective and necessary. As we teach our toddlers about fingers, toes, noses, and eyes, we must also normalize that their penis or vagina, nipples and breasts are all similarly normal, healthy, and beneficial to their overall bodies. These particular parts are private and not meant to be shown to everyone, but not because they are bad or dirty. When we talk about them, we need to lump them together with all the other parts of their bodies: normal and designed for certain purposes![63]

Parents often hesitate to use biological or sexual terms, likely out of a fear that they will be sexualizing their children too early. While I understand this fear and see the reasoning behind it, it is a myth. This myth comes from us mixing up sexual development with eroticism or adult sexuality. Children who have not been exposed to adult content, haven't been abused, or have not hit the biological stage of puberty yet, do not think erotically. They may be curious, but not in the same ways that teens and adults are. A 6 year old does not normally look at another kid their age and think about behaving sexually towards them. They may want to understand the differences or see a part of their body that they don't have, but this is not erotic in nature. This is exploration. They may try to touch their sibling in the bathtub or be silly with their private parts. This is curiosity. Of course, sometimes curiosity is dangerous, it can definitely "kill the cat," but this normal curiosity is why supervision and using proper terms for body parts is so crucial. This is why we need to help them set boundaries with their own bodies and indulge their curiosity with healthy answers and guidance all along the way. Shaming them or punishing them is not a helpful deterrent.

Our kids look to us (whether parents, guardians, or mentors) to tell them what is weird, scary, strange, or taboo. When we call a penis a penis, they will not typically go running through the grocery store or down the aisle at church yelling it out. I mean they might, but that's another person's problem to deal with, not your confident and protected child's.

---

[63] A great resource on this particular topic is the book *God Made All of Me* by Justin and Lindsey Holcomb

When you implement these conversations and tools in your household, you will become more aware of people who never had them. You will notice discomfort in society at large regarding such topics, which I would say is the root of our issues. I have had grandparents and teachers cringe at the idea of saying penis and vagina out loud. I have had rooms full of clinicians and educators turn red from me teaching on this topic. Many of them have reached out to express their appreciation for helping them confront their own trauma and fears. You might be turning red in the face right now just reading it. I still feel discomfort sometimes, and I get it. I would love to keep everyone feeling safe and secure at all times, but the reality is that this is impossible. Having taboo conversations takes courage. If it were easy, everyone would be doing it. We need to be extremely sensitive, but we must talk. If we cannot then how will we expect children to talk about it when something awful happens. When we do not talk to children about these things we unintentionally teach them that, "no one should talk about these things," but we need to teach them how and when to, in an age appropriate way.

If biological terms become common in your home, your child will likely not think much of it in the moment. Then, as they grow and their penis itches or their vagina is irritated, they will know the proper terms for them and come to you without shame or fear. As childhood itching or touching of private parts leads into other developmental things like arousal or masturbation, you can tackle those things as they arise with a better assurance your child trusts you and will ask you questions using accurate terms and with the certainty you will tell them the truth.

With that in mind, proper terminology for all body parts is crucial for another reason. With the biologically accurate words, if something happens or someone touches them, our kids are able to tell us where, how, and on what body part specifically. Not to mention that they are more willing to share such incidents with us if a bridge of confidence has already been built over time.

There have been horrible instances where a family called their daughter's vagina a cookie, and for years the daughter would say, "Uncle tried to touch my cookie." Because it seemed like a game she was playing, family members and teachers missed the abuse happening right in front of them. We want to give our children the right terminology to prevent someone manipulating them into something because they are confused. Using terms like cookie, teetee, nunu, or anything else we decided to make up, morphs their idea of private parts into something silly or strange to talk about. It would be like if I called a giraffe a spotty-spotty-long-neck. It is a giraffe. Call it a giraffe. Let's not confuse our children by projecting onto them our own insecurities and fears. It's a penis, call it a penis.

THE PENIS RULES

1. I am the boss of my body, and no one touches me without my permission.
2. My private parts are to be kept private except when washing or at the Dr. (you will not be washing me).
3. We keep our clothes on except around our closest family.
4. We do not keep secrets.
5. I will never get in trouble for telling.

Body Safety

Not only does your child need to use and feel comfortable with correct body terminology, but they also need to know that these parts are private. *God Made All of Me* by Justin and Lindsey Holcomb is a great book to walk your children through their body safety rules and private parts if you want a more specific guide. The book also covers the differences between secrets and surprises. If you're feeling frustrated that your parents didn't walk you through these things, try to remember that our parents didn't have the same books and resources we have now. We have the opportunity and the responsibility to do better.

In my home, we have a body safety checklist that our boys know backwards and forwards. We call it "The Penis Rules," but the list covers all body safety themes. This is something they can lean on when they are being watched or kept by a grandparent, babysitter, or friend. Here is our list:

When our friends' kids come over, we all talk through the rules of the house. When our boys go to my neighbor's house to play, I talk to them about the rules. One day our boys were going to ride bikes and play at our friends' house next door. I said, "Boys, come here before you go."

They both sighed and said,"WE KNOW. Be gentle, be respectful, no one touches our privates and we dont touch anyone else's, and don't use potty words." I stood there shocked. I wanted to hug them both and make a big deal of it. Instead, I nodded and said, "Yep, I love y'all," and I went inside and thrust my fist into the air!

They did not act weird. They were not ashamed. They lumped all the rules into the same category. "Things Dad Reminds Us of ALL THE TIME."

My boys know these rules apply at all times (at church, with friends and family, with a sitter), and their care providers know this list, too. Our boys also know what to do if someone tries to touch them, asks them to be alone with them, or asks my kids to touch their body. They say "No!" and run to tell the closest adult or safe person. If they cannot find someone, we taught them to yell and run until someone comes. As they get older, they can obviously walk away without screaming, but the same level of intensity and immediacy needs to take place. Then they (or a trusted person) will call me or their mom, and we will immediately handle the situation. Above all, there will certainly be no "brushing off" of the event or invalidating their experience no matter how small it seems to us or anyone else. If you are confident internally then you will be able to be confident externally with your children.

If something happens to your child, or even a friend, it is important to get all the information you can without interrogating the scared child or making them feel ashamed. You do not need to overreact, but act you must. Next, follow up with the person who attempted the violation to make sure the proper protocols are followed and that the situation is contained and under control. The most important things you can communicate to your kid are that this was not their fault, the adult or child that was responsible has consequences, and that there are things put in place to make sure this never happens again. Then simply make space to have small talks over time to ensure the child is okay. Allow them to go see a play therapist or a child life specialist to make sure a baseline is noted, but equally crucial is allowing them to move forward if you feel they are no longer experiencing fear or damage from the event. Trauma doesn't need to define any of us.

Building Better Bridges

This same type of calm needs to apply to the potential aggressor and their parents. Grace needs to be shown and empathy and understanding extended. That child is most likely just playing out or exploring something they have seen before. In the case in which abuse has been confirmed to have happened, that child needs support and help to recover. Boundaries and expectations can be set without dumping shame on everyone involved.

Both body safety and using proper terms for body parts can reduce sexual abuse by a massive margin. One of the main reasons that we find it difficult to learn about sexual abuse in children is that just thinking about it makes us sick to our stomachs. This is another reason that I'm writing this book. These fears have cost me years off of my life, taken away the joy of certain experiences from myself and my children, and given me intrusive thoughts, anxiety, and fear that I couldn't have imagined. This is the cost of helping others find freedom. No wonder many of us avoid it.

The simple truth is, when we dwell with such dark thoughts, it is hard not to be attacked mentally, physically and spiritually. But, nevertheless. Someone must think about the scariest parts of childhood abuse in order to protect our children from those things. I, of course, am not the only one ready to face such fears, and I have no moral high ground and no purer heart than the next person, but by the grace of God and the word of my own testimony, I do have something. Something I feel is important, helpful, and that demands to be shared. Whether you think so or not, you have something to share too, and I am certain you have the courage to do it!

So here I am, after wading into the deep waters to explore how the bad guys think. I think I mentioned before that I am an Army veteran. One of the ways that we protected ourselves overseas was to learn the mind of the bad guy. We knew how, when, and where they would attack and their strategies, and this is the way we combated them. Such are the methods we must use when it comes to sexual abuse prevention. We have to know why and how an abuser might attack. We also must know who these people are and how to stop them before our child is in harm's way. After listening to victims my entire career, one truth is clear: the number one reason an adult or child will leave your son or daughter alone is that they do not want to be caught. Opportunity is the most dangerous element. An offender, even a young one, looks for children who they can manipulate. They look for children who they can "explore" or "experiment with." They target homes without rules and without supervision to replicate what they have seen or what has been done to them. Regardless of who or how old, if your child uses proper terms for private parts, knows how to stand up for themselves, and knows their own body safety boundaries, the abuser will flee from your child and look for another person who is more vulnerable. Prevention is possible with the proper awareness and support.

Consent

With language to accurately name their private parts and structures in place to know about body safety, we now can teach them how to talk about consent. The first two topics are essential in discussing this third topic.

Consent means affording someone their own choice about touch, behaviors, and then respecting whatever answer they give. With kids, we can use language such as, "Ask permission, and respect the answer."

As with other sections, I want you to know there are other resources that dive deeper into many of these topics that I am covering with broad strokes. Krystaelynn Sanders Diggs' *The ABC's of Consent* is one of those, and I highly recommend checking it out.[64]

Consent can be as simple as allowing our kids to turn down a hug or kiss from grandma or Aunt Suzanne. They don't have to sit on anyone's lap that they don't want to. Consent also means that *we* will ask them permission before we touch their bodies in any way. Safety issues or health concerns obviously require a bit of leeway, but most every other time, ***it is appropriate to wait for a yes or accept their no***. Now, listen. I can hear what you're thinking. "What about this situation? What about that scenario?"

---

[64] There are amazing books out there on almost all the topics I cover here, and you can find my list of suggested resources at the end of this book.

Building Better Bridges

I trust and hope that you are a good parent and that you know your children well. Use your judgment. We do not want to be manipulated or set up for failure. Sometimes obedience is necessary, and our young kids do not get to ask why or how. I have certainly picked up my screaming toddler and carried him to the car after a full on meltdown on the toy aisle. However, I do believe these situations are fewer and farther between than we assume. We can all do a better job of treating children with the same respect we would expect when it comes to our own bodies. Every situation is different and calls for different responses, but you get the picture.

Indulge me in a quick story to show you that I have been on a journey to learn these things, just like you are now.

I remember times I would attempt to discipline my oldest son, and he wouldn't listen. One of these times, I remember he ran to his bedroom and told me I was "the worst father ever" and "a monster." For the first time ever, he slammed the door to his bedroom. He was probably 4 or 5 years old at the time. We had been talking about how no one should touch his body without permission and that if they did, he should tell me right away. I told him his dad would always try to keep him safe. Well, this time I was the bad guy. The door slamming was a shock and triggered anger in me. I walked in, snatched him out of his bed, and made him stand in the corner. I was full of blind anger. Here I am, a grown man with a fully functioning brain and all the training in the world, and yet in frustration, I snatched my 4-year-old up simply because he slammed a door to go cry in his bed. That is the thing about being a parent. We all have our own trauma and baggage. None of us do this thing perfectly, and we all fall short. The amazing thing is that with every hurtful mistake there is an opportunity for repair. With every repair, there is a chance to grow and build trust.

As I turned to walk out, the Holy Spirit lovingly reminded me of all the conversations I had with my son about consent and body safety. The Spirit also reminded me of all the grace God gives *me* on a daily basis when I throw a fit (adult tantrums can be even uglier than a slammed door). I broke. I realized that my job is to show him how to process these big feelings and fears. I turned around to go back, and I got on his level to apologize. I asked his forgiveness and assured him I would never touch his body without permission again, unless it was a safety issue. Nothing is worth violating that trust. Since that experience, I try to say something like "Okay buddy, I am asking you to follow directions, and I am going to give you a chance to move your body or I will have to help you move it." This doesn't always go perfectly, but I have very rarely touched him without permission since that day. I tell you this humbly to remind you that we will all mess up as we learn new tools, conversations, and behaviors. None of us will do it all perfectly. Building a foundation of health and trust, however, can keep us from causing lifelong wounds that will take decades to heal. I fully believe our kids don't need our perfection, just our honest guidance, trust, and love. That is what authenticity looks like. Remember that people trust authentic people, and they fear fake ones.

Teaching consent is a healthy and straightforward way for kids to learn about boundaries and to make those boundaries for their bodies. If they say yes to something and then change their mind, then that "no" is enough to end the game of tickles, wrestling, or whatever is going on. When "no" is said, everyone should stop immediately without explanation or shame being projected on the child. We don't call them names, belittle them, or make fun. When someone has had enough, it means enough.

Additionally, consent is relevant from birth to adulthood. Ask your child if they would like to be picked up. Ask them if you can change their diaper. Ask them if it's fine to wipe their bottom. These might sound silly or even counterproductive to say to your child, especially when they're infants, but such language will get you into practice, and shows your child that their body is their own. Obviously, I am not saying children are capable of being fully in charge, nor should they be. But this kind of autonomy does set a precedent for their understanding that they choose who can enter their personal space and that being asked is important. For example: If you are about to move your baby to another room or change their diaper you could say, "Would you mind if mommy changed that poopy diaper?" or "Would you like to get out of this room and come over here to the playset?" When we are changing food out or taking things away we can say, "Do you think Daddy could take this bowl or food from you and replace it with this one?" We of course have to do what is best for the child even when they say, no or cannot speak, but it is an amazing opportunity to try to give them the feeling of autonomy and confidence in their own choice. Not that they always have one, but that their choice matters to you as parents.

If we set consent as the norm, then they learn that *not* asking is a red flag. Another amazing consequence of asking your child's permission is that once they learn the choice is theirs to make, they will likely make healthier choices regarding their own body later, as well as treat other peoples' bodies with that same caution and respect. If it's theirs and they are proud of it, they will probably want to take good care of it. This can seem counterproductive, but that is only because having conversations and debating with a child is difficult and tiring some days. It would make our life way easier if we just told them what to do and they listened and had no opinions, but in the long run I can tell you this creates healthier humans. If your child grows up to be a believer, they will also come to realize the Holy Spirit lives within that body! That is really cool!

Consent can be taught many times over their childhood and through endless different methods. Use toys or games, use the ordinary moments where they interact with doctors or teachers. There will be many opportunities to teach these lessons and empower your child to know they are the boss of their body! In theory, of all the topics in this book, teaching consent will likely be one of the easiest to discuss with your child because their body is important to you too, and you want them to be able to protect it.

Unfortunately, the more difficult part will be teaching family, caregivers, and other adults about your child's boundaries. Many adults who were not given the same boundaries, lessons, or safe space are often the ones that give pushback. They say things like "when I was a kid" or "this weak parenting stuff is making them soft." Unfortunately, they just do not understand and might frankly be a little jealous. Regardless of how everyone else feels or reacts, we have to do what is best for our kids in the long run. We can no longer parent our children for the affirmation of others or to avoid hard conversations. We cannot build weak bridges, because the people in our lives have never experienced strong ones and live in fear.

Although consent is basically the same no matter how old we are, there are some differences in how we talk about it as our children grow. How you approached consent with your toddlers and young children will determine how difficult those conversations will be with your teen. If you have consistently taught about body safety and consent, this road will be easier. If you have not, don't panic. It will be okay. We can start figuring out how to share this information now. Maybe that should be our motto here...***better to start now than to never start at all.***

With teens, there are several opportunities to teach consent. Dating and sex being one of the primary ones. This is a spot that society and religion as a whole needs a little critique. Even if you believe teens should not be sexually active it is important to teach them the basics of dating and consent. This way they have all the information and can make the healthy choices to protect themselves and others. Teens must know that YES means YES, and NO means NO. No response or silence also means NO. *Anything* but YES means NO. To do something sexual with someone without their consent is abusive, and if you have sex with someone without their consent, that is rape or sexual assault. I tell teens all the time that unless someone is explicitly saying "Please have sex with me," then it is a NO. I also tell them the pros and cons to premarital sex and the research behind it, but if they choose to ignore the truth and take a risk, I want them to understand how to with as little harm as possible. Hopefully by now you realize I'm definitely not condoning teen promiscuity or sex. As a Christian, I teach my boys that sex is meant for marriage and marriage only. All forms of sex. I tell them that God set these rules in place to protect us as His children, not to prevent us from enjoying life. Sex is a gift, an amazing one, but I believe it is its most wonderful and is best enjoyed in the safety and love of a marriage. Scripture is clear, God wants us to have amazing and healthy sex. Why would anyone compromise 40 years of amazing sex for a few years of promiscuity and temporary pleasure? We can see even within the research, with all the trauma and exposure that we have, having sex before marriage brings about a lot of pain and suffering for everyone. Marriage is an amazing way to heal all of that and bring sexuality back to the way God designed it in the first place. I also know that every household has its own beliefs and therefore its own rules. Whatever your values might be, surely we can agree these conversations with our children are vital. Regardless of the different ways we raise our kids, discussing healthy sexuality, boundaries, and consent is a major way that they can keep themselves and their peers safe, whether we are there to protect them or not. However you choose to speak to your teens about consent and sexuality, I hope this gives you a path and plan.

To neglect these topics and discussions is just that - *neglectful.* It is to leave our children lacking a strong foundation of truth and health. When we leave them to figure it out on their own, we allow society, films, and pornography to shape their beliefs around sexuality, consent, and their own bodies. This wave of neglect causes a life of damaged relationships and leaves broken people in its wake.

In addition to dating conversations, social media and sharing content also provide great avenues to teach consent to your teens, or in this culture, your younger kids too. Shared content doesn't have to be sexual to be embarrassing, inappropriate, or a violation of someone's consent. They need to learn to think before they screenshot something that was meant to be private and think even harder about sharing it with anyone else, much less a group. A conversation about your child's motives might also come into play here. What is our intent in sharing something? A laugh at someone else's expense? Are you trying to get attention and be liked? A good rule of thumb is just because someone posted or shared something doesn't mean that you have free range to comment, distribute, or poke fun at their content, whatever it may be. Sharing a private email or text thread can also be a major violation of consent. If you have videos or pictures of your ex girlfriend on your phone you should delete them. We can teach them that taking videos and pictures in the first place is unsafe and extremely risky, but at a minimum they need to know that pictures of other people are not their property even if they are on their devices or were sent to them. They are not open for sharing or showing others. Celebrity leaks are a prime example of how our world is extremely toxic in this area. Just because the internet enables us to do these things doesn't mean we *should.* This goes for all of us...not just our children. Your kids, just like mine, will be most likely to learn and repeat the behaviors that you exhibit or choose to ignore and not speak about.

The burden is on us to create a culture of safety and responsibility online and stop teaching toxic behaviors through our own activity on social media. As parents or leaders, we have to stop acting like other people "have it coming" or are "asking for it" just because they posted something we don't like or agree with. Likewise, we must teach our teens that they don't have the right to blast anyone publicly. Well...they have the right. Free speech and all. However, what we have the *right* to do and what leads to a life of *success* are not always the same thing. In fact, if you catch yourself justifying something by saying "I have the right to..." you should probably go ahead and toss up a red flag in your brain. Usually that phrase is followed by some cruelty or selfishness we know we shouldn't be doing. It's like saying "I don't mean to sound harsh but" and then saying something super harsh....yeah, you probably meant to.

All this boils down to self-control. However hard this might be to exercise in our own hectic and demanding lives, it is our job to teach our kids to have self-control, how to be kind even when they have the right to do otherwise, and even when they feel fully justified in their retaliation or retribution. The most powerful way to teach this is by modeling such behaviors for them. Our best tool for teaching consent, or any of the other topics discussed here, is living out these lessons ourselves.

A Few Other Safety Rules

You made it through this chapter (almost)! You have bravely faced the sad statistics and truths regarding sexual abuse and boldly ignored the awkwardness of teaching proper body terminology, body safety, and physical/virtual consent to our children. Not so bad, right? Especially given that a few awkward moments throughout your kid's childhood might save them from untold harm. **Lots of people say they will die for their kids, but will you live for them? Will you fight for them through uncomfortable conversations?** Before we move on to other important and challenging topics, I have just a few other suggestions to share about keeping your children safe from certain traumas. Your house is your house, and I am certain you will choose your own rules and structures. I just share mine as a way to tell you what has worked for my family and many of the families I counsel.

1. *Limited Sleepovers (none is the safest option)*

Building Better Bridges

I know that this is a big trigger for some people, but more and more people are realizing what a poor idea this is, especially for kids under 14. Either the child is too young to protect themselves, or they are in the midst of hormone changes and puberty. Even one of those should be reason enough, but I am fairly confident you have experiences of your own that support this rule. If a trustworthy parent or chaperone will stay up with the kids, then go for it. But, again, I just don't see the risk to reward ratio paying off. Especially since I know all my friends with kids would not be any good to the world after 10 pm. If you can be certain of a home that has no risk of unsupervised time, screens, or inappropriate conversations and content, then you can make that choice. Sleepovers in my house are a no-go unless I have real trust in the things we cover in this book. For me the risk outweighs the reward. Seeing our childhoods in rose colored glasses can really cause problems. If we think about what happened at the sleepovers we attended and remember that we didn't have phones, the internet, or social media ....then we might rethink being so casual about them. If you are reading this and you did have all of those things during sleepovers then you also know the dangers are everywhere.

2. No Closed Doors

There should be no closed doors when young children are over playing. They do not need privacy from adults. We should be able to hear and go see what they're doing whenever we want. They should know that we might pop in at any moment. This keeps their brains aware that they are safe, able to call out, or able to leave the room when they want to. This also lets them know there is supervision, and there are boundaries being enforced. Remember you will have to remind them every time. Even if they do not have any schemes or ideas, they will shut doors 100 times for the fun of it. If they do shut the doors just gently remind them of the rules.

3. No Playing Under Blankets

Maybe it sounds odd to you, but we make it a point in our house to not allow children to be under the same covers together. An open blanket fort or a camp-out is fine, but snuggling and rolling around under a blanket can lead to friction and biological responses that are unnecessary and which lead to exploration that is too early and unhealthy. This is especially true from 10-13. The simplest things can become problematic when hormones are at play. Again, this is about limiting experiences and problematic behaviors, not doing away with them entirely. They are going to roll around, wrestle, and make up silly kids' games. My boys love to get "squishy" with their grandmother, but we just have to be mindful of what is happening as they age and other children are involved. They are not doing something wrong, it's about we as parents being mindful of what could happen and having a baseline of expectations.

4. *No Unsupervised Play for Long Periods*
Simple and pretty easy to execute. We must let our children know that we will be popping in and checking on them on a regular basis. Staggering your "pop-ins" is always a smart tactic because it keeps them guessing on when you will be there and limits their risk-taking. Let's be honest: kids are crazy, and there are enough YouTube videos and reels of kids painting a wall, opening a bag of flour, or cutting their own hair to tell us we need to check in.

5. *Secrets vs. Surprises*[65]
My last rule is more of a clarification that I have taught my boys. At our house we started from a very young age teaching them that secrets keep you sick. We want them to understand that Mom and Dad do not keep secrets from each other, and they do not keep secrets from us. Surprises are fun and meant for good, but secrets are dangerous. We teach this distinction so that when another child, adult, or friend tells them to keep a secret, a red flag goes off in their mind. They immediately know something is not right or safe. It may seem like an extreme position to take, but ask yourself when keeping secrets *ever* goes well. What is the point of keeping secrets? Privacy is one thing, but secrecy and withholding are entirely different. Once learned, this intense type of honesty and integrity extends into other areas of life for our children. Grades, relationships, addictions – transparency and trust in childhood builds a framework for our children to know their parents are trustworthy, and they can feel safe talking to them about any topic or situation. It also teaches kids to say what they mean and stand by it, in Biblical terms, "Let your yes be yes and your no be no."[66] What a valuable lesson about

---

[65] This idea is articulated in *God Made All of Me* by the Holcombs, which I have mentioned before. Truly a great children's book!

[66] "Let what you say be simply 'Yes' or 'No'; anything more than this comes from evil." -Matthew 5:37 (ESV)

staying true to our word and not lying or withholding. We can help instill such honesty by 1) being honest to our children, spouses, and friends, and 2) showing love and compassion when our children tell us things.

Given all these rules and strategies, you might feel like your house is about to be sucked dry of any fun. Maybe this all seems like...too much. But listen. Children should be allowed to be children. They are wild and funny and will do things they don't even realize are inappropriate. They will run around with their pants down or pee in the yard. They will show their private parts to one another out of silliness and playfulness, because they don't have the boundaries and awareness that we have. They will say penis or vagina or boobies and make us silly songs that will drive you crazy. Do not fret. Do not panic. Just laugh and redirect. Teach them calmly and respectfully how, when, and where these things are appropriate and move on. The human body is beautiful and designed by God to be good and glorifying to him. We do not have to respond in panic or anxiety while our children are learning boundaries, but we must make clear our expectations so healthy habits form as they grow up. You will do great if you pay attention. Only then will you pick up on cues that something may be off. Each child is different and each family has more flexible or rigid boundaries depending on their situations and experiences. The goal of this is to give you safety railing. Feel free to change things up as you feel best and based on the uniqueness of your child and family system.

Alright, let's bring this chapter home.This pervasive lack of age-appropriate conversations regarding sexual development is one of the root causes for sexual abuse in children and teens. The three main topics we covered here are three of the most commonly avoided conversations in our homes. Yet, such talks are paramount in guiding our kids through a safe and healthy childhood. By the time they make it to puberty and beyond, we will have built a foundation that can handle almost anything that is thrown at them. We can build these better bridges, create lifelong trust and honesty, and set them up for success and health for decades down the road.

As you take the steps to talk with your children and educate them, I challenge you even further to tell everyone involved in your child's life these new rules and expectations. Let them know that your children are not prey, and no matter how trusting you are, you are also vigilant. If a child or an adult ever has a problem with you establishing boundaries, that would raise a red flag. Anyone with the mere inkling to victimize or experiment with your child will run the opposite direction. Anyone else will be incredibly understanding and would probably feel inspired to implement something similar in their own homes, even if it takes a little education. That is kind of the whole idea. I would love nothing more than an eruption of these conversations, a generation of children who have tools in their own hands to prevent abuse or traumatic situations. Heck, buy everyone a copy of this book for Christmas so they don't have to keep asking you "Where did you get this all from??"

I want to be very honest. Educating our children is not foolproof. Sadly, there will always be a chance for outlier situations and fringe cases where someone kidnaps, abducts, or abuses a child who has every possible resource and tool at their disposal. Your child might explore with another child or do something that goes against everything you have taught them. Please do not shame them or freak out. Talk with them and build better boundaries. None of us can control every situation, so let's give our kids the space to learn and grow safely with us, because eventually we won't be with them. Bad things can happen. The likelihood of those things happening is very low, however, when your child is equipped with knowledge and is confident about their body and their choices.

Last note. Not every family has two parents, support, or resources. This is why community is so important. Single parents need healthy males and females to help them have these conversations with the opposite genders. Moms can talk with sons about these things, but it would be nice if a healthy male could guide your son in the areas of manhood and development and the same would be said for women and daughters. As children get older it is appropriate for both parents to be able to talk with their children together.

All that I have shared in this chapter is aimed at starting conversations early and preventing the trauma and exposure that often lead to abuse. I hope this content helps you achieve that protection and prevention in your family. The truth is, though, sometimes exposure happens, trauma happens, and someone we love gets abused in one way or another. While not a single one of us ever wants this to happen, I want to share ways to notice the signs of abuse if it is happening, and what to do if it does take place.

Reflection & Discussion

1. Have you experienced abuse in your own life? If yes, what are your thoughts on therapy or your own method for healing?

2. How have any possible traumas from your own life affected the way you see yourself now and how you relate to your kids, spouse, or peers?

3. Did you learn about consent and body safety when you were young? Is it a priority for you to walk your children through these things?

4. As an adult, do you think your arousal template was disrupted by anything in your youth? What can you learn from that to pass on to your kids?

5. Do you tend to believe when someone reports possible abuse to you or to doubt it? Why?

6. What are the protective rules in your own home?

10. Abuse: Seeing the Signs and What to Do

*Sexual abuse can happen to anyone, regardless of age,
gender, or background.*
- Jennifer Marsh

Following our discussion on abuse, I wanted to add this short section that I pulled directly from an organization I am really grateful for – RAINN (Rape, Abuse, and Incent National Network). All the information in this brief chapter is from their page on abuse warning signs, and we can all benefit massively from being cognizant of these signs and red flags in our circles of influence. Your gut instinct as a parent, or even just a friend, combined with knowledge and awareness, is the best asset you have.

Warning Signs for Young Children[67]

Every 9 minutes, government authorities respond to another report of child sexual abuse.[1] Child sexual abuse can include sexual contact with a child, but it may also include other actions, like exposing oneself, sharing obscene images, or taking inappropriate photos or videos of a child. These crimes can have a serious impact on the life and development of a child, and often continue to impact them later in life. Learning the warning signs of child sexual abuse is often the first step to protecting a child who is in danger.

It's not always easy to spot sexual abuse because perpetrators often take steps to hide their actions. Some signs are easier to spot than others. For instance, some warning signs might be noticed by a

---

[67] Starting here and going through a couple of pages, all of this content is pulled directly from an incredibly helpful organization called RAINN that I mentioned above. Thanks to RAINN for all the amazing work of your team.
(https://www.rainn.org/articles/warning-signs-young-children)

Clint Davis

caretaker or parent, and are often red flags that the child needs medical attention. Listen to your instincts. If you notice something that isn't right or someone in a child's life is making you uncomfortable—even if you can't put your finger on why—it's important to trust your gut, continue to watch for signs of abuse, and **talk to the child** who may be experiencing abuse in age-appropriate ways.

Signs of Abuse

Physical signs:

· Sexually transmitted infections (STIs)
· Signs of trauma to the genital area, such as unexplained bleeding, bruising, or blood on the sheets, underwear, or other clothing

Behavioral signs:

· Excessive talk about or knowledge of sexual topics
· Keeping secrets
· Not talking as much as usual
· Not wanting to be left alone with certain people or being afraid to be away from primary caregivers, especially if this is a new behavior
· Regressive behaviors or resuming behaviors they had grown out of, such as thumbsucking or bedwetting
· Overly compliant behavior
· Sexual behavior that is inappropriate for the child's age
· Spending an unusual amount of time alone
· Trying to avoid removing clothing to change or bathe

Emotional signs:

· Change in eating habits
· Change in mood or personality, such as increased aggression
· Decrease in confidence or self-image
· Excessive worry or fearfulness
· Increase in unexplained health problems such as stomach aches and headaches

· Loss or decrease in interest in school, activities, and friends
· Nightmares or fear of being alone at night
· Self-harming behaviors

This list may seem overwhelming to keep in mind when looking out for a child in your life, and some signs seem to contradict each other, such as being overly compliant or oppositional, or showing regressive behaviors or advanced sexual behaviors. The most important thing to keep in mind when looking for signs of child sexual abuse is to keep an eye on sudden changes in behavior. Trust your gut and don't ignore your feelings if something seems off. If a child tells you that someone makes them uncomfortable, even if they can't tell you anything specific, listen."

Be cautious of an adult who spend time with children and exhibits the following behaviors:

· Does not respect boundaries or listen when someone tells them "no"
· Engages in touching that a child or child's parents/guardians have indicated is unwanted
· Tries to be a child's friend rather than filling an adult role in the child's life
· Does not seem to have age-appropriate relationships
· Talks with children about their personal problems or relationships
· Spends time alone with children outside of their role in the child's life or makes up excuses to be alone with the child
· Expresses unusual interest in child's sexual development, such as commenting on sexual characteristics or sexualizing normal behaviors
· Gives a child gifts without occasion or reason
· Spends a lot of time with your child or another child you know
· Restricts a child's access to other adults

It's not always easy to identify child sexual abuse—and it can be even more challenging to step in if you suspect something isn't right. Keeping a child away from the perpetrator may mean major changes in your own life, even if you are outside of the child's family.

"As it started to settle in, I replayed it in my mind. How could this happen? I had so much shame, so much guilt that I had brought this man into my house to molest my child. What kind of mother am I?" said **Lisa***, a mother of a survivor and member of the RAINN Speakers Bureau. "The guilt and the shame were deafening—but at the same time I knew I had to do what was necessary for my daughter."*

If something seems off, pay attention to that feeling and look into it further. If a child tells you that someone makes them uncomfortable, even if they can't tell you anything specific, listen. Talk to someone who can help you figure out if this is something that must be reported, such as a staff member from your local sexual assault service provider. In the meantime, if you are the parent or have influence over the child's schedule, avoid putting the child in a potentially unsafe situation.

Remember, you are not alone. If you suspect a child in your life may be experiencing sexual abuse, you can talk to someone who is trained to help. Call the National Sexual Assault Hotline at 800.656.HOPE (4673) or chat online at online.rainn.org.

Hello, it's me again now.
I include this resource directly because they covered the signs far better than I could have. The RAINN site also provides many other amazing resources and facts to help notice, prevent, or deal with abuse. I highly recommend visiting their page if you are experiencing difficulty with this issue and you don't know who to turn to or where to start.

If the unthinkable happens and abuse does happen to your child, I want to first of all say that I am so sorry. Your pain, anger, fear, and despair are valid emotions, but I also want you to not blame yourself. The best way you can help your child through this is to be there for *them.*

The first thing you can do is make sure you have a support system around you so that you do not make their struggles and issues about *you.* Then, as you forgive yourself and try to avoid those intense feelings of shame, make sure you do the same for your child. It was not their fault either, so don't shame, blame, or judge them. Maybe it seems impossible to blame a child for their own abuse, but in a very emotional time, some parents blame the child because they just wish the whole thing hadn't happened. They just hope it's not real, but this can translate badly to the child whose experience was very real.

Many children who experience sexual abuse already feel confused, ashamed, angry, and depressed, as well as feeling like they are to blame. Victims often blame themselves and take responsibility for things that are not their fault in order to create a sense of control and protection in an out-of-control situation. Also, many abusers threaten or deceive children into believing they liked it or asked for it. Please don't make the mistake of adding fuel to that fire.

Talking to your child after you find out abuse has taken place can feel like the scariest and most daunting thing in the world. Just breathe and know that most of all, they just need you to be there. Try to limit the amount they have to repeat the details and get them to a professional so that memories don't get confused or details do not get missed. There are local agencies that can take your child's case and follow legal protocols for the best possible outcomes. We have a local agency called "The Gingerbread House" here in my town. They are an amazing group of professionals. Their goal with forensic interviewing is to get the right information so that they can prosecute the criminal and get the child the help that they need, without having them more traumatized by telling their story to the cop, the parent, the lawyer, the judge, the therapist, on and on. The poor kid needs to tell their story, but not to multiple people. This information can get confused by the child and then manipulated in court. The child's mental health should be the primary focus with a close second being prosecuting the perpetrator. Make sure you know the agencies and trust them, because this can be a very devastating experience for a family if it does not go well. Make sure you get a referral from a trusted source.

Here are some practical things you can do and say if this situation arises in your home.

Clint Davis

What does my child need from me?

-Empathy – Be empathetic and warm towards your child, understand that this is a nuanced situation and very complex. Ask questions and don't assume anything.

-Stability – Do some grounding work with yourself before having these talks with your child. Make sure you are solid and supported before opening your mouth.

-Focus – Do not share a whole lot of your own feelings or make the situation about you. You can share some to try to connect and help them understand you are upset, but do not trump their experience with your own.

-Praise – Point out the things they have done well to manage this impossible situation. Let them know you are still proud of them.

-Guidance – Ask how you can help them, and don't overuse words. Just sit beside them, listen to music with them, or even cry with them.

-Space – Do not put pressure on them or ask for too many details. It is important to limit the number of times the child has to tell their story. We do not want them having to explain it to you, the cops, the interviewer, child services, the lawyer, etc. We want them to share it with one person so they can document and get accurate information and to avoid making the child relive the experience so often.

-Protection – Make sure you find out if the abuse has stopped and show the child that you will take drastic measures to ensure it won't happen again.

What does my child need me to say?

-   I believe you.
-   It is not your fault, and we do not blame you. The person who harmed you is responsible, not you.
-   IF you want to talk about it, we will set up a counseling appointment.
-   I want you to talk to whoever you feel most comfortable with even if it is not a counselor.
-   We can make it through this together.

161

- I do not think any differently about you.
- You are still loved and cherished.
- You are not broken or dirty.
- I am here for you at any time you want to talk.
- You can write some private thoughts in a journal, and I will not show anyone.

How do I report abuse?

- Call your local police station and file a report.
- Call a therapist or counselor and set up an appointment.
- If there is a forensic interviewer in your area, reach out to them and get that set up.
- Call Child Protective Services in your area.
- Set up an appointment with an attorney to cover you and your child's rights.
- Call DCFS 1-855-452-5437 and make a report immediately.

Facing abuse with children is an incredibly hard thing, bordering on impossible. You will never hear me say otherwise. But you and your child *can* recover from it. Try not to lose yourself to despair, and above all, believe in yourself and your ability to handle this. You can do it. I have personally walked many families through this and I promise there is hope!!

Clint Davis

11. Gender Roles
(Yeah, We're Going There)

God's view of gender is not based on stereotypes or cultural norms, but on his perfect wisdom and love."
- Timothy Keller[68]

If private parts, body changes, and sex weren't enough to contend with, we also live in a world thrown into chaos regarding sex, gender, sexual orientation, and identity, especially as it relates to children. In every form of media, across religions, and in multiple cultures, we see great confusion and differing opinions. I will not (and cannot) try to solve all of those problems in this chapter, and honestly gender dysphoria, gender fluidity, or trans persons are not the focus of this particular book. I personally believe God designed us to be boys and girls, men and women, male and female. The science is pretty clear, but I also accept that other people have different beliefs or experiences. There are babies who, during their gestation period (time in the womb), get different levels of androgen and other hormones. This has been shown to affect their emotional and physical predispositions about gender and sex after they are born. This imbalanced level of hormones is very rare. There are also people, although even more extremely rare cases, born with both sex organs. Ambiguous genitalia is a rare condition and extremely difficult to manage as a parent and growing human.[69] We should honor and respect these situations and expect others to show love and compassion to one another.

---

[68] Mr. Keller passed away in May of 2023 before this book even hit publication. He has impacted countless lives and marriages with his Biblical and philosophical wisdom. Rest in peace, Tim.
[69] Berenbaum, Sheri A, and Adriene M Beltz. "How Early Hormones Shape Gender Development." *Current opinion in behavioral sciences* vol. 7 (2016): 53-60. doi:10.1016/j.cobeha.2015.11.011

Building Better Bridges

Even when we disagree or do not understand. As Christian's we believe sex and gender to both be gifts from God. There is a helpful book for Christian parents titled *God Made Boys and Girls: Helping Children Understand the Gift of Gender* by Marty Machowski. It helps explain gender and sex in a healthy way without stereotypes and without biased comparisons of girls and boys. This doesn't mean that people do not struggle with their gender identity. They do. For decades, we have done a great job of creating a toxic and confusing understanding of the difference in gender and sex. If you are of another faith, there are other suggested readings to help have these conversations.

I want our children to grow up understanding and respecting differences, even if they do not agree with the philosophy or ideologies presented to them. Information is power, and empowerment can help people feel safe and loved, even in disagreement. Below is a segment of an article by Carolyn Mazure from the Yale School of Medicine that I find to be massively insightful for the world we now live in and where we will be moving in the future.

"In 2001, a committee convened by the Institute of Medicine (IOM), a nonprofit think tank that took on issues of importance to national health, addressed the question of whether it mattered to study the biology of women as well as men.

The IOM, now embedded within the National Academies of Science, Engineering, and Medicine (NASEM), concluded there was more than sufficient evidence that, beyond reproductive biology, there were major differences in the biology of women and men that greatly affected their health and influenced treatment and prevention strategies.

Importantly, the committee emphasized that neither the health of women nor men is simply a product of biology but is also influenced by sociocultural and psychological experience. To differentiate between these broad areas of investigation, the members created working definitions of "sex" — when referring to biology — and "gender" — when referring to self-representation influenced by social, cultural, and personal experience.

The committee advised that scientists use these definitions in the following ways:

In the study of human subjects, the term **sex** should be used as a classification, generally as male or female, according to the reproductive organs and functions that derive from the chromosomal complement [generally XX for female and XY for male].
In the study of human subjects, the term **gender** should be used to refer to a person's self-representation as male or female, or how that person is responded to by social institutions on the basis of the individual's gender presentation. In most studies of nonhuman animals, the term **sex** should be used.

Here are some current terms defined in Yale's "Guide to Gender Identity and Affirmation in the Workplace" that can help us all be more precise and respectful of everyone.

Cisgender: A term used to describe an individual whose gender identity aligns with the one typically associated with the sex assigned to them at birth. This is a term that is preferable to "non-trans," "biological," or "natal" man or woman.

Gender nonconforming: A person who views their gender identity as one of many possible genders beyond strictly female or male.

Transgender: A term that may be used to describe people whose gender expression does not conform to the cultural norms and/or whose gender identity is different from their sex assigned at birth. Transgender is also considered by some to be an "umbrella term" that encompasses a number of identities which transcend the conventional expectations of gender identity and expression, including transgender man, transgender woman, genderqueer, and gender expansive. People who identify as transgender may or may not decide to alter their bodies hormonally and/or surgically to match their gender identity. Sometimes shortened to the term "trans."

Intersex: Describing a person whose biological sex is ambiguous. There are genetic, hormonal or anatomical variations that can make a person's sex ambiguous (e.g., Klinefelter Syndrome, Adrenal Hyperplasia)."[70]

---

[70] Mazure, Carolyn. "What Do We Mean By Sex and Gender?," Yale School of Medicine, 2021.

Building Better Bridges

We are in the early stages of understanding what is shaping these cultural shifts and biological changes. If you refer back to "talking to the right brain," I think you will see that listening and empathy will go a long way. Finding truth is important, but will not happen outside a safe and loving relationship. For those people who struggle with their sexual identity, gender, or that feel opposite of the sex they are born with, I feel deep empathy and sadness. You can imagine with all the trauma, neglect, and confusing information we have covered, why some of these conversations get heated or go off the rails. There are many traumas to trigger us. If you struggle with the body you live in and the sex that you were assigned at birth, please seek support and help. Be patient. Above all, please hesitate to make permanent decisions about your body based on what could possibly be temporary problems or psychologically temporary. Make sure you have worked through all the root causes and influences with the support of a professional team, before you make permanent decisions. As an adult, you have the free will and right to make whatever choice you wish, and far be it from me to infringe on God's gift of free will. You do not need my permission or validation, and I know the world is cruel and difficult enough that you don't need me adding to it. I just want to state what I believe God says and to tell you, that you are loved and worthy of love, and your identity and worth aren't based on your orientation or gender.

When it comes to children, clinical research shows we should all be conservative in making any critical changes, while being extremely emotionally supportive along the way whatever issues they face. As children grow into adulthood, clarity will come from maturity and professional support. If your child is confused about their sexual identity or gender, seek professional help[71] and guidance, but most importantly, please do not shame them. Do not focus on the symptoms, but get to the root causes of their issues, fears, and doubts. I hope this book can help with that.

Many people believe that sex and gender identity is absolutely an important conversation to have, but despite how the media makes it seem, gender confusion, particularly as it relates to becoming

---

[71] I should have mentioned this earlier, but now seems as good a time as any. I repeat this refrain about getting help so much because 1) Duh, I am a clinician myself and 2) no matter how much you want to help, sometimes we have to count on professionals to do the things we can't.

transgendered, affects a very limited population of the country. In America, Federal and state population studies from 2016 estimate that 1.4 million to 1.65 million U.S. adults – or 0.6%-0.7% of the U.S. population – identify as transgender, according to the Williams Institute at UCLA School of Law.[72] It is best to take these situations on a case by case basis. I am not an expert in gender dysphoria or LGBTQA+ research. I'll leave that discussion for someone else. I do know clinicians say that the number of those struggling is on the rise since 2016, but it would do us far more good to have these complicated conversations about gender with our children from early on so that they are not confused or manipulated by social media, 24 hour news networks, or other toxic messages. I know this is a very nuanced and sensitive topic so hear me out.

Regardless of if the root cause is trauma, biology, psychology, or some mix, gender identity struggles are on a spectrum. In some ways, we all struggle to understand what men and women are "supposed" to be. The ways boys and girls present themselves on an emotional, physical, and psychological level are definitely on a spectrum as well. Historically, the way we have talked about gender hasn't been super healthy and in many ways extremely toxic. It is imperative that we allow boys and girls to express themselves without demanding they stay within certain stereotypes. The range is very wide, and we have tried to force kids into boxes for too many years. When we teach our children things like "Boys shouldn't play with dolls" or "Girls can't have short hair," we shame them and make them believe their interests are somehow wrong. Shame like this in some cases can lead a child to think "Maybe I am meant to be a different gender" or "I'm not like other boys or girls, something is wrong with me" when that is not the case at all. In many cases it can make a child feel not good enough, unworthy, and ashamed of their preferences. This is no different than a teacher making assumptions about their students' learning abilities based on gender. There has been lots of research done about these types of gender biases in school and the effects it has on effort and long term performance. I read an essay from a young female student on this very topic, and she makes a great point: "Gender bias sets rudimentary limits on future potential and creates

[72]Flores, A.R., Herman, J.L., Gates, G.J., & Brown, T.N.T. (2016). How Many Adults Identify as Transgender in the United States? Los Angeles, CA: The Williams Institute.

inequality in the classroom."[73] In a 2022 *Forbes* article, we see similar phenomena:

> "The gender gap is a common feature of education systems around the world. In standardized tests, girls tend to outperform boys in humanities, languages and reading skills, while boys tend to do better in math, but when grades are awarded by teachers, girls do better in all subjects."[74]

I also remember reading some research long ago that there is no "math gene."[75] Neither gender is more or less disposed to being good in school or at any particular subject. Parents, childhood experiences, even the epigenetics we discussed earlier can have an impact on how children learn and what they like to learn. But gender? The research says, nope.

The range of how boys and girls play, act, and express themselves is massive. It is only natural that boys and girls will fall into certain categories of play, but that won't be the case 100% of the time, and if our children do not fall into the typical bell curve, our response certainly shouldn't be shaming them or putting them at odds with the opposite sex. Where there are patterns, there will be people that fall outside those patterns. We do not need to make more out of these differences than is necessary. God has designed each one of us to be beautifully and wonderfully made, but in a world that is broken, none of us come out wired perfectly. We are all on a spectrum in some ways, and a great many of us face unresolved trauma, attachment issues, or neurodiversity of some sort.[76] This is why judging children based on their sex or gender is a problem. We should get to know children as individuals, and we as parents have a front row seat to watching who our child becomes.

---

[73] Baltimore, Sharyn. "Gender Bias," One World Education, 2021.
[74] Morrison, Nick. "Teachers Are Hard-Wired to Give Girls Better Grades, Study Says." *Forbes*, 18 Oct. 2022.
[75] Campbell, Patricia. "Girls and Math: Enough is Known for Action," *WEEA Digest*, June 1991.
[76] Don't even get me started on the gendered diagnoses of neurodiversity in children. ADD, ADHD, and other brain disorders do not favor one gender over another, but girls are far less likely to receive such a diagnosis than boys. Having one of these conditions is not a death sentence for your male or female children's attention or functionality. Being wired differently doesn't mean being wired *badly.*

We can and should allow our children to express themselves in many different ways, regardless of gender stereotypes, but, like anything else, there are limits. You have to decide for yourself what those limits will be in your home. Avoiding shame, though, still ought to be a priority when setting those boundaries. We have to hold the tension of living lives as individuals with different views and beliefs and also how our beliefs and actions have consequences to our surrounding community, especially other children who are easily confused and influenced. For example: You may think spanking your kid is a good idea and helpful for discipline. You may have the right to do that in the middle of Target or at a birthday party, but that doesn't make it right or helpful to those around you that feel the opposite and not very helpful for your child either. Just because we have the right to do something, does not mean it is what we should do or allow. You may not mind that your child watches certain shows, dresses in the clothes of the opposite gender, or wears makeup, but your child is involved in a school, a culture and a community. What you choose to do does affect those children around them and does open the door to confusion and risk of bullying. ***Just because you have the right to do something, does not mean it is always the right thing to do.***

In American culture, we tend to swing to opposite extremes depending on the traumas and abuses of our past. While learning from our past can be enormously helpful to our own children, to be so consumed by it that we alter our worldview or manipulate those of children does little good for anyone. Everyone's voice is valuable, but the voices in the fringes seem to be the loudest, and our perceptions are being muddied. Yes. Every person should have a voice, but I don't think outlier situations should dictate the changes made to an entire society. Certainly not without addressing the long-lasting ramifications for that society. This touches the social media topic a bit, but trauma and gender identity conversations are best suited for a therapist's office or with your religious leader, not Fox News or CNN, TikTok or Instagram. As I said, I can't address every possible trauma here, but I do want to talk briefly about my own sons and the way I see parents and adults causing confusion in children regarding gender identity.

I have two boys. One of them is extremely rough and loves to wrestle. He is very emotionally driven, but he is not naturally in-tune with the emotions of others. He has some sensory issues and focus problems at times which affects this. He loves taking care of little kids and is learning to be a great leader. My second son doesn't like being rough, and he gets his feelings hurt very easily. He plays with "boys and girls" toys at church and would play with characters from any movie or cartoon you put in front of him. Barbie, trucks, my little pony, it doesn't matter. He will play with anything. They may be missing an arm or head and they certainly won't have any clothes on by the end, but play he will. He picks up on everyone's feelings and is very in-tune with other peoples' emotions. He is also the one who is more likely to punch you and run off to pee in the yard. Children are unique and dynamic. I hear this from hundreds of clients.

Both of them adored *Frozen,* love dance parties, and enjoy snuggling. They also both play violin, take Jiu-Jitsu, and love to sing. They both love to break things and figure out how they go back together. They love dirt and destruction. I haven't forced any of this on them or tried to get them to be a particular "type," they just are that way. They are loud and aggressive and gross. They eat their boogers and love a good poop joke and potty word, no matter how many times I try to shut it down. But – I know plenty of girls who do all of those same things and plenty of boys who love things on the more sensitive side. The most important thing? *Anybody* can love a mud pie or dance party.

Stereotypes are there for a reason. Even though girls and boys are on a spectrum, there are common experiences for many. Research and practical experience show that girls and boys are not the same. I remember when we first had my oldest son, all of our friends had girls. 90% of them loved arts and crafts and would sit at parties and decorate cupcakes or make artwork. My oldest would run around destroying everyone's art, and he never once colored until 4 years old. I remember we were doing a music class once and he was supposed to be sitting in my lap doing "quiet mommy time" (I happened to be there this particular day in place of Mom...see I'm breaking stereotypes), but instead, he was ripping the history of the Bible pictures off the wall. My youngest, though, came out of the womb coloring, and he will sit for hours doing crafts. He loves his "quiet mommy time" and both are very sweet and kind. My boys are boys who just happen to have a wide variety of interests and find fun in lots of different things.

Clint Davis

Gender bias from parents can occur unintentionally and often stems from societal norms and long ingrained beliefs. Here are some examples of gender bias that parents may inadvertently exhibit:

Differential chores: Assigning household chores based on gender, such as expecting girls to do more cleaning and boys to perform outdoor tasks like mowing the lawn.

Clothing choices: Restricting clothing options based on gender, such as discouraging girls from wearing pants or hats and boys from painting their fingernails for fun.

Toy preferences: Encouraging boys to play with traditionally masculine toys like cars and action figures, while steering girls towards dolls and domestic playsets.

Academic expectations: Setting different academic expectations for boys and girls, such as assuming boys will excel in math and science while girls will be better at languages or arts.

Sports and physical activities: Discouraging girls from participating in sports or physical activities that are traditionally associated with boys, or vice versa. Providing more opportunities and resources for boys to participate in sports activities, while limiting or not supporting girls' involvement in sports.

Emotional expression: Discouraging boys from expressing emotions other than anger or stoicism, while encouraging girls to be more sensitive and nurturing.

Career aspirations: Subtly steering children towards gender-stereotypical career paths, such as suggesting that boys become engineers or girls become nurses.

Communication styles: Interrupting or dismissing girls' contributions during family discussions while giving more attention and value to boys' opinions.

Risk-taking behavior: Discouraging girls from engaging in adventurous or risky activities, while encouraging boys to take on challenges and explore their limits.

Punishment disparities: Applying stricter disciplinary measures or punishments to boys while being more lenient towards girls for the same behaviors.

171

Building Better Bridges

Some of these practices are so subtle you may not even realize you have done them. And maybe your son loves raking leaves outside, and your daughter loves to fold warm laundry...that's fine! But tightly contorting our kids into predetermined boxes because of our own fears and "traditions" is a problem.

We should not force gender stereotypes on our children or make them feel weird or ashamed of their interests, but I also think that gender is real. There is a clinical and biological difference between males and females, but those differences shouldn't be used to make concrete judgements about what children should play with or enjoy or how they should or should not do with their educational goals. Additionally, and perhaps most importantly, we should never treat those gender differences as negative. I truly believe this is where we get into trouble. **_Neither males nor females are objectively better than the other, and our differences in personality and physiology should be celebrated as complementary, not disdained as "unequal."_** We certainly shouldn't compare ourselves to another gender as a joke or insult.
This common experience sets children on a trajectory of unhealthy views of sex and gender.

When we tell a little girl she's a "tom-boy" or we call a little boy a "sissy," we confuse them and paint the other sex as either more desirable or less so. We reinforce this all the way to adulthood when we describe a man as a "p***y," communicating that women are weak and lesser than men. Ideally your children, grown or otherwise, wouldn't be using such language, but nevertheless it gets used and needs to stop. Another small note on this. Why do we all gravitate to such intense extremes? A woman is either considered gentle and timid or is written off as a bossy or sassy drama queen. A man is either a three-a-day, truck-driving tough guy or is ridiculed as soft and effeminate. Did we all of a sudden lose the ability to have personalities? Just like my sons - can we not accept someone who has all sorts of traits? I know dads who love to hunt but can have just as much fun braiding their daughter's hair and moms who love to cook for their families that equally love taking their sons fishing. One more time: _interests are not gendered._

Despite your thoughts on this, and even if your beliefs are quite different from mine, it is incredibly unhelpful in any instance to project culture changes on children. They are children. Science tells us that before puberty they do not know what they like, who they want to be, or even who they really are. Their brains are developing at a rapid pace, and their main concern should be playing and connection to safe people. To preemptively coerce, manipulate, or expose them to content that can confuse them or force ideas into their heads is a bad idea. We have already done *a lot* of damage over the years regarding gender issues.

Think about if a girl is faster than a boy, and Dad gets mad and makes his son feel small. He says something like, "Don't let that girl beat you!" (I am certain you have either witnessed this happen or sadly been part of it yourself). This reaction teaches that a little boy losing to a girl is not okay or even makes him less of a man. This is the type of toxicity that has been in our culture for *ages*. This is also such an American issue. If you are from another country or culture, you may be confused about this topic or at least the level of toxicity discussed. In the Native American culture for instance, they talk about people having both female and male spiritual components. They teach that both are equal and valuable gifts.

We must learn to value the differences between men and women without implying one gender is better than another. We should be showing our children how to respect those differences, to see them as strengths, and to see them on a spectrum. We must also show them that in reality we are devaluing both genders by saying they are identical or blank slates. We're not! These are nuanced discussions to have, but when we don't teach these things, we create problems in an already difficult stage of life. We can look around at our culture and see the damage already done. Boys and girls and men and women are desperate for answers because they grew up believing they weren't good enough or that they are supposed to be something different. This is how trauma, neglect and forcing gender roles, based on that trauma and neglect in our own past, is creating a vicious cycle. Let's stop this cycle today. We can show boys and girls how to honor and love one another as individuals, and in doing so, honor themselves. All this without shaming them into thinking they have to change their bodies or their interests.

Last thing on this topic.

Building Better Bridges

Guess what, moms and dads? Your children are *not* going to be exactly like you. And thank goodness for that! They are going to be different and better humans if we model good choices for them, if we show them how to be kinder and more informed than we were. Just like racism and sexism, gender confusion, and the embarrassment that comes with it, is a *learned* behavior based on unhealthy conversations and shame brought on children by adults. We need to change our expectations, find out who our children are supposed to be, and stop trying to mold them into who *we* want them to be. Parenting out of fear has caused enough problems. Let us parent out of hope. Hope that our little boys and girls are valuable and different in many different types of ways. There are sensitive boys who love music, art, and dance. There are rough girls who like to play sports, roll in the mud, and chase frogs. And then there is everything in between.

I will say it again: I do not have all the answers. I just know that the gender or sexuality of a child should not be confused, controlled, or altered based on bias and fear by the culture or the parents. They should not be compared to another child or even a sibling. Their identity should be focused on one thing: they are a child loved by you and safe in your care. Gender is just one small piece of a huge puzzle. It should not be their entire identity. We as parents should walk alongside our kids through the big maze of growing up, helping them learn who they are with loving guidance and direction. This is not a perfect world, and there will be difficulty and brokenness along the way. Be patient. Seek counsel. Be a safe place for your child to learn and grow. Don't make this about you. Dads, if your son wants to try ballet, then go buy a ticket to see one with him, research and learn everything you can about it. Maybe even put on a leotard. Moms, if your daughter wants to go hunting with her dad, you should encourage that relationship and buy her all the best camo.

If your little boy wants to be in the school play and not on the football team, then we should celebrate that and encourage him to be the best actor he can be. If your daughter wants to get a job and be a professional, you should tell her you are proud of her, support her, and will always have her back as she follows that dream. Sure you can make suggestions about motives and help them look at the big picture. Yes, as a parent it is your job to guide them in areas and help them make the best choices, but mandating it or shaming them because it doesn't align with the "norm," will only cause worse problems, more confusion and pain.

On a similar note, give me a second to share a personal pet peeve of mine. Comparing body sizes and body parts to others. I absolutely hate this. This tendency to compare leads to tons of mental and emotional unhealth in children and adults. Which in turn is the cause of many of the childhood surgeries and horrible transformations we see in our society. You are beautiful and valuable the way you are! I can only speak as a male, but apply this however you want as well ladies. I know there is enough money made off of people changing their physical features in America these days. To give an example: As a man, the insecurities around penis size are *appalling*. As young boys in locker rooms, there are constant jokes and jabs about small or larger penis sizes. (Someone will probably make one about me having a small one since I'm writing about this haha) The average length of an erect penis is 5 inches. Let us move past this please. Can we just evolve already, guys? Between porn culture, pride, and male ego we have caused enough problems and confusion. I know both males and females deal with comparison of body parts. We need to educate our children as they develop that size and shape comparisons are nonsense and have nothing to do with their gender, standing in society, or their ability to please their partner. This deep and toxic trend leads to all sorts of issues and abuse in marriage and relationships. It also attributes to all the body shaming and body dysmorphia going on around us and in our hearts. I'll link a couple studies if you want to know more of the history of phallic insecurities and how this started all the way back with the Vikings of Iceland or beyond.[77]

---

[77] The following two links are great reads if you want to take the time to read! For those reading a hard copy, sorry, but you will just have to go old school and type this into your phone.
https://amp.theguardian.com/world/2004/oct/10/artsandhumanities.research
https://amp.theguardian.com/commentisfree/2015/mar/04/men-too-insecure-about-penis-size-ever-stop-worrying-if-its-big-enough

Building Better Bridges

So, here it is. As a clinician, the best advice I can give you is this: the more your child feels known and valued by *you*, the less likely they will be to stray, seek attention from unhealthy groups, or run further from you. When they feel confident in who they are and that they are securely attached to you, then things generally balance out, and any stressful seasons will likely pass. Just love them and educate them as much as you can, and accept nothing less from anyone else. Make sure you speak positively about your body, all its parts, and the parts of others. Teach your children that differences and preferences are good and that valuing themselves or others less, because of those differences is toxic and unacceptable.

Lastly, when it comes to sex and gender. Be patient. There is a lot going on that we do not know. **BUT**, there is a lot more going on that we do know. Search for the truth. Get to the root causes if there is confusion or unique challenges. Get them to a professional who is aligned with your values and is supportive of your parenting. Be open to correction and guidance. Do not let society dictate what you know to be true. Focus on your child and walk with them through struggle and you will be way more successful in the long run. If we do this, I believe they will grow and heal. I know our society still has a chance to be better and keep our children safer when it comes to sex and gender. I know any healthy caregiver or parent wants that too!

Reflection & Discussion

1. What are your beliefs about gender? From where did you establish those beliefs?

2. Do you find yourself being nervous of your child participating in certain activities? Do you think this makes them more or less male/female? Why?

3. How was gender and sexuality treated in your childhood home? How do you think that influences you and your parenting now?

4. As an adult, do you allow yourself to enjoy whatever interests you like without rethinking your gender identity?

5. What does your child enjoy doing, and how could you participate in that with them more?

12. Sex Talk Foundations

Talking to your kids about sex is an opportunity to share with them the beauty and goodness of God's plan for sexuality and intimacy.
- John Piper

After discussing topics such as sexual neglect, menstruation, erections, how to talk about penises and vaginas, what consent means, gender roles, and several other things, my hope is you feel emboldened to talk to your children about these things that maybe seemed too scary or awkward before. At the very least, I hope you reflect on the ways simply talking can really change the course of your kids' lives. As far as the ever frightening sex talk goes, if you have built a habit of discussing all these topics with your children as they grow, I honestly think it will be relatively easy. You will have likely prevented a great deal of awkwardness and built trust along the way that will create an open door with your child for any other conversation.

But maybe that's not how it is for you. Maybe you are thinking "Clint, my child is a teen already, and I haven't really discussed any of this stuff with them. What do I do now, is it too late for me?" Well, first, I want to remind you that just like many generations before us, we were likely not talked to or trained on how to have these talks. So, first and foremost, please don't shut down or beat yourself up. You are not a bad parent. Maybe you have missed some important things, but the most important thing is to start now! The goal here is not to point out all your failures or to be the bearer of bad news. The truth is, even if you have missed all the opportunities of your kids' early childhood, there is still a great amount of hope for you and your sons or daughters. God can redeem anything, anyone, and any situation to bring about blessing and joy and restoration. Your child might act awkward and uncomfortable, but they need you to be open and honest. They need you to make a safe space for them to talk and explore their experiences and desires. I have learned that when we *know* better, we can *do* better. We can't put into practice that which we don't know.

So, if you're reading this and feeling behind, that's okay. I want you to forgive yourself for the things you didn't know and for the parts of parenting that weren't modeled for you. Then, even if it might be an odd conversation, ask forgiveness from your child. Be candid, and tell them you have learned new information that you didn't know before. Start slowly having conversations and opening the door to healing and education...for both of you. Seek counsel and wisdom and for heaven's sake don't do this all alone.

In the entire history of my clinical practice, I have *never* had anyone come into my office wanting to talk about the parent that asked for forgiveness and tried to make things right. So, take heart. If you missed some chances, or if you regret some of the mistakes of the past, make amends. Your child will very likely forgive you and be thankful for the chance at reconciliation. The people who do come into my office with anger or resentment towards their childhood, do so because their parents harmed them, neglected them, or abused them and never once said they were sorry or took any responsibility. I can promise you this: your children don't want perfect parents, they want authentic and trustworthy ones. They want parents who own up to their mistakes and make positive changes. Parents that are willing to sit in discomfort in order to protect their family.

Wherever you fall on this conversation spectrum, if you have had lots of honest and informative conversations or very few, you still need to talk. Then your children will pass down these talks to their children, and your bravery can make changes for generations to come! You still have the power in your hands, my friend. We can be the wise counsel for our children and their children that we never had.

Preparing for The Talk

Understandably, a sensitive or emotionally charged topic like sex, or any of these other developmental conversations, is most effective if you have already built trust and strong systems of support between you and your child. Whether a toddler or a teen, your kids will be more receptive to your advice when they truly believe you have their best interests at heart and will not deceive them. Maybe you feel your lifetime of provision for your children will suffice, but that is not what earns their trust, I'm afraid. Instead, they need our consistency and diligence in the areas of sexual development, biology, and online safety. We must talk about these things, repeat what we said, and live out what we say. Whatever age you might be starting at, all of this happens over time, as issues or questions arise and new stages of development come up.

My years of clinical practice and psychological background have shown me that children who talk to their parents, in an age-appropriate way, about sexual health and relationships are less likely to take dangerous risks or make bad choices in their future relationships. They are also more likely to talk to you, ask you questions, or come to you about problems when they happen.

Take for instance this lovely question: "Mommy, where do babies come from?" Maybe this question hits you out of left field, and you are tempted to make up a story or just ignore the question altogether. Now, this might come as a shock. But the better approach is to be honest. Insane, I know, but honesty is the best policy, after all. Naturally, you will start more broadly and not give graphic details to a 6- or 10-year-old, but as they grow and mature, you offer more information. If you have an especially curious child with lots of questions, you can redirect their questions or figure out why they might be so keen on knowing.

With the proliferation of the internet, your child may hear about sexual topics from a friend at school or online before you are ready for them to know these things. This type of exposure always expedites the process of question-asking and sexual development conversations. Sometimes exposure, trauma, or just negative experiences force our hand to talk about things sooner than we would like. Even still, it is best to be as honest and open as possible, guiding them towards what is appropriate for them to know and discuss at their age.

Honesty is obviously the most important thing, but it's not the only important aspect of these conversations. I have given many parenting seminars, and nearly every time, parents will ask me for a sheet of *exactly* what to say. When I am in a session with a parent, I will sometimes write down examples for them, and they will often want to read it word for word to their kid. Here is the deal. That doesn't really work the way you think it will. You need to be *you*. The best version of *you*! Your kids know when you are being sincere, and they know when you're not. Using tools and relying on your resources is one thing, but reading verbatim off a script will not have the same impact as being candid and real with them. I will do my best to give you guidance on how and when to have these talks, but there are so many variables for every situation and every child. No two conversations should go the same way. The principles may be the same, but the application varies. Despite being rooted in research and experience, think of these conversations as an art, not a science. Conversations are a dance between two people. The flow, cadence, and steps will be different depending on who is partnered together and how much trust and comfort they have with one another. (check the appendix for a breakdown of how to manage crazy questions)

Bringing It Up

"Okay, Clint, that's all great, but how do I bring up such an important and scary topic?" I get this question all. the. time.

First, we must clarify: are we talking about the *act* of sex or sexuality as a whole? Those can and should be two different conversations. Quite likely, your child will have questions related to various sexual development topics before you have to sit down with a PowerPoint presentation and outline every possible subject. (Please don't do that, well actually, some kids might love just that!) So, first and foremost, don't jump to conclusions when a question comes up. Once more, this is likely your own traumas or experiences at play in your mind. Instead, clarify with your child what they are really asking. Make clear what they want to know before revealing too much information that they may not have even been asking for. When our anxiety flares up, we can sometimes jump the gun and lower our chances of having small and helpful conversations over a greater amount of time.

Building Better Bridges

Though sometimes circumstances will require us to have the whole conversation at once, typically this is not the case. Realistically, we will have ample opportunity to teach our children about human development and sexuality in stages and at various points in their growth. Here are just a few examples:

- When you or your child overhear negative comments about gender stereotypes such as "You throw like a girl," or "Boys shouldn't cry." Have a conversation about gender and how God designed males and females in incredible ways. Speak up when you hear this on a tv show and constantly speak truth and life into subjects of gender.
- When you see edited pictures of models or people on social media, billboards, or TV ads. Have a conversation about expectations vs. reality, especially in the digital age. They need to learn early and often what is fake and how to spot it.
- When you come across ads for hygiene products (condoms, tampons, pads, etc). In older children, use this as an opportunity to introduce puberty or changes in their bodies that will be taking place. This is great to do when they see you shaving your beard or they stick pads all over their clothes and come walking into the living room. Just my kids?
- When your child reads news stories, books, or articles that discuss sexuality or sex. Use these moments to determine what they know, and then, where appropriate, ask what they want to know.
- When a family member is pregnant or has a new baby, you can discuss conception, birth, and where babies come from. Babies are an amazing way to stagger the information as they get older and more mature. This will happen more often, between siblings, when mommies privacy is zilch.
- When animals at the zoo or the farm are mating. Have a talk about how sex is normal, natural, and is a gift from God used to create life.
- When your child sees someone breastfeeding, you can explain what's happening and tell them about the special

bond between a mommy and baby and reduce shame
around nursing mothers.

There are a *multitude* of other moments where an opportunity will
present itself, or your child will come to you with questions. The thing is,
we have to be alert to the rhythms of life to catch them.[78] I can assure
you, answering questions as they arise will be much more comfortable
than a 2-hour long talk of shock, confusion, or awkwardness. If all these
conversations are commonplace, you will be ready when the heavier parts
come, and you can enter into those discussions with more trust, grace,
and confidence.

Daily life and experiences will provide situations, both good and bad, that
enable you to pivot to teachable moments. Just like your child, you'll find
that *you* gain confidence from these conversations, and they will get more
natural over time. Our gender and sexuality are, after all, a natural and
life-long part of our being. They are also gifts that have been twisted and
corrupted by the world and other humans. We have to do our own work
to redeem our view of these things so that our children can see them
through healthy lenses.

As you find and utilize your teaching opportunities, don't be afraid to
simultaneously explain your family values or religious beliefs to your
children. I've said it before, but if you aren't guiding them in these things,
the world will be sure to do it for you. They will hear "truths" about sex,
their bodies, porn, and so much more without even looking for it. Our job
is to walk alongside them and help prepare them to know the real truth.
Obviously, we give our children some freedom and space to establish their
own faith, but when a particular message is against your values, it can be
helpful to say, "Some people believe these things, but here is our
perspective on that and here's why." This method is useful for all things
related to faith or intrinsic values, but can also be the way you set the
standard in your home for things related to sexual development. The

---

[78] Just a few days ago, I saw a TedTalk given by a young little girl named Molly Wright. It
shook me to my core, and I really suggest giving it a watch. The video is called "How
every child can thrive by five," and Molly talks about the opportunities parents have as
long as they are paying attention.

older our kids get the better our why's have to be and the more consistent we have to be living them out on a daily basis.

Just like in therapy, it is best to ask simple questions to gauge your child's comfort level and knowledge concerning their sexual development and other topics. You may be surprised by what they already know from school, church, or daycare. Here are a few examples (you guys like lists, right?):

- What do you know about where babies come from?
- How do you think babies get there?
- What do you think about the changes that were made on the magazine cover to make them look more muscled, more thin, or more tan?
- What do you think are toys meant for boys or girls? Why?
- What would you do if someone you liked treated you like the character in this book or TV show?

For teens it could be something like, all of the above and:
- Why do you believe people are LGBTQ?
- Why do you think sex before marriage is ok?
- Do you think porn is ok or unhealthy?
- How do you think gender plays a role in relationships?
- How does social media affect your mental health?

Our own past experiences might make these conversations feel daunting or too awkward to face. You may or may not know the answers, or we may just not want to answer it in the middle of the grocery store or doctor's office. First, take a deep breath, and remind yourself you can do this. Then, take a step back and recognize that they are asking *you* these questions and desire to know what you think and believe. This means that you have done an amazing job showing them they can trust you, and they feel safe doing so. It is always good to take a pause, say a quick prayer, and ask God to give you the wisdom to teach and disciple your child well. Kids can (and will) ask you some crazy questions, so here are some tips for when your child starts asking questions about sex:

184

- No matter how easy it would be to do so, don't immediately shut the conversation down. Leave the door opened. Do not slam it shut. After answering the first question, ask them if they have anything else they would like to ask about.
- Make sure to clarify that they learned the lesson you were trying to teach and that the conversation finishes at a place of understanding.
- Use the Post-It Note test. Don't say more at a time than you could write on a post-it. Or use KISS (Keep it Simple, Stupid.) Not saying you're stupid – I didn't make the catchphrase.
- Ask them what they know about the question and what they have already heard. Maybe ask them who they heard it from and follow up with that child or adult to see what was actually said before jumping to conclusions.
- Wait for the other parent of the same gender to come in and answer questions. This is not always possible, but when you can have someone with the same parts and the same experience talk to them, it can make a big difference.

The answer is yes, these conversations can be a little uncomfortable, cause some anxiety, and flush your cheeks (on both the parent and the child). This is okay. Just take a deep breath, work through those nerves, and handle this like the pro you are! Awkwardness is non-life-threatening. Admit it is awkward and scary to your kid to normalize the situation and show them how to push through.

Unfortunately, I can't guess every topic and scenario that might come up in your home, but conversations will range over a variety of topics. Here are some of the top FAQs that I have heard from my own sons, from another family, and that you will want to be prepared for:

- Breastfeeding
- Differences between boys and girls
- Growth of breasts or penis
- The mechanics of sex
- Romance between the same sex (Can boys marry boys, etc.)
- Does sex hurt?
- Why would you do *that*?
- When can I date?

Building Better Bridges

- Why does my penis get hard or grow at certain times?
- Why do boys have a penis and girls have a vagina?
- Why do I have so much skin down there?
- Where does all the stuff come out?
- Why is there liquid coming out, is something wrong with me?

The truth is, countless questions and conversations, both simple and complicated, will come up at a million moments throughout your child's growth. The most important thing to remember is just to be genuine and honest, and remind yourself that you are doing this for them, to give them the best chance possible when they face the world. I am certain you will be better at this than you realize.

But nevertheless, let's walk through this thing together.

Reflection & Discussion

1. Does thinking about the sex talk with your children scare you or your spouse? Why or why not?

2. How did you hear about sex when you were young? Was that a positive or negative experience?

3. When you had questions, did you ask them? If you didn't ask, why not? If you did, who did you go to for answers?

4. What are your goals for trust in your home, surrounding sexual topics or other things? How do you plan to build that trust?

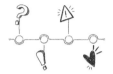

13. *When* to Talk About Sex and What to Say[79]

*"I flip ahead in the textbook. There's an interesting chapter about
acid rain. Nothing about sex. We aren't scheduled to learn
about that until eleventh grade."*
-Laurie Halse Anderson, *Speak*

Childhood sexual neglect, as we have defined it here, means not having
age-appropriate discussions of sexual development with your child. As I
said before, this leads to lots of potential problems, one of the main ones
being that our children will arrive at certain stages of their body
development and experience changes and sensations for which they were
completely unprepared. As you embark on having these conversations,
you'll want to try to stay just ahead of the next developmental stage your
child is about to enter and gently prepare them for it with information and
support. A little boy does not need to have his first nocturnal emission
without knowing that it's even a possibility. Children do not need to have
their first experience with masturbation and not know the names or
functions of their sexual organs.

A lack of preparedness in such crucial topics can lead to shock, fear,
shame, or confusion. Such negative emotions can in turn lead to a life
marked by secret-keeping, anxiety, even addiction and depression.
Almost every sex addict I have worked with has a story of being exposed
to sexual content early, being touched by an adult or another child, or
being shamed or laughed at when caught masturbating.

Kids are smart. If we do not talk to our children about these things, we
are teaching them that *we* don't talk about these things. Your son,
daughter, or a youth in your care will be less likely to come to you for

---

[79] For even more specific resources or books that will help your journey of talking to your
child about sex, check out the list of books here!
https://littlebookbigstory.com/9-christian-resources-help-teach-child-sex/

help or advice when something happens, because you have unconsciously and unintentionally set that precedent. I'd say 90% of the time, if you teach and model transparency and honesty to your children, they will reciprocate those things to you. **Build bridges, not walls. Trust me that it takes time, money, and suffering to knock those walls down later.**

I don't want to fill your heart with sheer panic, I just implore you to see how important it is to avoid childhood sexual neglect in your home. I'm hopeful this chapter will take some weight off your shoulders and give you a guide (not a script) for what to discuss, when to discuss it, and how to do it in an effective and loving way. I have broken it down in stages.

2 – 5 Years Old

We will call this the "Toddler Age." These early years are a great time to start teaching your child proper terms for private parts, who can touch them, and when this is appropriate. Teaching these things early is very important – they are simple but profound and set the foundation for many of the other things you will teach them as they get older. This is the developmental stage where children start to learn to set boundaries and also learn about consent. Years 2 – 5 also tend to be the stage where we have historically taken away our children's consent by forcing them to kiss a relative or sit on someone's lap, even if it seems like they don't want to. We also force children to share toys just to prevent other children from crying. Now I am all for teaching sharing and generosity, but not just out of obligation for someone else's temper tantrum. I think that sends the wrong message.

At this age, your details don't have to be super explicit, but these are perfect years to start establishing the basis of your family rules and values. Supervision is very important at this stage as well. Toddlers cannot always articulate what happened, and they are extremely curious and impulsive. Make sure they keep their clothes on when playing with other children, and limit the random acts of nudity as they get closer to 5 years. Nudity is not bad and certainly nothing we should shame them over, but we also need to be careful about what we share with others in person or online. I beg you. Never post pictures of your children naked on the internet, and do not force them to change in front of anyone. If they ask to put clothes on, let them. Don't force them to bathe with other children even for convenience sake.

You might hear your toddler ask where babies come from, and you can be as vague as you think is warranted, although I strongly recommend you don't lie to them. Doesn't matter if the lie is white, blue, green, or rainbow. You wouldn't want your child disrespecting you by lying, right? For example, you could say a mommy and daddy lay together, and a sperm and an egg come together to make a baby. Or you can simply say, a baby gets into a mommy's belly and comes into the world after 9 months. Usually a toddler will move on. If they don't move past the question, simply say you will be able to tell them more details as they get older, and gently redirect their focus. Just no stork nonsense, okay? Awesome.

If for some reason your child does explore sexually with another child or exposes themselves or touches another child, please do not freak out. I know that it can be overwhelming and that the other parents might get worked up as well.[80] It is normal for a child to explore the various parts of their environment. The worst thing we can do is yell at them, spank them, or punish them for this type of behavior. It is our job to supervise them and guard them, not theirs. Again, if you have responded this way, you have not ruined their life, but you must work to repair the damage and write the proper narrative for them. However, if the sexual behavior continues unchecked or occurs in an aggressive way, that may be a red flag. Employ play therapy[81], or consider an assessment by a professional. If it is a one-time thing, a single instance of silliness, or just an attempt to explore, simply redirect your child away from the situation, state the rules gently but firmly, and move on.

My oldest son is more bashful than my youngest. So when they turned 3 and 6 years old, we started limiting their time in the bath together and

---

[80] If abuse is occurring, head back to our section about abuse resources, hotlines, and how to talk through what happened.

[81] Play therapy is a therapeutic approach that utilizes play as a means of communication and healing for children. It employs the use of toys, art materials, or games to explore a child's feelings and help the observer understand and address a child's underlying issues. It is an amazing tool that I totally suggest researching if you are interested!

made sure they were keeping their private parts private. Every now and then they bathe together out of necessity (siblings are the exception), and I make sure that I am right there the whole time. Our house is not formal and stuffy, these kids are just crazy, and sometimes my youngest tries to poke the oldest in the butt or grab his penis, and they are both laughing hysterically. They are soaking wet and slippery and making a total mess. I am alternating between internally freaking out and laughing hysterically as well. These things happen. It won't be the end of the world. The goal of handling such a situation is to make everything relaxed and calm because, as the parent, you know what is healthy and common and how to respond accordingly. When we don't know what to do or what is appropriate at a certain age, we end up punishing our children for normal play and make the entire situation more complicated. I am sure many of us have memories of being caught in some behavior as a child and getting yelled at or spanked. This leaves a lasting impression on us not that we shouldn't do those things because they are bad, but that we are bad for doing them. This is a direct root cause for many peoples mental health struggles and sexual proclivities.

In this toddler stage, if there are any suspicions of abuse, don't panic or attempt to ignore it out of fear. Go straight to a therapist's office, and get help. Don't minimize when your gut tells you there is a problem. It might sound like I'm talking out of both sides of my mouth, huh?
Don't freak out. Chill. But also report. Well, growing up in a broken world is complicated, and sometimes it is a knife's edge we walk. You are likely the best judge of the situations in your own home, and I just want to offer how things *should* go nine times out of ten and what to do when they don't go like that. This is why I recommended finding a group of friends or other families who will try to follow this path with you. Lean on an objective party or a trusted professional when you feel lost.

6 - 8 Years Old

At this stage, which we'll name the "Kid Stage," it is important to start reading books similar to *Good Pictures Bad Pictures*, by Gail Poyner and Kristen Jenson. There is a Jr. and regular version. See, age appropriateness matters! We started this book with our children around 4 or 5 years old, because we wanted to get a jump start. *GPBP* is about how to keep our kids safe from explicit images online or in magazines. For better or worse, our children are exposed to technology and devices earlier and earlier. They need to know that there are things online that can hurt their brain, hearts, and bodies. They need to learn what to do if they see one of those pictures, what will happen to them, and who to go tell.

The steps *GPBP* teaches are to STOP, COVER YOUR EYES, TURN, RUN AND TELL.

The kid stage is also a good time to continue the private parts conversation. As I mentioned before, I am a boy dad so I continue to talk to my oldest son about his penis getting larger and what is happening to it when he rubs it against the bottom of the tub or pulls it while he is on the potty. I respond gently and simply say "Your penis is filling with blood, and that's called an erection. Stop doing that because it will hurt, and use your penis for pottying."

By 8 years old, it's normal for children to start exploring their bodies and trying to figure out what their different body parts are for. This might include placing a finger in their rectum, rubbing their clitoris, or stretching their testicles and penis. Please know that at this point your child is just exploring. They are not being erotic in the adult sense. Remember, they do not have the pasts we have, and they possess no images or ideas of sex between themselves and another person. Unless a child is exposed to adult content, is abused, or has had inappropriate child-on-child interactions, they will not think of their bodies in the same way as they will post-puberty. It is a good idea in the kid stage to begin discussing how your child's body will change when they get older, and specifically how their bodies will be changing over the next few years. You can use a growth chart or pictures to help explain how these changes have already been happening in small ways. Lots of times kids will point out the hair on mom's or dad's body that they do not have on theirs yet. Instead of brushing these comments off, use them as an easy introduction into how God is preparing their body for teen years and adulthood. If you are a research and resource person, this is a good age to read *God Made All of Me*[82], as well as other books on gender, secrets, and body safety

---

[82] Can you tell I love this book yet?

protocols, many of which I will list in the resource list at the end of the book.

These are also the years where children start learning from other children at school. Some of these processes can be sped up by friends with older siblings. Try to limit terms and phrases about dating, crushes, boyfriends etc. These years are very crucial to setting up good ideas and expectations and not rushing them into pre-teen and teen years. This is also the time to try to build up positive ideas and correlations for the other gender. Promoting good relationships through conversations about the positive aspects of the other sex is very important moving forward. One tactic I use with my sons is if someone is wearing something revealing or breastfeeding in public, I look away and express to them that we are going to respect women and not stare regardless of the circumstances. This might seem like an easy and small task, but in a world where men are more likely to point or catcall a woman when she walks by, I want my boys to grow up learning how to respect women and men, even if they don't know how to respect themselves. It is not our job to judge, but it is our job to learn to control our own eyes and responses. If we start young it will make our jobs much easier in the future.

9 – 12 Years Old

Preteens give us the greatest years of all: the beginnings of puberty. (Catch that sarcasm?) Girls will often start puberty before boys. In America especially, puberty is starting earlier and earlier. It must be what we are putting in the chicken. Girls can start as early as 9 years old, and boys at 10 or 11 years. Obviously there will be outliers and late bloomers, but these are not the typical case.

Preteen years can be some of the most difficult years if we don't have healthy and open conversations, and, as with many things, the most crucial conversations can be the most daunting. Even still, these are the years to start talking about the actual mechanics of sex. You can put this conversation off until you feel your child is ready or can understand it, but don't put it off for very long. Face those fears, because remember: we always want to be one step ahead of the season our children are walking into. If your child is about to enter into puberty, it is essential you tell them about the body changes that are about to happen.

For girls, their first menstruation is a vital part of them entering into womanhood. The last thing they ought to be feeling is shame, fear or confusion. Above all, they don't need to be surprised, something that I fear happens all too often. The best person to deliver this conversation would be a mother or another trustworthy female in a girl's life. As I mentioned earlier, some families and friend groups are offering or encouraging "period parties" to lessen the stigma and shame surrounding periods. As you talk to your daughter about menstruating, or if you are a leader sharing with young girls in your mentorship, here are some of the topics that need to be covered:

- Periods are good and a sign of healthy growth
- What will happen on a period and different levels of blood flow
- Differences in tampons/pads/cups and how to use them
- What hormone changes will occur and how those might affect their mood and body
- How menstruation relates to pregnancy and ovulation
- Sexual activity during a period

Before 2010, I would have said that the major conversations with boys needed to be around pornography and masturbation, but based on the way things have changed in recent decades, these are topics affecting boys and girls almost equally. Due to advances in technology, social media, and the introduction of the smartphone, kids are viewing pornography and adult content, on *average*, by age 10 or 11. Whether your kids own their own devices or not, I recommend revisiting *Good Pictures Bad Pictures* and *God Made All of Me* at some point in these preteen years.

Another must-have conversation between the ages of 9 and 12 is the discussion on internet safety and social media use. We have to stress to our kids that it is not okay to send or receive nude pictures. Teaching your children about proper etiquette for texting and online gaming communication is vital. Set up and describe what your family rules will be regarding these issues. Over 40% of children between 14 and 17 years old have sent or received a nude picture through the internet, sometimes

194

as early as 9 years old when older kids or siblings are involved.[83] Children need to be monitored, and they need to understand the seriousness of these actions. Beyond how their brains and hearts will be affected, they could also be charged with making or distributing child pornography. This is not the time to be relaxed on sleepovers, campouts, or unsupervised play dates. It is vital that the parents and adults around your children know *your* rules and expectations. If you do allow your preteen to take part in such events, make it known that you are having conversations before, during, and after in order to protect your child. I honestly advise against overnight stays, but they can be done in rare and highly protected situations with people you trust implicitly.

In this area, middle schoolers can be the most difficult age. They are just old enough to know things might be dangerous but too young to understand the social and emotional consequences of their actions. They seem like big kids, but really they are just overgrown toddlers when it comes to many things. As parents, we must keep our guard up and make it through these preteen years with as few scars as possible...for ourselves and our kids. Be wise as serpents and gentle as doves, my friends![84]

13 – 18 Years Old

As your child enters teenager-hood, the conversations you have with them will change a bit. The topics, the tone, and the details you share. All of this, of course, depends somewhat on the conversations and trust you have already established. If the bridges you built are made out of steel and iron then they will be able to hold heavier things. If the bridges are made out of twigs and construction paper, then we might have to do some reinforcing and use supports. The more trust between you and your teen, the more effective these more serious discussions will be. None of this is to say you are without hope if your child is a teen and you haven't had the previous conversations over time. I've said it before: meet them with honesty, ask forgiveness for not talking about things sooner, and build trust now; it's not too late.

---

[83] "Sending nudes and sexting." *eSafetyCommissioner* (esafety.gov.au).
[84] "Behold, I am sending you out as sheep in the midst of wolves, so be wise as serpents and innocent as doves." -Matthew 10:16 (ESV)

Building Better Bridges

With teens, the vital topics to start talking about are porn, using social media, dating, and sexuality. Asking them about when they think they will be ready to kiss someone or have sex is important, though it may seem counterintuitive. Teaching kids about the consequences of unprotected sex is a must. This is *not* giving them permission, but you are simply equipping them with all the knowledge and tools to keep them safe and assessing where they are. If your family values align with waiting until marriage to have sex, then teach that to your children. If you think that is too conservative or does not matter then all I am asking is for you to have a robust reason and philosophy and teach your kids *something*. Avoiding the topic altogether, shaming them, or inadvertently teaching them to hide the truth will only ensure you are never part of that conversation in their lives. Leaving them to figure it all out on their own is also a road to disaster. If you do not teach them your reasoning and values then they are guaranteed to fear coming to you and will find the information from a far less reliable and more toxic source.

If you ask me, sex education has fallen into two camps: 1) we assume you'll have sex, so here is how to do it semi-safely, or 2) we demand abstinence with no explanation as to why.

The problem here is that very few people have taught teens anything *logical* about waiting until marriage. Our culture or church culture has not taught them how to date, how to set structures and boundaries to protect their minds, bodies, or hearts. It is either no sex until marriage or just go for it whenever. There is great need for a balanced perspective on this topic. I hope to be at least one voice that helps with this. Here's the kicker...God wants us to have great sex. No, seriously. He wants us to be free to explore and find enjoyment in a safe and protective way in the bonds of marriage. Even if I didn't believe in God's commands regarding sex, I feel I would still fall very much on the same side. As a clinician, I would say that it doesn't make very much sense for a young teen with no experience to have either monogamous or open relationships in which sex is common. The risk to reward ratio is so extremely skewed toward risk during teen years. This goes back to teens having no frame of reference for how to date or what healthy dating is separated from sexual behaviors. In today's society it is getting even more skewed towards risk.

Clint Davis

One of the things I teach teens in this stage of their sexual development is that if they can't *talk* about sex before, during, or after in a mature and healthy way, then they shouldn't be *having* sex. The statistics actually show that fewer teens are having sex today, but they have replaced sex with porn during their teen years. So it is not that children are having a healthier view of sex, it is that they are building a bad relationship with sex and their bodies, on their own and then bringing that into their young adult lives. This is why I also use the illustration of the Frankenstein monster of sex and porn. When a person exposes themselves to a variation of men and women before they find their life partner, either online or in real life sexual situations, then they are constantly comparing their spouse to the best parts of those images or people. This sex frankenstein has the best body parts, does the most pleasurable things, brings them on the best dates, has the best family, enjoys the best music, etc. We can't help but to compare our spouse to all the best parts of our previous partners. No one can live up to that. It is an unrealistic expectation and only causes conflict, resentment, bitterness, and disappointment later on, for everyone involved. I've seen this in clients all too often, even if many years have passed. Our brains are quite incredible, and they don't just discard those images or sensations. Things will come out of nowhere right in a moment that is supposed to be pure and enjoyable.

Then, as we stay married, we look at our spouse getting older or after having a few kids, and we revert to this backlog of data and memories we've stored away. This is never good. This could be how a spouse looks physically or acts in the bedroom or it could be how our spouse pursues us emotionally. Both men and women fall into these camps. When we are not getting what we want or what we got early in marriage or our numerous past relationships, it is easy to start feeling entitled and looking for the next best thing to make us feel that way again.
Maybe you've heard the excuses and crude comments before?
"You have to test drive the car before you buy it, dude" or "I gotta know what I am getting myself into, sister." OR "He doesn't make me feel like so and so."

I hate to break it to you, but men and women are not cars, and as humans, we change and evolve throughout life and experiences.

Building Better Bridges

Sex was given to us by God as a gift that will grow and be the most enjoyable within a committed relationship with *one* person. Teens and young adults should know the truth about dating and sex before marriage, the hard facts and the emotional truths as well. Because humans likely have numerous romantic partners before marrying someone, it only stands to reason that pre- or extra-marital sex with those partners most often ends in conflict, difficulty, and disaster. Notwithstanding that any of that baggage can and will enter into a future relationship.

In his article for the Institute for Family Studies, Scott Stanley references a surprising (or not-so-surprising) 2018 study by Michael Rosenfeld and Katharina Roesler. They note in their study that despite sociology's recent claims that premarital cohabitation produces a lower rate of divorce, there really is no substantial difference in those who cohabitate vs. those who don't. In fact, the trick is that cohabitation decreases the likelihood of divorce in the *first* year of marriage only to skyrocket the chance for divorce further into the relationship, which mimics the research from earlier decades that cohabitation before marriage produces poorer outcomes long term.[85] The research is clear. Go back and watch the Marshmallow Test again. We are better off when we defer our reward and lead healthy sexual lives than to take what we want now. The costs in doing so are painfully high and long reaching. As your teen gets older, this is something you must impress upon them. They need to be able to see the long term consequences. The problem is their brains are not wired to be capable of it, so you have to give better reasons than just don't do it.

I also think it is important to teach teens that sex is not about seeking the most pleasure or chasing the best orgasm. It is about intimacy and security. It is about love and mutual submission and respect. It is about way more than making ourselves feel good after a bad day. Yes, this is a deep and nuanced discussion for a teenager, but the reality is, if they are mature enough to be able to make babies, then they are mature enough to understand the hard truths of sexual expression and consequences, good and bad. As a Christian parent, this is part of the discipleship that

---

[85] Stanley, Scott. "Is Cohabitation Still Linked to Greater Odds of Divorce?," The Institute for Family Studies, 12 January 2021.

has been missing in our communities and families for far too long. The bible addresses this clearly, but because we are too scared, traumatized or ill equipped to apply this in our culture, I feel the need to have this conversation here and now.

Okay then. What did we just cover in the last several chapters?
Let us briefly recap: We walked through discussing private parts and boundaries for body safety and consent, the differences between men and women and how we ought to celebrate those differences, how to lay the foundation for discussing sex with our kids, when to have those talks, and how decisions related to dating and sex as a teen affect us deep into adulthood and marriage. Not to mention all our earlier chats about brains, hormones, trauma, development, and avoiding abuse. It's not like we've covered much, eh? I hope you have also discussed even more than these things with the questions at the end of each chapter to help provoke reflection and inspiration.

These are the deep and meaningful conversations that our toddlers, kids, and teens desperately need. Despite what you may think, they are dying to have these conversations with you. Someone they can trust without having to navigate life alone or feel embarrassed when their peers know something they don't. We have to model and teach them how to have healthy relationships because in a world that is broken and hurting, "healthy" is not the norm. In fact, *normal* gets further from healthy every single day it seems. Unfortunately, due to changes in technology and social media, our chances of informing them before they are exposed on their own is slowly slipping through our fingertips.

As we trek forward, I want to talk about some of the things that are making all these topics and conversations much more nuanced and difficult. I will address the increased risk of exposure for children, how the internet contributes to the risks they face, and what we can do to change it before it is too late. The first topic we'll tackle (while I am feeling brave enough to do it) is likely one of the most uncomfortable sexual topics out there. Something your kids might face even before they reach puberty.

Part III:
Hurdles and
Healthy Changes

Clint Davis

14. Pornography & Masturbation: The Two-Headed Monster

There is no dignity when the human dimension is eliminated from the person. In short, the problem with pornography is not that it shows too much of the person, but that it shows far too little.
-Pope John Paul II

This is probably the most difficult chapter for me to write besides the one in gender because the word itself, let alone the topic, is rarely discussed. Maybe you are cringing at this word too. Masturbation. There I said it again. It's just so incredibly personal and private, and perhaps a lot of you reading this have your own experiences with masturbating, whether positive or negative. All of this to say, I am a bit uncomfortable here, and maybe you will feel that through the pages. Mainly, this is because I don't have all the answers, and the number of differing beliefs and amount of shame around this topic is extremely high. The last thing I want to do is trigger someone or set them up for failure. I wouldn't exactly call this subject controversial, in the sense that I believe we rarely talk about it in a healthy way, if at all. There is no controversy if we are just silent. Masturbation is either alluded to in a TV series or movie, or it's celebrated in porn. Many times, we make light of masturbation, or it is mentioned in whispers at middle school campouts or sleepovers and met with snickers and laughs. I mean *American Pie* was a wildly popular movie about a highschool student who had sex with an apple pie, and everyone went to watch it. How is it that we can address it in that popular of a movie, but we don't know how to speak about it with our own kids. As far as hearing about it from parents or leaders in the Church, it is my experience that it is *rarely or never* mentioned. I got curious about what other people thought, so I started asking around to my friends and clients. Almost all of them confirmed that never *once* did they hear about masturbation from a trustworthy and safe source. Only through media or a secondhand conversation from a peer. Person after person. Client after client. Friend after friend. Very few people were educated and taught about

201

masturbation. Almost all of them had experienced this event, but alone, afraid, confused, and in many cases ashamed.

As you'll see, though, this chapter involves porn as well. I put the masturbation and porn subjects together in this chapter because I honestly don't think we can talk about one without the other in the times that we live. *That is why it is double the trouble.*

Recently, our culture has been discussing porn and its effects more and more, but there is still a huge population of people who think pornography is fine, harmless even. As of 2018, according to a Gallup Survey, 43% of Americans polled said they consider porn to be harmless, up 7% from the year before. Those percentages get even more disturbing when broken down into subgroups.[86] I shudder to think what those percentages might be in 2023. Now, those stats seem stressful and discouraging to me, but I am not your parent or your life coach, so whatever you do as an adult in your own time is your right. My main concern, though, is the continued exposure of explicit or adult content to children as soon as they are old enough to hold a device in their hand.

Let's talk about masturbation first. For thousands of years masturbation was something that almost every human experienced throughout their natural development. Both boys and girls experience masturbation through itching or rubbing themselves, or grinding their private parts on something or someone, all of this usually before puberty and often inadvertently. It was not usually paired with porn images for most of human history.

Even the thought of accidental masturbation might frighten you, so I want to take a moment to distinguish the difference between normal sexual development and erotic pleasure. Before puberty, when a child masturbates or explores their body, this is normal sexual development. Especially when your child has not yet hit puberty, there are many ways to redirect them and help them explore their bodies in a safe way. Here are some of the things I either recommend or have seen:

---

[86] Dugan, Andrew. "More Americans Say Pornography Is Morally Acceptable." *Gallup.Com*, 6 Feb. 2023.

- You can ask them to stop, and tell them their private parts are for using the restroom.
- You can employ something called Body Mapping where you trace their body on a huge sheet of paper and color and draw certain body parts, describing their function and purpose.
- Depending on age, you can redirect to the activity of dressing and undressing to familiarize them with their bodies, body coverings, and development of fine motor skills
- You can stand with them in the mirror, clothed, and point out different facial or bodily features, describe what those parts do, and compare them to you to point out how we are all unique and beautiful. This also helps create a positive body image early on.
- You can tell them to go to their bedrooms and explore their bodies in private.[87]
- You can tell them proper ways to stay hygienic and to not harm themselves and why certain body parts require different care than others.
- Or you can do the two options I flat out reject, which is that you can say nothing and let them figure it out on their own or accept and celebrate it without assessment, boundaries and healthy advice (this is the experience of 98% of the people I have talked with and helped. This does not go well.)

As they go through puberty, many, if not most humans experience masturbation in order to explore their bodies and release hormones. According to Healthline (where we all go for our medical questions these days), there are pros and cons to the practice of masturbation. This is a much longer discussion, but as society is moving marriage and committed

---

[87] Understand me here. I include this as a last resort and only with great caution. I am not saying allow them to freely masturbate simply for pleasure, but more to help them understand their body in a tactile way, which may be especially needed for certain children who need help understanding their body's uses and how to grasp self-control. Exploration should *not* be confused with masturbation. Although that will happen and they should not feel shame for it.

relationships further and further from the puberty age, this means there is more time between a child being biologically ready for sex, babies, and masturbation and their actual ability to engage in these behaviors without major risks. For most of history you didn't have to wait 10-20 years to follow your biological or emotional instincts. Marriage might have occurred earlier, but the maturity level of a girl who could actually have a baby came much later than today. "Between the 1890s and the 1950s, the average age at menarche – the medical term for first menstruation – fell from 17 to 12. The age at which most girls get their periods has fallen much more slowly since the '50s, but it remains a topic of medical interest and concern – among other reasons because earlier menarche conveys increased risk of breast cancer."[88] This 5 year age drop primed girls to be ready for babies way earlier than in the past. Increasing the need for earlier birth control and increased risk of children being pregnant without protection. I explain this to help us understand that biology, psychology, and spirituality all make an impact on when and how sexuality works out in our children. As culture changes, we have to look from a micro and macro level.

In today's society a teen's body may be physically ready for sexual things, but emotionally and spiritually, these children are far too immature for them. There is a big difference between a 12 year old and a 17 year old. We have to do a good job as parents to prepare our kids in all three areas - physical, spiritual, and emotional. This need makes resources, tools, and support so much more important! Managing the natural instincts of the body and forming a healthy relationship with ourselves and others, becomes more difficult the longer we hold out. It is important to teach our daughters and sons self control. Let us not forget that some people will not get married or be in a committed relationship. It is vital that they have a healthy understanding of sexuality so that they do not live in toxic shame for their entire lives.

It is not my job to tell you what to do or exactly how you should do it, but I do want to give you some good options and stress to you that the last one listed is *not* one of the good ones. A child should not be shamed or shunned for normal developmental behavior. They are going to feel

---

[88] Scott, Cameron. "What drives earlier menstruation in girls?," Department of Epidemiology and Biostatistics, 2021.

feelings of pleasure with their body, because God designed it to work that way. We distort our children's view of their own bodies when we react viciously or out of fear. There are several amazing clinicians and coaches out there who can help people with the shame they feel around masturbation or sexuality in general. Please seek help for yourself or your child if this shame and trauma has been your experience.

If a child has not been abused, exposed to adult content, or touched by another person, the likelihood of masturbation becoming a major problem is very low. Unfortunately, according to everything I have written in this book and all of the research we have, that percentage of children is getting lower and lower. This is why it is vitally important to talk to our children about the consequences of using masturbation as a self-soothing tool or using it as a way to lust after men or women, whether that's online or people they actually know. This is where that behavior turns dangerous and addictive, especially when merged with violent or abusive pornography. I am not going to say that fantasy is all bad or that self pleasure is all bad, but I will say that it is extremely risky when taking into account the totality of a child's knowledge and experiences or lack thereof.

When I talk to parents about discussing masturbation with their children, my biggest piece of advice is to have the conversation over time. It will go better for both parent and child this way. This way, when you get to puberty and have to explain masturbation and your beliefs about it, you won't be using these terms for the first time with your child. Another tidbit of advice is that it helps to have your own thoughts and feelings sorted out. If you're a parent of a young child, go to a professional in your area. Get some training. Listen to some podcasts or read books or articles that align with your beliefs and values concerning the topic, and talk to your child about their private parts and anatomy in a healthy and age-appropriate way. This will allow everyone to feel more at ease and a great deal safer. Not completely, but more so. It's not an easy thing to talk about, after all.

In an earlier chapter, I gave the example of explaining to a 3-year-old that their penis is called a penis. Then as they get a bit older and they notice their first erection, we call it an erection. As they progress and continue to explore their body, we can explain the mechanics of sex at age 9 or 10. This allows for us as parents to build upon multiple conversations that have hopefully built trust and understanding between ourselves and our child over a decade. Then, just as our child is going into puberty, those conversations regarding sex become more frequent, and we add in the topics of nocturnal emissions, pornography, and masturbation.[89]

If you are the parent of a teen and have never had these conversations or anything close to what we've discussed in earlier chapters, it is time. Yes, at this point, it might be more awkward and a little more complicated, but they will most likely thank you later. I can almost guarantee that if you haven't talked to them about porn and masturbation before, they are either extremely confused based on what they have heard from peers or these issues have gotten out of their control, and they need your help. They are likely just too ashamed to ask or seek guidance from anyone. Whether you meant to or not, you have probably sent the message that "We don't talk about those things in our house." Start now. I have had so many clients finally muster up the courage to talk to their child about these things, only to find out their child has been struggling with the two-headed monster for years and has been living in shame all that time. You have to bust these awkward lines of communication wide open so that if your children are feeling ashamed, scared, or out of control, they can come to you or a trusted adult for help and resources.

Earlier I stated that masturbation prior to puberty is a typical part of sexual development and exploration, which is not to say that masturbation at this stage doesn't need to be talked about, addressed, and monitored. When puberty hits, however, or if a child has been exposed to adult content or been harmed, this is when that act becomes purposefully erotic in nature. Merriam Webster defines erotic like this: "of, devoted to, or tending to arouse sexual love or desire."[90] If a child is prepubescent and has not been exposed to any adult content then they will have no images or ideas to fantasize about. They can make things up

---

[89] If these things are happening earlier than puberty it is usually an extremely rare case and may be a medical issue or sign of abuse.

[90] "Erotic." Merriam-Webster.com Dictionary, *Merriam-Webster*, https://www.merriam-webster.com/dictionary/erotic.

in their heads, but they won't be able to make up what they haven't seen or do not have the biological wiring to explore yet. They are basically exploring a simple physical sensation. After puberty, or after exposure to sexual acts, this will change, and they will start to recall, reinvent, fantasize, and put themselves in those scenarios.

This is when things can become extremely dangerous and risky. If a child has already been harmed or exposed and subsequently masturbates to those types of thoughts and feelings, then they are at risk for being aroused by unhealthy things and ideas, which can cause serious problems for themselves and others. If a child or adult masturbates and simultaneously looks at pornography or fantasizes about a friend, another student, or an adult in their life, it will start an unhealthy cycle which links erotism, abuse, and self-gratification in their minds. This can lead to tons of shame if it is not addressed and explained in a supportive way. It can also lead to seeing others as mere body parts to be lusted after and objectified for our own pleasure. This touches the arousal template discussion we had earlier. Those templates are fixable, but only through lots of time and effort.

Unfortunately, the statistics tell us that, thanks to the onset of the internet, smart devices, and social media, unhealthy arousal patterns are becoming the norm for more and more young children.[91] I want parents to understand that in the world that we live in, exploration and physical arousal are the least of our worries compared to what else is going on. It is masturbation to violent and graphic porn or to their own abuse that we have to address immediately and through a whole community of support.

I am certain children from many past generations have experienced abuse and exposure to explicit content. I know this is not a brand new phenomenon. People have always masturbated and sought pleasure, but with the advent of the internet, the link between early exposure to porn and frequency and intensity of content that is used for masturbation is mind-blowing. It is also the self-soothing and self-gratifying way masturbation is being used by our children that has not been explored

[91] There is lots of wonderful content about arousal patterns in the following paper: Carnes, Patrick. "Cybersex, Courtship, and Escalating Arousal: Factors in Addictive Sexual Desires," *The Meadows*, 2001.

very much in the general public. We don't want to talk about it ourselves, so we definitely don't talk about it with our kids. If we live this way we are ignoring the impact of this subject simply because we are uncomfortable discussing it. What's wild to me is that I fully believe this discomfort stems from the fact that most of us have been neglected or traumatized regarding masturbation in our own lives. We don't even seem to have enough *un*-traumatized or *un*-exposed people to form a control group in research that would help us understand what it would be like to not have been overly sexualized, abused, or sexually neglected. Geez, that feels like something that has been weighing on my chest for ages now. I am writing this whole work, to some degree, as a way to continue my own healing, but mainly so you too can face your discomfort and past experiences in the service of preventing such things in your children and for generations to come. If we avoid looking at the facts because they are ugly, change will never happen.

I don't want to try to give you answers I don't have. My aim is just to point to the facts, statistics, and clients I have seen and to try to bring awareness to the correlation between this data and the realities we see taking place. I hope that this sparks new and healing conversations in your home, with your friends, or with your therapist so you can explore how your beliefs or personal history is affecting you and your family in the here and now. I pray and hope that anyone reading this can get help and recover from any exposure or trauma of which you have been a victim. If you find yourself addicted to masturbation or pornography, don't despair. Help is available, and not a single one of us has to be defined by our addictions, nor do we have to

ASK YOURSELF:

· Can I do it without lusting?

· Can I do it without random thoughts and images popping into my mind?

· Do I masturbate without sexual or erotic images?

· Can I do it and not allow it to become a coping skill or addiction?

· Is this good for me?

· Do I feel ashamed or disgusted?

208

stay trapped by them. Of course, not everyone who masturbates or looks at porn is addicted, but it is important to assess your own health in every area, especially if you are attempting to discuss these things with your children.

A note for my Christian readers, or for anyone who simply wants to get a clearer picture of the morality of masturbation:

People always ask me if masturbation is a sin. That's difficult to answer with a yes or no, and I think that has to be dealt with on a case-by-case basis. I don't know of a particular verse that *directly* addresses masturbation, but I know for certain that God calls us to flee sexual immorality, and the scriptures are clear that lusting after others is unhealthy and sinful.[92] If you search the web for articles or other Christian speakers who have an opinion on the topic, you will find people that lean in both directions.

Instead of one hard and fast answer, what I try to remind us all as believers is that there is *no condemnation* in Christ.[93] However, if we make Christ our Lord and King, then we have to be willing to submit to that Kingship, giving up anything that we have made into an idol, and seeking all our comfort and support from the Holy Spirit. If we become reliant on any earthly pleasure to meet all of our needs or support us emotionally, we will find a road of only emptiness.[94] Even for those who don't subscribe to that belief system, I think we can agree that addiction of any sort can be incredibly dangerous. Such a dependence is toxic for any human being and only stands to cause us harm. I would put masturbation in this same category.

---

[92] "But he who is joined to the Lord becomes one spirit with him. Flee from sexual immorality. Every other sin a person commits is outside the body, but the sexually immoral person sins against his own body. Or do you not know that your body is a temple of the Holy Spirit within you, whom you have from God? You are not your own, for you were bought with a price. So glorify God in your body." -1 Corinthians 6:17-20 (ESV)

[93] "For God so loved the world,that he gave his only Son, that whoever believes in him should not perish but have eternal life. For God did not send his Son into the world to condemn the world, but in order that the world might be saved through him." -John 3:16-17 (ESV)

[94] "You will never know the fullness of Christ until you know the emptiness of everything but Christ" -Charles Spurgeon

Building Better Bridges

Additionally, I find that people usually know if they are doing something harmful, have felt the conviction of the Holy Spirit, and they are simply trying to find a justification for their actions. If you are feeling unsure about masturbation in your life, ask yourself a few things for me.

My guess is after just a short amount of self-reflection, you will be able to tell for yourself if that's a habit you should continue. All that being said, the absolute worst thing we can do is to become so ashamed that we just shove our emotions down and keep our struggle a secret. Conviction to change your behavior is one thing, but in my experience, shame only ever leads to more sin and more shame. I would say that the conviction offered by the Holy Spirit is there to remind us that we are children of God, loved and secure, no matter what sin struggle we have and to guide us back to the path we were designed to walk. In fact, a friend of mine,[95] a woman in her early 30s, suffered under the weight of her masturbation for a decade. She felt ashamed, and she convinced herself she was the only woman in the world dealing with this temptation. Didn't even tell her closest friends. Not until a sermon she heard at her college church group that mentioned this verse: "There is no sin that is not common to man."[96] Same night, she called her mom, confessed, and was met with only grace and love, not one *ounce* of anger or disappointment. Only after this was she able to overcome her addiction. In one of our sessions, we talked about how, for her, masturbation was a problem. A sin. The solution, though, was to open up about it and free herself from the weight of her shame. You might not feel that it is a sin or even believe in sin. It is not my job to tell you what is or isn't moral, but I want you to think about it and teach your children to think about it and process out any shame or guilt that is found.

In my own life, masturbation and porn feel like they have always been there. Through my early sexual trauma, my parents divorce, high school bullying, 9/11, war, hurricane Katrina, and so much more, that two-headed monster was certainly always there, lurking. They were

---

[95] Just FYI, I got permission to include this story. She wanted her story to be able to help someone else.
[96] "No temptation has overtaken you that is not common to man. God is faithful, and he will not let you be tempted beyond your ability, but with the temptation he will also provide the way of escape, that you may be able to endure it." -1 Corinthians 10:13 (ESV)

coping and survival skills that got me through the most difficult times in my life. They also led to such deep shame that it caused me sleepless nights and massive anxiety. By the grace of God, I went into marriage with honesty and openness with a woman who showed me understanding and forgiveness, but this does not mean I have handled these things perfectly or that I haven't caused damage over the years to my wife and myself. This can be a lifelong battle for some, but I promise you that you are not alone. You can overcome these things and you can find freedom. Freedom from shame. Freedom from a secret life of brokenness. Freedom from behavior that makes you sick. In turn, you can help your children walk a different path that leads to freedom from the very first step. You have to take responsibility for what you can and heal by doing the work of recovering from your own early exposure, trauma and childhood of neglect.

I tell these stories because regardless of your particular thoughts on masturbation, the safest course of action is to talk about this topic openly and give our kids the opportunity to tell us if they feel ashamed, out of control, or uncomfortable with the act. As believers we guide them to a relationship with the Lord and a community of Spirit-filled believers, that will guide them and support them to find what is healthiest and most glorifying to God. Again, I don't have all the answers, and I know not everyone reading this believes in Jesus. I suggest, as your beliefs dictate, you should speak to your pastor, priest, rabbi, or therapist about what is being laid on your heart regarding this topic. Just please, wherever you land, do not shame your child, make them disgusted with themselves/their bodies, or call them names. I can promise that won't be helpful and like so many of the men and women I have worked with, they will need years of recovery. Also, as you love and support your child through these struggles and conversations, love yourself while you're at it. Maybe you can't form an honest and healthy relationship with the body God gave you.

Here are some dos and don'ts that *can* be helpful if you see your child masturbating:

> - Do not interrupt them and scare them; address it at a later time

- Try not to be reactionary; if you do react badly, apologize
- Do not shame them or call them gross or disgusting
- Do not laugh or joke about it in any way
- Do not tell anyone about it in their presence
- Do not spank them or punish them over this behavior
- Do have this conversation slowly and over time
- Do follow up with them and say something like "Hey, I know you saw that I noticed what you were doing. Please go into your room and pray about it, and so will I. I want to talk to you about it, but you *aren't* in trouble."
- You can normalize and validate their experience without accepting or approving of their behaviors

Obviously, this book is predominantly about parenting tools, so I won't go too deeply into my thoughts on masturbation within marriage. That is an entirely different can of worms. What I do want to say is that couples should be open and honest about their past experiences, traumas, and opinions. Transparency, especially in the difficult things, can prevent shame, compulsion, or addiction creeping its way into a marriage, as well as bringing healing or restoring broken trust from an individual's past. The truth is, if we as parents cannot talk about these things with each other, how are we going to seem confident when we talk to our children? We must be on the same page, united, and as healthy as possible on this sensitive issue.

Before looking at some of the ramifications and statistics of pornography as well as its drastic evolution, I have one last reminder. It is *really* helpful to have the sex conversation before the masturbation and pornography conversations. When your child already knows certain terms and understands the basic mechanics of sex and the purposes you subscribe to, you will have a much easier time explaining masturbation to them. Yes, yes, I realize I make this sound relatively simple. I also realize there are two types of people reading this book: those that want to prevent future sexual neglect or abuse and those that need to recover from them. Either way, we have to choose to be brave. If we find ourselves scared to have these discussions, we must let ourselves be scared and have them anyway. We simply have to do it scared. If you have young children, prevention is possible. If your child is in their teen years and you're thinking now about missed opportunities, do not shame yourself, give in to despair, or convince yourself it's too late. Just breathe, take a step in the right direction, and start talking. They are resilient. Every mistake or missed opportunity makes space for repair. They do need help to recover from what is now such a common addiction in teens and young adults. Find a clinician in your area who can help with addiction to masturbation or pornography. Make sure that person has a robust understanding of healthy sexuality and that their beliefs pair with your own.

Reflection & Discussion

1. Have you ever established your thoughts and values regarding masturbation? If so, what are they, and have you expressed them to your children if age-appropriate?

2. When you express your thoughts on masturbation to your kids, is it a reaction out of fear and anxiety?

3. Do you have any private sins or habits that are weighing you down? Have you considered speaking about them to a close friend, leader, or counselor?

15. Is Porn Really *That* Bad?

"We pursue sexual sin not because our hedonism is too strong but because our hunger for pleasure is so small we settle for a cheap imitation of the real thing: porn."
–Benjamin Vrbicek

Let me answer my own question – the answer is yes, porn is *that* bad. Especially for a child's developing brain. Synapses are connecting and neurons are firing at an incredible rate. I guess we could just stop there, but let's not. Let me explain a few things, the first thing being that porn is *not* two people having sex. In most cases, porn is a toxic, unrealistic, and perverse corruption of actual sex. A stat I read from the National Center on Sexual Exploitation tells us that "Of the 50 most common pornographic videos, an analysis found that 88% of scenes contained physical violence, and 49% contained verbal aggression."[97] My stomach turns at the thought of children watching pornography of any kind, and what we see is that the content out there is even worse than we imagine. It is very difficult to find softcore porn online, and if you happen to click on an adult website, just the thumbnails are traumatizing to see. From what I have heard and seen, even universally accessible platforms like Instagram and TikTok are letting porn slip through the cracks for anyone to stumble across at any moment.

In most cases, if a child or teen is masturbating to porn, they are masturbating not only to fake sex, but legitimate physical violence against other human beings. So even if we believe that masturbation has no negative impacts, when paired with porn it has devastating consequences. There is a long list of porn that no human should ever be

---

[97] Powell, Tiffany. "Institutions of Higher Violence: The Influence of Pornography on College Sexual Assault," National Center on Sexual Exploitation (2021).

involved in, look at, much less become aroused by. Consuming pornography this way wasn't possible for most of human history and has only become so dramatically commonplace in the last few decades.

During my accreditation to become a Certified Sex Addiction Therapist, one of the most well-known CSATs, Rob Weiss, showed us a chart detailing the advances in eroticism and sexuality in a timeline form. I have included some of it here to show just how much and how quickly things have changed.

Pre-history-1860s	Recreational and intimate sex Cave Drawings and painted porn Infidelity and concubines Prostitution and harems Public bath houses and steam rooms (orgies) Masturbation
1860-1970s	Photographic porn Porn movies Porn theaters Adult bookstores Strip clubs
1977-1990s	All of the above plus.... Video and VCR Phone sex Softcore porn on TV at home Adult and escort sections in the newspaper, magazines, and yellow pages
2007-2010	All of the above plus.... Sexting Live video streaming Hook-Up apps (Tinder, Grinder, Ashley Madison, Scout)

2010-present	Sexting
	Social media
	Porn websites
	Online chat rooms
	Live chat rooms
	4k and virtual reality
	Virtual sex with Teledildonics[98]
	Bodysuits and sensory immersion suits
	Selective searching for specific fetishes (Only Fans, etc.)

Sexuality and sexual content are not new. Taking pleasure at the expense of others and our own mental health is not new. What is new, however, is the rapid increase of accessibility to sexual content, its violent trajectory, and the overall proliferation of exposure to such content for younger and younger viewers. The chart above illustrates that human nature has been the same all along, but access to dangerous content is skyrocketing. Not to mention that with this incredible increase the sheer lack of discussion about how things are evolving is pretty much the same. These factors are leading to the desensitization of our world and culture. The average human being in the 1970s was exposed to sexual content, but it was likely only when they sought it out and predominantly consumed by adults. Today, very little "seeking out" is necessary. Porn, in many ways, is delivered right to us and to our children. I don't have time to get into A.I. girlfriends and sex robots (don't google it), but we will have to tackle the wide range effects of this as well. I know this might sound like a Sci-Fi movie, but as we develop new technologies, we must keep our children and teens safe from the perversity that tech will bring into the area of sexuality. We must understand the risks and potential threats that seem "fringe" now, but will become more common in the near future.

I hate to break this to you, but we have always been perverse and lustful as a species, but we have *not* been as vulnerable and exposed as we are today. The last two generations of children and adults have been so

---

[98] Teledildonics refers to the use of technology to facilitate remote sexual interactions, typically involving wireless devices such as vibrators or other sex toys operated remotely by a partner.

over-exposed to this content that it has changed the way our brains are wired. Thanks to entertainment, social media, billboards, commercials, and just about every ad in magazines, the average person goes through life more sexually stimulated than any time before.

That's just a little of the external content we are seeing. Let's take a look at the internal side of things for a moment. Biology lesson time.

On the whole, men are driven by the hormone testosterone. We are also typically more visually stimulated. We were wired this way to have sex, procreate, and keep the race alive. Males or females alone couldn't accomplish this necessary goal. We have desires and hormones for good reason. None of this justifies abuse or watching porn, but I just want us to see that pornography appeals to boys and men to a greater degree because of its visual nature, playing to the testosterone that drives us. In recent years, though, we have seen some polls that reveal teen girls and women are watching porn just as much if not more than boys.[99]

Now, our biology did not change overnight, although as we discussed earlier, epigenetic changes are definitely affecting us all. Instead, the changes we see in men and women come from over-exposure and abuse of our brains, hearts, and bodies. We are also being influenced by our desperate attempts at keeping up with the desires of our partners.

Girls see guys they want to date or marry, they desire to learn the preferences of those men (or boys, as the case often is), and because of a lack of education, long-term trustworthy conversations, and

---

[99] Bustle's Lea Rose Emery wrote a 2017 article discussing 10 years of data from *PornHub* showing the rise of female use of the major porn site.
Emery, Lea Rose. "(Not So) Plot Twist: Women Watch More Porn Than Men," *Bustle*, (2017)

building a healthy self-image, girls are going to porn for lessons in how to be "desirable." Which, surprise surprise. Pornography negatively warps peoples' desires, and we end up in a cycle where sex is taken completely out of its original, wonderful context. It moves from developing over time and deepening intimacy, into chasing arousal, orgasms, and the most pleasure possible.

Because of the increase in adult content and stimulation, paired with children seeking pleasure to heal the pain of the emotional damage brought on by their parental relationships, we have become pleasure seekers (remember our talk about dopamine?). This is true when it comes to almost every area of life, but none more so than sexuality. Our films, books, movies, and stories have hypersexualized love, and we have turned and twisted a gift from God into a toxic mess. Children who do not grow up to experience healthy relationships and healthy sexuality do not even know what they should be looking for. They believe the chemicals sex brings fixes all and fulfills all their emotional needs. Sex is amazing. It should be. God wants people to have meaningful sex that brings unity, joy, and fulfillment with a spouse. Sadly, people are chasing empty pleasure and fleeting orgasm and calling that love.

I want to share my small tale of the effects of male biology mixed with exposure to porn. I have come to hear this same story from many men and women over the years. I share this to normalize this unhealthy and tragic experience to validate anyone reading this feeling loads of shame.

I, like many boys in the 80s, was exposed to pornography at a very young age. I can still remember the first magazine I saw and the first VHS tape that was played for me. I was less than 10 years old. I'm sure many of you can relate to what that feels like. Seeing something you know you probably shouldn't. I remember being confused, sort of horrified, and a little excited. Not really sexually excited, considering I had no clue what I was looking at or that it even existed, but there was some sort of excitement within me.[100] I was curious, and like every other

---

[100] I mentioned it before, but it's helpful to remember that, especially for children, sexual arousal and eroticism are not always the same thing.

little boy I knew at the time, I continued to go back to it whenever it was an option. Which, thank God, was not very often. I was intrigued by what I saw and curious to find out more. In my years in clinical practice, I have talked to thousands of men and hundreds of women who share similar stories.

A handful of experiences with masturbation or porn don't constitute an addiction, but new research shows that pornography is as addictive as cocaine, if not more so. According to a *Wired* article written by Ryan Singel,[101] this research was even brought before a 2004 Senate hearing to inspire change. Here is a quote from Mary Anne Layden, a clinician present at that hearing:

> "'The internet is a perfect drug delivery system because you are anonymous, aroused and have role models for these behaviors. To have drug[s] pumped into your house 24/7, free, and children know how to use it better than grown-ups know how to use it - it's a perfect delivery system if we want to have a whole generation of young addicts who will never have the drug out of their mind.'"

Layden goes on to express that:

> "Pornography addicts have a more difficult time recovering from their addiction than cocaine addicts, since coke users can get the drug out of their system, but pornographic images stay in the brain forever."

The article mentions another clinician who reiterates the dangers of pornography due to its connection to masturbation and that such an act results in the "release of naturally occurring opioids," something not even heroin can do.[102] Which takes us right back to our discussion of instant dopamine versus long-term serotonin.

The volume of hormones and neurochemicals released when we have sexual experiences is massive. Again, this is possibly tied to a survival

---

[101] Singel, Ryan. "Internet Porn: Worse Than Crack?, *Wired*, 2004.
[102] Ibid.

mechanism, ensuring our continued existence. Simultaneously, though, this rush of chemicals is what makes things like masturbation and pornography so addictive. Put into perspective, imagine someone who battles emotional trauma and poor coping skills getting addicted to cocaine. The risks would be huge. Porn and masturbation don't get the same attention as substance abuse, but just like hard drug use, these sexual addictions are similarly providing escapism, dissociation, pain reduction, self-gratification, and pain avoidance all in an instant. This is why linking porn and masturbation is a recipe for disaster. Especially for children. So, with as much passion as we try to warn our kids against drugs or alcohol, we ought to pour the same effort into preventing porn addiction. There are of course people who push back against even the facts and research. I am concerned about adults who dismiss porn as harmless, but my focus here are the harsh and tragic effects such content and practices have on the developing minds, hearts, and spirits of children.

Let's not forget the main point of our whole journey through these pages: to protect our children and start them off from the best and healthiest possible place, with as few future hurdles and hang-ups as possible. To do that, some of us may need to address and recover from our own pasts and unhealthy coping tools.

I don't write this from a perspective that says "Just pick yourself up, and do better." As we have seen above, porn or sex addiction is *extremely* difficult to overcome in our world. No one is above getting trapped in that cycle, and no one can defeat it without community support. If you are one of the rare parents that haven't seen or struggled with pornography, good for you. Sincerely. You are the type of person I hope our kids can become in the future through some of the tips and resources I've written about here. I want to look up in a decade or two and see vastly improved statistics. I want there to be millions of people who haven't seen porn, haven't been sexually abused or neglected, and who don't let social media and smartphones ruin their lives and marriages. Just imagine that for a second. A world with far less sexual addiction and trauma. Maybe it will take some time, but I know we can get there! We all have a responsibility to share information once we know better, even if it goes against the grain.[103] While everyone is tucking their tails between their legs or sticking their heads in the sand, we have to step up. Starting today.

Porn in the American Church

To any believers reading this, you are not exempt from the pervasive reach of pornography addiction. In some ways, I feel the battle rages even more in churches due to secrecy, shame, and massive fear of people finding out your hidden sins. Religion has done a great disservice to people by not helping its members understand the nuances of these struggles and therefore unintentionally leading people into deep shame. Statistics reveal an increase in the amount and reach of pornography in the Church that cannot be ignored. It is also not a problem that affects only men. Women, teens, and children are also being caught in the snare of pornography at alarming rates.

You may assume that the Church is immune, whether you're a believer or not. We see the smiling faces of the people who attend our churches. "Surely these people could not be battling pornography addiction," we tell ourselves.

The many studies and reports that have come out over the last several years, however, show quite a different picture. A disturbing one. Not only has pornography invaded churches, but in many cases, Christians – and even church pastors – engage in viewing porn at almost the same rates as the secular population.

The research studies I've mentioned, primarily conducted by the Barna Group and Covenant Eyes[104], reveal that initial exposure to porn begins in childhood and only progresses from there. Porn, in many forms, is increasingly easy to access due to the wide variety of platforms which now make it available: printed materials, the internet, smartphone apps, DVDs, television, and more. Porn is packaged in many forms from

---

[103] Suzy Kassem gives us this charge: "Stand up for what is right, even if you're standing alone."

[104] The Barna Group is one of the premier Christian research groups I frequent for information. They were started in 1984, and have since conducted thousands of research studies through millions of interviews.
Covenant Eyes is the app I mentioned that seeks to help save people from porn or aid in their fight against a porn addiction.

softcore to hardcore to childporn. Not all porn users look at all types, but all types are available.

Let's look at some data to see the scope and effects of porn in society and the church. This is from the Conquer Series 2022.

- Over 40 million Americans are regular visitors to porn sites. The average visit lasts 6 minutes and 29 seconds.
- There are around 42 million porn websites, which totals around 370 million pages of porn.
- The porn industry's annual revenue is more than the NFL, NBA, and MLB combined. It is also more than the combined revenues of ABC, CBS, and NBC.
- 47% of families in the United States reported that pornography is a problem in their home. Pornography use increases the marital infidelity rate by more than 300%.
- 11 years old is the average age that a child is first exposed to porn, and 94% of children will see porn by the age of 14.
- 56% of American divorces involve one party having an "obsessive interest" in pornographic websites.
- 70% of Christian youth pastors report that they have had at least one teen come to them for help in dealing with pornography in the past 12 months.
- 68% of church-going men and over 50% of pastors view porn on a regular basis.
- Of young Christian adults 18-24 years old, 76% actively search for porn.
- 59% of pastors said that married men seek their help for porn use.
- 33% of women aged 25 years and under search for porn at least once per month.
- Only 13% of self-identified Christian women say they *never* watch porn
- 55% of married men and 25% of married women say they watch porn at least once a month.
- 57% of pastors say porn addiction is the most damaging issue in their congregation.
- 69% say porn has adversely impacted the church.

The last statistic that is heartbreaking is that with all of this information less than 7% of those churches have a plan to deal with this now or in the future and less than 10% of churches are talking about mental health.[105]

I feel weary just typing those facts out. These statistics are staggering and heartbreaking. These are the numbers within the church community. In fairness, I would argue that the majority of people who took these surveys, might attend church and call themselves Christians, but are not necessarily mature believers walking with the Holy Spirit, but nevertheless. These stats might be way lower if we had a deeper, open, more connected community. That is another book, one which myself and my friend Tyler Hennessee are currently writing called "Wild Branches: Uprooting Discipleship." Find our podcast or socials to get more information. The thing is we cannot wait to make these changes. If the damage done by pornography is this pervasive in the Church, where people understand and claim that porn is harmful and wrong, how much worse are the statistics in secular environments where porn and obsessive masturbation are deemed acceptable and even celebrated? It seems like every year there are new ways to use the human body and technology for self-gratification and radical and harmful emotional coping. At what cost? I shudder to think about it and fear the long-term ramifications it has on our hearts and minds. We must not stay comfortably numb! I do not list these statistics to shame the American Church goers, I am one of them, I point them out to challenge us to step up. Read a book, listen to a podcast, get some training and join the fight for the future of our children.

Pornography's Link to Human Trafficking

As a part of my career, I have had the wonderful opportunity to work with ministries dedicated to stopping human trafficking. In my role as Director of Recovery, I wrote programs and training for individuals and community members to both prevent and recover from human trafficking. My dear

---

[105] All of these data points come from Jeremy Wiles, CEO of Soul Refiner. Wiles, Jeremy. "15 Mind-Blowing Statistics About Porn And The Church," Conquer Series, 05 May 2022.

friend, Cassie Hammett[106] and I wrote Louisiana's first John School Curriculum. This is a program supported by our local government and the DA office. It seeks to help men who are first time offenders of sexual solicitation of adults get the help they need to stop harming themselves and others. In the span of a year or more, we worked with 80+ men that had been arrested for trying to purchase a prostitute, and we attempted to help them understand their behavior through the lens of their own recovery and trauma as well as the lens of the women and children they were soliciting. We hope to continue this course in Louisiana and throughout the country for years to come if possible. All that to say, my experience has helped me grow deeper in my understanding of how porn culture and human trafficking are linked. Hundreds of first hand accounts give better information and clarity than any documentary or book could ever provide.

One of the things that can help us stop viewing porn or increase our urgency to keep our children from viewing it is to understand how closely pornography is correlated to human trafficking and all sorts of other atrocities. Don't hear me say that if you view porn or struggle with porn addiction that you traffic human beings or that you are even in that same universe. What I am saying is that by viewing porn you are silently and even inadvertently casting a vote for child porn and human trafficking from a consumerist perspective. It is all about supply and demand. If no one was buying and viewing porn, there would not be teens and girls being used and abused to create such content. Because that is what is happening. There are enough porn stars leaving the industry and telling their stories to confirm this is true.[107] Porn actors and actresses are usually high, drunk, or on pain medication to be able to get through the difficult scenes and sex acts that they have to produce. They get paid very little, and in order to earn more for themselves, they have to do more exotic and deplorable things. This is the content we don't want to

---

[106] Cassie is the founder of the Hub's Urban Ministry, and she is such a force for good. You rock, Cass.

[107] I strongly recommend going and listening to some of these incredible and powerful stories! One in particular that I will suggest here is Alia's story, which you can find on YouTube by searching "What Led Me into the Mainstream Porn Industry" - Thanks for sharing with us Alia! There are countless stories like her on *Fight the New Drug*'s channel!

talk about, and these are the things we shy away from. I could list these things in detail, but I am sure the worst you can imagine is not too far from the truth. However painful and however much we don't want to, we must talk about these things. Our silence means blinding our children to the facts and the risks they will face. As you address the dangers of porn in your home, we must also mention the brutality of the industry and what it means for human beings. We must give them good reasons and context for not watching porn and help them to see that it is not always a victimless act. It is our job as parents to educate our children, protect them as much as we can, and to prepare them to make their own healthy choices in a very unhealthy world. Their joy, their emotional health, and their minds are all on the line here.

There is a cultural argument that porn is not bad. Maybe you've heard this, and maybe such arguments are appealing to you in that they allow us a justification for our selfishness and lust. If you ask me, this thought process would be like removing the warnings from all tobacco products. The proof that porn is hurting us is there, but we aren't putting a Surgeon General's label on porn sites. And why not? As we've seen, we can be addicted to images and sensations just like the high people chase with substance abuse.

The porn epidemic is getting increasingly worse and more unmanageable, and there is little being done to slow it down. The consequences are widespread. For example, the number one buyer of Viagra or pills like this, are males 19-24. There have been dozens of erectile dysfunction pills produced and companies created in recent years because of the increase in both erectile dysfunction and anxiety around pleasing partners.[108] We, of course, are not addressing the root cause, but treating the symptoms. This increase in erectile dysfunction in young men is in large part due to the last decade of ruining their brains, bodies, and arousal templates with content, over-stimulation, and poor coping skills.[109] A real girl with whom they are in a real relationship can no longer help them reach climax or arousal because of the amount of content they have been viewing for the past decade on their phones and computers.

---

[108] Hinde, Natasha. "Erectile Dysfunction Forums Offer Raw Insight Into How Millions Of Men Cope With The Condition," *The Huffington Post UK*, 2016.
[109] Check out the site https://www.yourbrainonporn.com/ if you want to read more on these topics!

Our children, boys and girls alike, are growing into adults who have toxic views of sexuality, other people, and themselves. They will become adults who will face incredible challenges and obstacles in their romantic relationships. Just look at our current cultures views on sexuality. Look at the amount of affairs. Look at the amount of divorces. Look how popular "Fifty Shades or Grey" became. If we do not act, this entire crisis will only get worse.

I want you to think about it this way. All of the depravity and erotic content that we are seeing now was created by men and women whose porn exposure was through magazines or fuzzy VHS tapes, viewed sporadically when they could find the chance. **Ask yourself...what will be created by the teens and young adults who have been looking at hardcore abuse pornography in clips and videos nearly every day for the past decade? Think about it like the origin story of a supervillain. Kids become sexually broken, because they experience sexual brokenness.** We have to wake up, make some changes, and turn the tide. We have to save our communities and our children. We have to create superheroes. Boys and girls who will stand up for what is healthy and right, because they were taught what is healthy and right. I hate that this information is scary, but the truth is scary. Fear can be a powerful motivator for good. Conversely, in some phrasing or another, the scriptures tell us over 80 times not to fear.[110] So, the point isn't that we should never feel the emotion of fear, but that when we find ourselves being afraid we need to act in spite of that fear. We need to run toward God, community, and health. We can learn to act in faith and trust that hope is here and now.

Alright, I know. That was a bunch of scary information with no action steps. We are getting there. It is horrifying that we have no foolproof way to prevent 100% of our child's exposure to inappropriate content, but we can limit it in an extreme way. They will still have times when we are not with them, times when they are at school or are using another friend's device. The goal is to shape their hearts and minds so they can resist this temptation and, if exposed, they can come to us and ask for help. I

---

[110] Matthew 6:25, Philippians 4:6-7, Deuteronomy 31:6, and Joshua 8:1 just to list a few of them!

promise we still have power in our corner. We can do a lot. Here are four ways I suggest for helping keep your children safe from accessing and viewing pornography online:

1. *Limit their Access:* Despite the temptation, you should wait to give your child a phone until they are mature enough to handle it. If and when they do get their own phone, try to limit their ability to search the web and to download apps on their own. Apps such as Bark, Net-nanny, Disney Circle, Covenant Eyes, Ever-Accountable, and others are good tools for blocking pornography or allowing you to more closely monitor the content your child sees.[111] Whatever method or app you use, your child's phone should certainly be more limited than it is.

2. *Increase Accountability*: Think about enforcing device check-ins. Kids should learn to be open and honest about what they are exposed to. We must teach them that confessing their struggles and failures leads to freedom, trust, and support, not shame and abandonment. This means as parents we have to be equipped and supported ourselves, as well as modeling trustworthy behavior in our own lives. Covenant Eyes is a great app for this. You will get screenshots of their phone and what they are viewing every day. This allows for open conversations about over-consumption of not just porn, but anything through their device that they might be obsessing over.

3. *Affordability:* Devices are not free, and they are not a right. Phones are a privilege, and they are not their own. We must make them earn their devices, pay for them, and build up trust over time. This should not be as easy as asking for a phone, getting one, and thinking that it is theirs with no questions asked. Consider building a community and network of parents on the same page about these things so you are not alone.

4. *Seek Advice:* Have the humility and take the preventative steps to ask for help. Ask a therapist. Ask a pastor. Ask a professional. We will spend 10,000 hours learning about our

---

[111] If you want to know how to do this, contact our clinic at 318.562.6903, and we have a specialist to walk you through it!

new iPhone, Mac Book, bass boat, fitness program, or job, but we won't take the time to learn about protecting our most precious commodity from a life full of disaster.

These are helpful practices that reduce your child's risk of being exposed to the alarming breadth of harmful content they could stumble upon online. Setting up boundaries and rules early on will be most effective, and if you want the truth, it can be helpful to include your children in your own accountability. Let them know that all of us can be hurt by what's online. From simple jealousy and insecurity from social media to more damaging porn and violent content. All of my suggestions are great tools, but the most beneficial thing you can do to help protect your children is to earn their trust and be consistent with them. None of us is 100% perfect, but if your child trusts you, they are far more likely to be open with you about what they are watching. As a dad myself, I know what a fine line we walk as parents. It is our duty to set up firm rules, no matter how painful, but we also have a duty to forgive and show gentleness. Just like I have, I encourage you to find a support system of other parents and friends that share similar values to you, a community who can spur you on, keep you accountable, and who are willing to be honest with you. We cannot do this alone. I know I can't. We also cannot do this in a community filled with people unable or unwilling to make changes and have braver conversations.

I pray and hope that we can gain insight and resources into our children's lives so that we can help them recover from this horrible disease and behavior. Porn might sound like the punchline to some joke, but the truth is, it's not okay, and the consequences for sweeping it under the rug are vast and far-reaching. Yet, our culture is becoming more and more numb to it because we see small versions of porn nearly every day. Billboards, music videos, commercials, and magazines are numbing our eyes, hearts, and minds. These things are normalizing highly erotic content meant for private consumption for anyone looking. As we turn our eyes from this content, we have to open those same eyes to our children and open our mouths to speak truth and life.

We have to wake up and fight back against the normalization of pornography and the sexualization of our children at younger and younger ages. We are fighting over the line between exposure versus education. Though it seems strange, our ability to help our children avoid the erotic ideas, explicit content, and biased misinformation flooding the internet is to equip and educate them on those very things. We must show how healthy development, understanding sexual terms, and being confident in their own bodies provides protection against society's warping of those subjects. We minimize and ignore these issues at the expense and demise of our children. As I have clearly laid out, this does not mean putting them in bubble wrap or overprotecting them. I know this is a hard balance and a painfully fine line, but the more mindful we are, the more confident we are, and the more resources we have, the more we will hit the mark.

As I wrap up this chapter and reflect on my own experiences with violent and sexual content as a young boy, I am all the more motivated to put structures in place and have regular conversations with my boys. I long for them to have a confident and complete view of their bodies, how to keep themselves safe, and how to look out for the well-being of their own minds. I long for the same things in your children.

*****

Hey. If you have made it to the end of this chapter and feel discouraged or scared because your child or teen has already been exposed to pornography, the next few pages are for you. I included a short set of questions from a resource I trust that will guide you through a conversation with your child regarding what they saw, what the next steps are, and tips on how you should be reacting as their parent or caregiver.

The following 8 questions come from Defend Young Minds, a company founded by an author I have mentioned here already, Kristen Jenson. She's a brilliant leader and advocate for preventing childhood sexual abuse, inspired by a very traumatic story from her own family. Feel free to come back and reference these questions anytime you need. You aren't alone in this.

1. **Can you tell me what you saw?**
   a. Children may not have the words to explain so be sensitive and patient. They may be scared and think that they will get into trouble.

2. Did you understand what you were seeing in the pictures or videos?
a. This is gauging how serious the issue is. It is important to understand the child's or teen's understanding of sexuality. Make a plan to follow up with a book or resource.

3. How do you feel on the inside, and how did it feel seeing those things?
a. Expressing emotions is important. Some young kids may say that it was "gross" or it made them sick. Explain that it is normal to be curious and for those images to excite you or bring you pleasure, but it is also normal for them to make you feel gross at the exact same time.

4. How did your body feel when you saw those images?
a. Make sure you explain there is no right or wrong - our bodies will respond in all sorts of ways, and it is important for us not to shame ourselves. It is natural to be excited or to have physical responses. We do, however, want to wait until we are older and more mature to engage in those behaviors and feelings.

5. Are you replaying those images in your mind like a movie or film?
a. Our brain is so cool, and we are able to remember things, but this can get us into trouble as well as stress us out when we cannot make them stop. Reassure them that they have tools and resources to take charge of their brain and thoughts. (any book by Dan Siegel or Tina Bryson is great)

6. What activities could you do to help you move your brain off of these images and thoughts?
a. Go outside.
b. Drink water.
c. Draw some pictures.
d. Write in a journal.
e. Talk about it.
f. Go see a counselor.

7. What do we need to do to keep this from happening again?
a. We can take responsibility and apologize for not protecting them.
b. We can close the loopholes on their phone or device.
c. We can talk to whoever showed them the content or made it available.

d.   Get updated apps and resources. Covenant Eyes, Fortify, and many other apps I listed earlier will help you.
8. Is there anything you want to ask mom or dad?
a.   Continue to keep lines of communication open.
b.   Do not be awkward.
c.   Do not make jokes.
d.   Do not pressure them to talk.
e.   Make them an appointment with a counselor if you are concerned.[112]

I hope you find the opportunity to use this chapter here on porn to educate your child on the pitfalls and dangers of pornography. Help them to see what is really going on, how they are being preyed upon, and what is real vs. fake. Let them know the science behind what they might be feeling and the problematic ways in which porn affects their brains and bodies. Try to find that line between normalizing and understanding what they are going through, without justifying the behavior. Make a plan as a whole family to protect each other from inappropriate content, mom and dad included, and help them to feel supported and empowered, not judged or shamed.

Here are some helpful resources related to pornography, addiction, and trauma in this area:

If you want to read more targeted information about sexual trauma, betrayal trauma, addiction, arousal templates, or the effects of porn on boys and girls, I will list some of the best resources here:

The Porn Trap by Wendy and Larry Maltz
Your Brain on Porn by Gary Wilson
Life After Lust by Forest Benedict
Facing the Shadow or *Shadows of the Cross* Workbook by Patrick Carnes
Always Turned On by Jennifer Schneider and Robert Weiss
Closer Together, Further Apart by Robert Weiss

---

[112] Dittman, Stacey. "The 8 Best Questions to Ask When Your Child Has Seen Porn," *Defend Young Minds*, 24 July 2018.

At the end of this book, I have a list of many of the resources I have mentioned, as well as some additional ones, in order to offer the best possible breadth of information for you and your family. As far as clinical support, especially if porn addiction is a struggle in your home, I urge you to find a PSAP or a CSAT[113] in your area or online. There has been a lot of hurt and disservice done to children and families by untrained professionals and pastors in this area. Seeking out help is the bravest thing you can do for yourself or for your child. If you or your spouse struggles with sexual unhealth please seek proper help. I have seen so many people recover and heal from these issues, and you should always remember you are not alone. You are not gross or disgusting. You are a human worthy of love and peace. Worthy of freedom.

---

[113] Pastoral Sex Addiction Professional and Certified Sex Addiction Therapist, respectively.

Reflection & Discussion

1. Do you or someone you know struggle with viewing pornography?

2. What are the current methods you have for protecting what your child watches on TV, on a tablet, or on their cell phone?

3. How do you define 'pornography'? Are there ways in your life that "soft porn" is getting a foothold on your or your children? (TV shows, social media, etc.)

4. What changes would you like to see in your house related to what your household is watching? Would you be willing to discuss that as a family?

16. Digital Immigrants vs. Digital Natives[114]

Today's students have not just changed incrementally *from those of the past, nor simply changed their slang, clothes, body adornments, or styles, as has happened between generations previously. A really big* discontinuity *has taken place. One might even call it a 'singularity' – an event which changes things so fundamentally that there is absolutely no going back.*
-Marc Prensky

You know as well as I do that technology has changed our lives. We know that technology touches nearly every aspect of our waking lives. If you are over 30 years old, you also know that how kids, teens, and young adults use technology now is vastly different to how we learned to use it. I want to explain a little bit of what it means to be a native of technology versus what it means to have grown up without it.

VHS tapes vs. Netflix. AOL Instant Messenger vs. Snapchat. Running through the yard waiting on dial-up vs. filming a TikTok on the street in an instant. I had an entirely different childhood than my sons will have. The same goes for you and your children. The world has changed (and continues to change) at an alarming rate. Obviously, our broken human nature plays a huge role in porn consumption, addiction to masturbation, and sexual trauma in any form. Our internal desires, though, are not the only contributing factor.

We will dive deeply into smartphones and social media, but I wanted to take a chapter to talk about the cultural and technological changes that

---

[114] Unknowingly, I used these terms to describe me vs. my sons, but the terms were coined in a fabulous article by Marc Prensky. I use analog to digital converts but Marc does such a great job! I want to give him credit, because using these particular words is genius, and his work is incredibly insightful. I recommend giving it a quick read! Prenksy, Marc. "Digital Natives, Digital Immigrants," *On the Horizon*, MCB University Press, Vol. 9 No. 5, (October 2001).

make our teenagers wildly different from us, how our younger children will be even further removed from the realities we knew, and how understanding these changes is crucial in how we approach educating our children. Neglect and trauma can manifest in so many ways, big and small. As we walk through practical topics and questions, I am sure that it will be very overwhelming. Whether you are talking about menstruation to a little girl or about cell phone use to your teenage son, my hope is you will feel more equipped and aware of the conversations you can, and should, be having. The goal is to raise a child that is protected, confident and who can avoid abuse by seeing the signs and red flags.

I do talks all over the country to churches, schools, and businesses about social media, pornography, internet safety, and mental health. Through the course of all these speaking engagements, I have talked with more and more teens to try to get their perspectives and gain insight into their worlds. I want to be able to talk practically and precisely about how this new world is affecting them and to be able to pass that knowledge on to you. If I have learned one thing that stands out, it is that they need to hear some explanations.

Our tendency as parents, teachers, and leaders is to correct behavior and move on. Maybe your home is different, but so many parents are doing this to their children, whether purposefully or not. We focus on the "what," of the behaviors that scare us and that we are desperate to prevent. If a child has a behavior problem, we say "He needs to cut that out and straighten up. She needs to get off that phone." We don't usually stop to ask why. Why is he sleeping in class? Why is she constantly on social media? Why is he always on his iPad? Why is she distracted and fidgety? Why do they get so angry or throw those fits? As we discussed earlier, the "what" really won't be helpful until we get to the root of the problems our kids are facing, especially problems related to the internet. They need to feel known and seen to listen and hear.

Teaching the "why" and developing critical thinking skills in our kids deals somewhat with their IQ, but a great deal more with their EQ, or emotional intelligence. The Bible calls it wisdom. Psychology calls it insight. Whatever word you want to use, the way to build it is to have conversations and not just demand certain behaviors with no explanation.

Clint Davis

I think it will help more than you can imagine in achieving the behaviors you were after in the first place.

All of this, however, requires you to understand the context that makes you and your children different, and to acknowledge those differences aren't inherently bad. We are simply not the same as the children we are raising. Digital Immigrants vs. Digital Natives. These are terms coined by writer Marc Prensky if you didn't catch that footnote, and I have found them incredibly helpful. Native means "born into," and exactly like a native of a country grows up immersed in their surrounding culture and practices, so also are these children born into and shaped by technology. They are the first generation to grow up with social media and smart devices from infancy to adulthood. Most of their parents, including most of us reading this book, are not native to smartphones or social media - we are what we call digital immigrants or as I call them, "analog converts." We had physical maps, used pencil sharpeners bolted to the wall, lugged around books in backpacks, and some of us carried around a bag phone that weighed 15 pounds. We had math teachers tell us for 40 years, "you won't have a calculator with you everywhere you go!" Well guess what Mrs. Smith? You were so wrong. Think about it. None of the children in school today will ever hear that statement. It has been filtered out of society in just a little over a decade. What else has changed or has been lost?

If your experience was anything like mine, you had to call your friends on a home phone and talk to their dad for 5 minutes while your friend screamed in the background to hang-up while they picked up the landline in their room. Then you waited for the click to make sure mom and dad weren't trying to listen in on your conversation. Speaking of landlines, recently we ordered a home phone. We have been allowing our boys to make calls and answer the phone to keep their social skills growing and to make it easier for them to have access to their friends and grandparents. This has opened up conversations about etiquette. They have to answer and say "Davis residence, (insert name) speaking." It is adorable and so sweet. As we have been doing this, my parents have called the boys more than ever before, probably because they don't have to bother us or feel like they are interrupting our flow through our cell phones. This brought another realization of what we have lost unnecessarily. Cell phones have

237

caused us to move to texting and now snap chatting, instead of talking. Home phones can bring back the balance! You might want to try it before transitioning to any kind of mobile device or video call situation. You will be surprised at the skills your kids learn that they cannot gain anywhere else. It has been a hilarious process and also made me feel like a total dinosaur.

Many parents today are analog to digital converts trying to parent these digital natives, and let's face it, we are lightyears behind. Now, this obviously isn't our fault. We didn't have emails, smartphones, or access to so many people and so much information. Some of you reading this probably did begin to have access to those things early on, but not by much and if you are reading this in the future, I hope this book has changed the trajectory of our lives in some way. The other thing that is different about the childhood of digital converts is that people also didn't have such easy access to us. I mean for goodness sake, just 15 years ago, if a young child wanted to know what women thought about things they would have had to walk over to a group of grown women and ask them. Today they can find out what hundreds of grown women think in a matter of seconds about whatever content they are looking for. For the first time in human history a stranger can be talking to, sending images to, and influencing your child all while they sit next to you on the couch, and you might not even know. The problem is that this aggressive amount of access is all this generation has ever known. The click of a mouse or the swipe of an app has been releasing dopamine into their brains since they were babies. Think about it – even toddler toys are now phone-shaped with buttons, lights, and sounds. We didn't see the harm at first, because no one on earth could have seen what was coming. "It's just MySpace...what could go wrong?" (Who was in *your* top 10?)

Although, maybe some people did see it coming.
Steve Jobs and other Google and Apple employees have all publicly stated that they would not allow their families or their children to use these devices. And yet, they certainly don't seem to have a problem with our families buying them and becoming digital zombies. Food for thought.

I find it incredibly strange. We judge these kids and young adults for their lack of work ethic, their inability to hold a conversation, and their lack of resiliency or mental toughness, but in many ways, we are the ones that allowed this to happen. We are the ones that didn't safeguard them, offer them honest information, or educate them on the consequences of their actions. The truth is we didn't know what we were doing. Millions of kids didn't get up one day, go to the store, and purchase a $600 tablet or a $1,200 smartphone. We bought it for them, and we likely did this for any number of reasons. Because our neighbor's kid had one, because of the radical consumerism and individualism of our culture, or simply because of an increased pace of life that leaves adults mentally and emotionally exhausted. The phone or the screen has become the best babysitter we can buy, all for just a moment's rest from our children and the world and all for the low cost of our children's mental health. Which is not even mentioning that, psychologically, our kids will value what we value. A toddler tries to steal your phone, because they see how important it is to you and how often you reach for it.

I am not saying I am completely innocent on this front. I just think we need to take a hard look at what has happened in 15 years. I cannot go to a restaurant or a public place without seeing a family of 4 or 5 all with devices in their hands and not one person engaging in conversation. Sound familiar? I see couples at dinner both on their phones the entire dinner. Smart devices are the greatest pacifier the world has ever known, and just like an infant's actual pacifier, our phones and tablets are keeping our brains stuck in baby stages of development and relationships.

Do you know that when your child looks at a screen or swipes on an app that their brains are releasing neurochemicals that instantly change and rewire their brain forever? Same for when a teen views explicit content online. If parents were putting out lines of cocaine on the kitchen table and letting their kids snort it, we would have an all-out crisis. Instead, we allow their undeveloped brains to have more screen time than they need, and in doing so, trigger a similar dopamine response as strong as cocaine or other substances. Every click, swipe, or notification floods the brain with its favorite chemical. It is no wonder why teens react in rage when you ask them to get off their phone or turn off the computer for the night. It is also no surprise that I get parents telling me "I can't take their phone or game console away. They will have a complete meltdown." Parents even fear their child might hurt themselves over losing their devices, and honestly, I am not surprised. An addict reacts the same way at the loss of their next dose. Many apps like TikTok not only have ridiculously inappropriate content, but they are also designed like a slot machine at the casino. Psychology calls this "random reinforcement."[115]

Maybe that sounds extreme to you. Maybe it is extreme. Frankly, though, we experienced extreme change in a matter of just a few years, and we haven't stopped to ask if all that progress was in the right direction or if it was as fun and harmless as we thought. Technology is useful and very amazing, but it is also very dangerous in the wrong hands and at the wrong times.

Speaking of hands. One of the things I do when I speak at schools is to poll the audience. I usually get the most honest and real time answers in scenarios like this. Kids don't assume my questions have an agenda. I ask the kids to raise their hands if they have a phone. Then I tell them to keep their hands up if they have Snapchat, TikTok, or Instagram. All the hands go up and stay up. Finally, I ask them to keep their hand raised if their parents taught them how to use their phone or their social media accounts. 98% of hands usually drop. Research shows that only about 16% of parents utilize any monitoring or parental control apps for their teen's devices.[116] Imagine if only 16% of parents treated drug use the same way. Or how about if we allowed our 13-year-olds to drive our cars across town without any direction or supervision? They would crash. Well, that is what is happening to our kids and dare I say, society, they/we are crashing. At every event I go to, the kids interrupt me to tell me stories and describe exactly what I am there to teach them about. They already know the dangers because they are experiencing them, but because we are not preparing them or keeping them safe, they have thought it normal. They have been convinced there is no other way or that this is the way.

This lack of boundaries is a real problem. Especially when we consider that many of us did not grow up with these devices, so we have no clue what the dangers are or what red flags to notice. We are immigrants to

---

[115] Koetsier, John. "Digital Crack Cocaine: The Science Behind TikTok's Success," *Forbes,* 2020.

[116] Anderson, Monica. "Parents, Teens and Digital Monitoring," Pew Research Center, 2016.

our kids' digital worlds. We are flying blind in our own homes while our digital native offspring have learned every trick in the book. We have to gain some ground back. Hence, this whole book. One of my greatest hopes in writing this is to bring awareness to parents of all different backgrounds, and to validate you. You aren't alone in the chaotic and scary journey of raising healthy human beings. You aren't alone, and you aren't to blame. All these painful statistics and hard truths are not your fault. You didn't know the information necessary to create healthy structures and have crucial conversations with your children. Many of us lacked the resources and parental support ourselves. The consequences just were not so harsh. Yes, the world has changed drastically in just one decade, and it feels overwhelming. Guess what? We can all catch up.

First of all, give yourself some grace, and take a look around. The world has changed more rapidly in the past 30 years than at any other time in history. The space between one generation to the next is called an age gap, but with technology catapulting us forward at an alarming rate, that age gap is even more significant than it seems. We didn't gradually shift to a culture of handheld devices and social media over five generations – it happened in just one. In many ways, my childhood was more similar to my grandfather's than it is to someone just 15 years younger than me. Humans have and will continue to use technology to answer problems and find solutions. It will be up to our children to fight against norms and figure out solutions to making social media a safer place that can be used for good![117]

The differences between you and the children you are raising is staggering, and I write this section on technology not to send you into a blind panic, but to shed light on the ways we need to educate ourselves. All of us. We have to understand just how much things have changed in order to be successful parents. In fact, things are still changing as we speak, and we should show extreme caution in how quickly we allow our children to be exposed and indoctrinated by the next cutting-edge

---

[117] Kids today should be asking hard questions of their technology. "How will this be used, what is the future of AI, etc." One of my good friends and fellow Ted speakers Michael Trezza discusses this in his talk "The Broken Promises of Education." For more on that, check out his training program *Giant Leaps Learning*.

technology. We must learn how it works, how it affects them, and what are the pros and cons. We have to be even more mindful of the boundaries we enforce and more involved than ever before. Our margin for error is much smaller than in the past, and it is continuing to shrink.

What I am talking about here is the difference in exposure and immersion. A teen today isn't just exposed to sexual content, they are *immersed* in it. They are not just exposed to stories about violent crime, they are immersed in them. They are not just exposed to a few messages of fear and hate, they are immersed in them, constantly. They don't see the occasional sex scene in a movie, they are immersed in nudity and vulgarity nearly every minute of every day. This is happening younger and younger. In your child's hand lies access to 24-hour news, endless entertainment with very little limitation, and apps dictating to them what is valuable and worthy. If we don't learn that part of their world, we will have no part in it. They are digital natives, and we just aren't. When we stop treating our kids like they will have the same childhood as we did, and stop blaming them for the ways we're different, then we have taken the first step to helping them. I hope that this book will bring about amazing conversations between several generations. We will need multiple generations to come together to find solutions and create safety nets to catch us when we fall.

There is one more aspect we need to think about as digital immigrants trying to raise children in a fully digital age, something called "information overload." I don't know your history or the stories from your childhood, but as a 40-year-old father, I do know that the way we seek information and value it, is immensely different.

Digital natives have access to unlimited information. They have apps that tell them how to get from place to place, influencers that tell them what products to buy or foods to eat, and videos or articles that teach them about any topic they wish to learn. What they do not have, however, is any way of distinguishing what is true or false on the internet, what is good or bad. Those skills for assessing or measuring are lacking. Not only are there a million and one versions of the "truth" out there on the web, but even more fundamentally, our culture is starting to think there is no such thing as truth at all. Do you see the paradox?

Clint Davis

There is no truth, but live your truth at the same time. Oh, and I promise this product is the best...I am telling the truth. Don't believe me? Ask the list of paid actors or paid bots that have liked and followed my page.

If adults have a hard time making informed decisions in a culture swirling with unlimited options, a child or teen doesn't stand a chance in the face of the infinite opinions and information on their device.

There are many wonderful things that have come from our access to information, but like many of the topics in this book, there are consequences when we misuse our tools. If I handed my oldest son a power saw, I would *agonize* over every single instruction, making sure I was there to tell him to keep his fingers out of the way and be mindful at every second. I would also be there with him to supervise and watch out for his safety because he's 8 years old and using a tool he's never used before. It's dangerous.

Now, I obviously don't think my son is in danger of losing a finger from a smart device, but honestly, there is a lot more at stake. Maybe it seems silly to you, but this generation of kids did not grow up going to the library to pull out an index card to find a book on a particular topic. If a girl wants to know the capital of Brazil, she can simply pull out her phone and say "Hey Siri, what is the capital of Brazil?" Boom, she knows an answer she didn't know before. Which is an amazing ability, no doubt about it, but it also can risk making us lazy and less resilient. Children and adults alike. Okay, sure, looking up the capital of Brazil is probably not that big of a deal, but what about things beyond trivia?

One of the major issues with getting information instantly is that when we don't use our brains for problem solving or critical thinking, we will lose our mental strength. Time for another story.

I had a conversation with a local youth pastor the other day. He was taking kids around to lower income homes to do yard work for the residents. They made all the teens leave their phones in the van. One of the jobs was to mow the front yard with a push mower. The leader assigned this task to one of his stronger students, and then he left to go check in on the other sets of kids. He came back to check on this boy about 30 minutes later and see how much he had left to mow. To his surprise, the student was in the exact same place, standing with the mower in the middle of the yard. The leader was confused, so he asked the boy "Hey, you okay? Did you flood the motor or something? I thought you'd be halfway done." The boy responds, "I wasn't sure how to crank it, and you took my phone so I couldn't look it up on YouTube."

There are many consequences to this information era. One of the biggest being that Digital Natives, and now even us old digital immigrants, don't have to use their brains to problem solve anymore. YouTube and Google act as our brains now, which is especially problematic for children whose brains are still growing. Our children's minds are not firing synapses or making the neural connections in the brain that lead to true success in life. They are firing and connecting those synapses, just in some new ways that are not helpful for humans. They are not using their hands to build and construct, they aren't relying on their memory for how to spell and write a sentence, and they aren't learning to fail and try again without entirely falling apart. These different regions of the brain, then, are nearly impossible to strengthen and access later on in life. I'll be the first to admit that I love how I can YouTube how to put in a new toilet, how to swaddle a baby, or how to clean grease off of something. This saves me tons of money and frustration. The teenager from our story, however, did not even attempt to start the mower. He didn't even give his brain a chance to figure it out, and he didn't remotely consider asking for help from someone else. Which brings us to another tragic consequence of information overload.

Teens and young adults already think they know everything, as I'm sure you have seen. Now, they think they truly have access to every bit of knowledge. So...what would they need you for? Hormones, pride, fear, and a million other puberty-driven feelings already make it hard for a teen to be open and vulnerable with their parents. In 2023, a teen has all those reasons plus a tiny, palm-sized cheat sheet in their pockets that will give them any answer they want to know, answers to the questions they are no longer asking you. Children, teens, and even full-grown adults now seek advice from their phone instead of another human being, because they can just Google any question without needing to have awkward or difficult conversations. They do not have to discuss confusing content or debate controversial ideas. They can go online, find a group of people on a Reddit thread or on a YoutTube channel who will support them, and they can go on finding exactly the answers they want to hear. As I am sure you can imagine, this phenomenon causes a huge number of issues later on – not ever having to build mental toughness, assuming they are never wrong, only finding groups online and never building local community, the list could go on and on.

This generation has the ability to be the most connected, well-researched, and informed generation ever, but I look around and see mostly disconnection, misinformation, and loneliness.

These teens are desperately seeking connection, to be known, and to be loved, but they are finding it in all the wrong places. I express all of this as a way to show parents and caregivers that if we do not step into *their* personal, digital worlds and try to understand what *their* worldviews are like, we are going to lose them. You have a chance, if you choose to take it, to venture into your child's life and show them you are a place they can come to and trust for good and honest answers. If we can't meet them where they are with transparency or support, they will stop looking to us for guidance and instead will turn to their peers and to the internet.

Is it hard to talk about sex and abuse and social media to a 13-year-old? Yes, it absolutely is. That barrier might seem impossible to cross because we truly grew up in a different world than they are living in now. If you are the parent of a teenager and you fear things are too far gone or that you are too late, don't give up on them or on yourself. You will have to do some work towards healing and recovery, but there are answers for you. Some of those answers we will cover in the last pages of this book. If you have a younger child, prevention has got to be the goal. Every tool, suggestion, conversation, or rule I have mentioned here is a stepping stone. Talking about body parts and consent and gender at 9 or 10 years old builds the foundation for trust that will allow your teen to respect your advice regarding the internet years down the road. All of these things work together.

Digital natives and digital immigrants. This is who they are, and who we are. Arming yourself with an understanding of these generational differences will enable you to set boundaries that make sense for your family and that protect your children from getting too much access way too fast and with no structures in place. This chapter places us in better context. Let's move on and discuss the tool in question - the smartphone.

Reflection & Discussion

1. Reflect on your childhood. What was it like? What did you do for fun? How did you look up information? Reminisce on old stories!

2. Do you ever find yourself thinking your generation was just "better" or thinking negatively about newer generations? Why or why not?

3. How has your life changed since the technology and internet boom? How do you think it will affect your parenting either now or in the future?

4. Do you have any ideas or plans on how to address technology in your home?

17. Smartphone Plague

We steal their boredom from them. As a result, we're raising a generation of writers who will never start writing, artists, who will never start doodling, chefs who will never make a mess of the kitchen, athletes who will never kick a ball against a wall, musicians, who will never pick up their aunt's guitar and start strumming.
-Glennon Doyle, *Untamed*

The ways life has changed since the 80s and 90s are vast and pretty easy to spot, but there is no more obvious sign of the culture shift than the smartphone. I want to talk a little bit about smartphones, how they arrived in our hands, and how none of us, *especially* our children, got a handbook on how to use them.

Now, despite the possibly biased-sounding title of this chapter, I freely admit that the smartphone has brought about good things along with bad. I also freely admit that despite owning and using a smartphone in my own life, I think the bad outweighs the good. I call smartphones a plague because they came into the world very fast, spread to the population even faster, and they have a notable effect on us as humans. The evidence is new, and the studies on exactly how smartphones influence our brains and lives are still being done as we speak. Even still, the objective pros of such widespread use of smart devices are few.

The smartphone is the first piece of technology that has entered the culture in the way that it has. One night in 2007, we were playing the snake game on our Razr or Nokia, and just a few nights later, we could have a full screen device with an interface and abilities never before available. You might know it as the iPhone 1. In the blink of an eye, we went from no apps to endless apps. No internet in our hands to surfing the web in HD. We went from limited access to porn to instant access.

Clint Davis

From using our phones for utility to using them for dopamine hits and instant gratification.

This is the first piece of technology that advanced at this speed in the history of the world. For some perspective, let's take airplanes as an example. In 1903, the Wright brothers made their slice of history with a powered aircraft. Other people in other parts of the world were accomplishing something similar not long after them. In the decades that followed, people like Charles Lindbergh and Amelia Earhart braved flights across the Atlantic Ocean. But it was not until more than 70 years later that the technology and mechanics improved enough to achieve commercial passenger flight. 70 years of improvement and learning before flight was available to the world. Imagine if someone would have mass produced the plane before it was ready and before we had the proper safety protocols and mechanisms in place. It would have been a disaster.

Our smartphone journey has been the complete opposite.[118] We built a phone that was *vastly* different from any phone before it, something more computer than simple communication device. Nothing like a smartphone had ever been in the world before, and the tech world launched it into society with no clue how it would change us all. We started with a phone the size of a briefcase that needed its own handle to a Blackberry or Nokia that handled calendars and could take somewhat decent pictures and then jumped all the way to a cell phone equipped with countless apps, social media, faster internet access, private messaging, email, instant shopping and Amazon, instant porn, and instant information all at once. Not to mention that we did all of this *so much faster* than we did with something as big and dangerous as an airplane.

Tell me this. When you or your friends first got an iPhone or Android, did it come with a psychologist? Did it come with a pilot or flight attendant that sought to make sure you stayed safe? Were there teams full of

---

[118] Now, clearly phones were developing and changing before the smartphone arrived in our hands. I am speaking more so of smartphones and how vastly different they were from a normal phone that calls and texts. The discrepancy between a Nokia and an iPhone is so large they might as well be different products altogether.

249

people to make sure that your choices did not negatively impact everyone around you? Did it even come with a warning about the dangers of prolonged screen time or an info packet about how the phone's design was meant to pull you in and keep you online? Mine sure didn't. Oh, and by the time Apple added notifications about increased "screen time," it was far too late.[119] We were hooked.

We didn't train anyone or have a group of experts ready to fix the problems this fabulous invention would cause. To my knowledge, Apple, Android, Google – they weren't doing large case studies or focus groups to test the smartphone's effects on adults or children. They didn't follow people around for a few years to see if they would get more depressed, more addicted, more stressed, more confused, or more anxious. Neither did Facebook or Instagram. Although, at a recent congressional hearing, some evidence brought these companies' previous knowledge into question.[120] I am not trying to say we should have relied on those massive, for-profit companies to be any sort of moral or caring guide for us. I just want to point out that maybe the blind trust we placed in a cultural phenomenon was not really earned. Maybe, just maybe, our desire and need for connection was primed and ready to go, and our trauma and brokenness blindly ran into the arms of something for which we were not prepared. I realize that the smartphone is just a tool and it is the hearts of people that make choices, but what I am saying is that without knowing the risks, being educated on how to use them, and putting guard rails to keep us safe, things are not going well.

Again, adults are responsible for their choices. It is not Google, Apple, or the phone's fault. Keeping kids safe is my focus. In 2007 adults bought the first iPhone. And just as we are conditioned to do, they got the new one a couple of years later. Then what happened? Well people started passing down their old phones to their children! Between 2008-2010, we put a mysterious, dangerous, life-altering piece of technology in their hands for the first time ever, despite being total amateurs ourselves. We didn't know how it was going to affect our brains, our bodies, our social

---

[119] Just FYI, this screen time feature didn't get added until iOS 12, which came out in 2018.
[120] Paul, Kari and Milmo, Dan. "Congress grills Facebook exec on Instagram's harmful effect on children," *The Guardian*, 2021.

experiences, our families, or our communication skills. Nothing. Before we could possibly know the consequences for *ourselves*, we let children have this thing that none of us could fully understand. Those devices not only give our children access to potentially dangerous information, entertainment, and people, they give all sorts of people access to our kids. To include one more airplane analogy, this would be like if all those aircraft companies unleashed 10,000 jets into the sky without providing air traffic controllers, runways, satellites for tracking, or expert pilots to fly the planes. Can you imagine? There would be crashes everywhere! Not to mention, none of us would have ever flown anywhere. From where I sit, this is exactly what is happening with our society since the development of the smartphone or tablets. We are crashing and burning.

I want to make my stance very clear. I am not against technology. I have an iPhone. I wrote this book on a MacBook. I have social media and use many different apps. ***I am not against technology. What I am against is children having access to all this technology without being trained, educated, or protected which leads to misuse and screen addiction. I am against children being not only exposed to adult content before they are even in puberty, but immersed in it.*** I am against the way companies and politicians prioritize their agendas and bottom line over the dangers of exposing children to content that will change the way they live, feel, and think about themselves and others. Life is difficult enough for our kids without these devices being in their hands 24/7.

The truth is that smartphones are being given to kids earlier and earlier and for a whole laundry list of reasons. But think about it...this is a terrible introduction to communication, social life, and relationship building. It is no wonder that a child who gets a phone at 9 or 10, who has only ever sent Snaps or emojis, will end up with no clue how to have a real conversation. It is no surprise that their anxiety is at an all-time high or that their social anxiety is crippling them. They are learning to communicate and resolve conflict through text messaging and social media apps, not to mention how easy bullying becomes when we are anonymous. Even worse, kids are watching the adults in their life model this behavior. They don't learn how to resolve conflict in-person with an actual human being or develop the skills to persevere through uncomfortable situations. A relationship gets hard, and they end it with a "Sorry, we need to break up" text. They want to leave a job and will simply send an abrupt email to their boss that says, "I quit."

We are creating a society of people who have a lower level of social skills and less social capacity for empathy, open communication, and conflict resolution. There has been a huge increase in clinical anxiety in incoming college freshmen since 2010. More children seem to be on medication now than ever before, and that number isn't going down. This was before Covid hit. The research hasn't even come out about the damage the pandemic caused. I realize that there are a lot of factors causing mental health problems in teens and college students. These smart devices are not the only thing to point a finger at. The goal of these conversations is for us to see what damage **IS** being caused by them.

Do you know that some college campuses now have "parent orientation." This means that your 18- or 19-year-old college student needs you to come to college with them to help do the things they feel incapable of doing. This orientation is offered so that parents can intervene and talk with the guidance counselor or the professors if there is a problem. I have worked with teens and young adults with EMDR[121] and trauma therapy to help them learn to make a doctor's appointment, call in their prescriptions, or ask for help from a teacher. Sheer panic washes over them, and they are overwhelmed by unbearable shame and guilt. It's a painful thing to see unfold in their brains. But, honestly, how could this not happen when their entire culture uses pictures with 5-word sentences to communicate on Snapchat. I know this is not all kids, but it is very common in those who have grown up with devices in their hands and lacked appropriate supervision and guidance.

And what are our kids saying with their 5 words and a picture? Most likely if you are reading this, you are 21 or older. Have *you* ever sent a text or an email you wish you hadn't? Have you ever made a post you regretted later? Or how about posting a comment on social media and inciting a revolt in the comment section? I know I've made some of these mistakes, and I quickly vowed to try and never make them again. Even something

---

[121] For more information on the technique of Eye Movement Desensitization and Reprocessing, check out this resource: https://www.emdr.com/what-is-emdr/

as simple as sending an email too quickly. Once, I was in the middle of something at my desk, and when an email came in from a client needing help, I had 10 other things on my mind. I shot back a hurried reply: "Here is the number to our front desk where we have two people who will help you. Thanks."

No grace there, no patience or consideration for their suffering. I was mortified, so I immediately sent another email to them. "Also, thank you for being brave enough to reach out. I know this is tough, and we are really excited to help you on this journey." That client was gracious to me, and things turned out fine, but I would have *never* made that mistake in a real conversation with a person sitting in front of me. Naturally, none of us have absolutely perfect social skills, but most people can see a person's body language, facial expression, and hear their tone and would respond with greater grace and empathy. The anonymity and uncertainty of email and text allow so much room for error.

Even as adults, it can be very difficult to keep our composure, use proper online etiquette, or restrain ourselves from looking at or gossiping about things we shouldn't be. For goodness sake, one of the newest updates on the iPhone allows you to unsend texts and pictures as long as the person hasn't seen it. This speaks to the insane amount of things we regret sending. If we as adults struggle with these things, what are our children experiencing? They don't stand a chance of being responsible phone owners without causing great harm to themselves or others. Like I said earlier, 95% of them are not even being taught. It's the digital wild wild west, and we clearly need to try something different.

None of this information is a criticism against people 30 and under. I only want to point out that things have changed. *A lot.* If you grew up in the age of smartphones and social media, then it is highly likely that no one has taught you how to operate amidst all these changes. If you are a parent and didn't grow up in the digital age, this information is crucial for you too. A person might argue that since the entire world has changed, we need to just catch up and play along, but the research and evidence screams differently. Succumbing blindly to the call of the internet is not the way (any Mandalorian fans?). I also want parents to understand the difference between the humans raised before the 21st century, and those raised after.

We have talked about these digital natives, how smartphones arrived and changed things in a big way, and what sorts of problems unchecked device-use can cause in both us and our children. Not the nicest picture, I know. So, I want to take some time to really lay a foundation to arm you with information and tools to help you make healthy decisions for your child and family when it comes to devices and smartphones. One more time before getting into it, I want to assure you that I am not anti-technology or anti devices. These things obviously have brought amazing resources to our lives, but I am against giving children phones and devices *that they have no clue how to use.* Without children or their parents understanding the risks that are present and the boundaries that can be implemented to keep us all safe, we are in for a world of hurt.

I don't want to be shy about discussing the problems with devices because the ways we can do better are numerous and very simple. So, let's get into some of the changes we can make to help ourselves and our children. I also want to mention that a tablet or iPad is just as dangerous as a smartphone. People will tell me that their child doesn't have a smartphone as if they are not in danger, but in the same breath will tell me their child has a Kindle, iPad, or some other device that has apps and unfiltered access to the internet. Let's face the truth, guys...there is not really a difference in the danger level there. Kids are not getting into trouble by making too many phone calls.

One other main argument people make is that they want their child to be able to call and check in when they are out of town, at another adult's house, at an after-school activity, etc. I am not suggesting that your child shouldn't have a way to contact you. There are many devices available now that allow communication to happen without risk or with exceptionally lower risk. Obviously, waiting to trust your child with a device until they are much older is the most sure-fire way to protect them from device addiction and constant screen time. I'll mention this a bit more in a few pages. We'll call that method "smartphone-abstinence." But changing the *type* of phone we allow our children to use is also a way to majorly impact them so we can change their relationship to their devices. Just a few of the safer options out there include:

254

Clint Davis

- The Light Phone
- Gabb Wireless Phone
- Jitterbug
- Bark Phone
- Flip Phone (kick it old school, ya know)
- Smart watches

There are many phone alternatives in 2023 that lower our child's risk and still allow them their freedom in a safe way. The phones above are less dangerous in the sense that they don't allow unfettered internet access or streaming. If you are reading this in the future, I'm sure there are even more options. Heck, I hope we have solved all these issues by then. I know I am praying for that.

It is astounding to me how many parents just don't have the time or energy to find the better options that are out there. It seems easier (and often *is* easier) just to give them our old cell phones or go get the same one that we have because that's the phone we know how to use. Much like the awkward conversations we discussed earlier, our problem is that feeling overwhelmed can often stop us from taking the necessary steps to make devices safer for our kiddos. I empathize, and I get it. Work is busy. Kids are hard. Times have changed. These are all valid reasons for not knowing what to do with the new world we live in, but that is why I am writing this book. I want to change the paradigm.

The phones I listed above are especially helpful as a first phone. I know you might not be able to force your 17-year-old to use a Jitterbug, but introducing these simplified "dumb" phones early helps establish trust and good practices with less risk than a smart device. Remember our options are either prevention or recovery.

However, if you want my honest opinion (which maybe you do if you have made it this far), I really believe a child under 13 does not need a smartphone for any reason. That's it...my #1 solution for many of our smartphone troubles. Instead of a list of 10 million boundaries and complicated rules, this is the single best advice I can give. Just be patient, and hold off on offering a smart device to your children as long as you reasonably can.

Besides, this isn't just my solitary opinion; the research shows that enforcing such a rule limits the greatest amount of damage with the best possible outcomes for their mental health.[122] "Wait Until 8th" is an amazing group who have done lots of work in this area, helping parents take a pledge to wait until the 8th grade to give their child a phone. Maybe I haven't said it before, but I don't believe in these rules because they limit my child's happiness or freedom, but because we are very rarely the best judges of our own desires. Also, I will choose them being bound by our house rules which are enforced for their benefit, over them being held captive by the toxicity and addictive content on the internet. I would rather cause my sons frustration now than have them face emptiness, despair, and even trauma later in life.

My stance is to wait until after 13 years old before smartphones become part of the picture for my boys, but regardless of when your family decides to take that step, we need a new perspective on these devices. Treat them like driving a car and earning a drivers' license. Go with me on this metaphor for just a second.

A smartphone, much like a car, can be an incredibly useful resource when used properly or can become a massively dangerous tool when used recklessly. Remember when you were a kid and your parents taught you how to drive? It was probably on some back road or in a big, empty parking lot. For me, it was in a big field, and I remember my dad ended up getting so annoyed that he got out, slammed the door, and went back in the house. I'm sure many of you can relate to something similar – slamming brakes, jerking the steering wheel, and a lot of our parents grabbing the "Oh-Crap-Bar," to put it nicely.

Many of us probably started this homestyle driving education at 11 or 12 years old sitting in our parents lap. Then we might have upgraded around 13 or 14 to driving home from a friend or neighbor's house, very slowly with white knuckles and great gnashing of teeth with our parents giving guidance at every turn...literally. Then at 15, we got to get our learner's

---

[122] https://www.waituntil8th.org/

permit, and guess what? Our parents still needed to be right beside us making sure we didn't murder anyone on the road, ourselves included. They had to watch us, keep us safe, and offer corrections to make sure we could navigate this new and dangerous tool well, all before we got to take any sort of driving test. Even after all our learning at home, we took a driver's education class, drove the car with some random person in the passenger's seat, and then took a written test based on what we learned. Then *finally*, if we showed enough smarts, safety, and confidence, we earned that card of freedom – our driver's license. Even at 16, after we got our license, we had a curfew and rules. After 17 or 18, we were more on our own and free to make mistakes, back into polls, or run into a ditch or two. I am sure for many of us, though, that our parents still checked in or stayed up worrying about us until we got home, as well as staying on our case about car maintenance and cleanliness. Where are all my "I'll get gas tomorrow friends?"

I wanted to paint that picture because I believe that cellphones, especially smartphones or devices, should be viewed the same way: a life-changing and powerful tool that requires training and practice and guidance. To stick with the metaphor, our current culture is basically putting the car, the keys, and the license in the hands of 10- and 12-year-olds, without giving them any advice or instruction and then sending them down the busiest interstate in the world, just hoping they don't crash. Well, shocker – they are crashing. The data shows it. The kids show it. Our jam-packed counseling offices show it. They are dying in more ways than one.

So, that's the advice. We should treat the cell phone like a car that requires a driver's license to operate. This is the way that ought to play out.

Let your child use a device every now and then when they are 11 or 12 years old and under strict guidance and supervision. Teach them how to navigate the device, what it should be used for, and how to stay safe while using it. Talk with them about the dangers on the digital road and how to avoid running into unwanted pictures, videos, or people they don't know. Teach them the "rules of the road," so when they do need to use a phone on occasion, they don't get lost or hurt.

Then, when they hit 13 or 14, maybe give them a smart phone of their own that they can use at limited times during the day. Make sure you approve all messages, contacts, and social media accounts. As a matter of fact, to be safe, you should go so far as to receive and read all messages to and from their friends. I would say this sounds extreme, but I feel the age we live in makes it necessary. The risks are extreme, and no one seems to be lessening those. With new means of communication cropping up all the time, it is on us as parents to teach them how to communicate through these new platforms. Without guidance, how will they have a clue how to navigate this appropriately? How will they build trust if we aren't showing them how to be trustworthy?

Here are some helpful apps to use:
Net Nanny, Bark, Covenant Eyes, EverAccountable, Screentime, Aura, FamilyKeeper, WebWatcher, OurPact

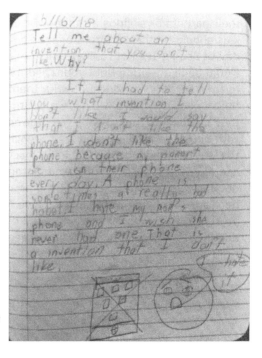

At 15, maybe they get their smartphone learner's permit. This step assumes they've shown you they can handle it and that you can give them their own personal phone and social media accounts. They have watched you drive; you have watched them drive. You have taught them the rules of the road and helped them stay away from the dangers. Now they are free to use their learner's permit and practice more hands-on learning, but you will still be right there every step of the way, with all the safety and mentoring in place.

Clint Davis

At 16 or after, they have grown in their maturity, and after 4-5 years of practicing and slowly building responsibility and trust, they earn their "license," and you hand over the keys. At this point, you must be able to trust them and allow them to make their own mistakes and learn from them. You don't stop being there for them, but you understand that you can't protect them from the world forever. They won't always have your hand to hold as they grow, and they need to know how to navigate these things with confidence on their own.

None of this is about depriving something from our children just because we can – I love bringing joy to my sons! In fact, take a look at this journal prompt from a child. They sometimes *hate* phones. Maybe because it wastes their time, causes bad habits, or because it steals all their parents or siblings attention. Besides, I don't necessarily think our kids should go their entire teenager-hood without *any* cell phone or device usage. It's not really feasible in today's world, for one. For two, it would be like waiting until your child had their driver's license to do any form of car/driving education with them. Practice is crucial. When the time comes, my boys will have a car that they drive and a phone that they can use on their own. I will be worried, but I will learn to trust them with big responsibilities and try to teach them to be trustworthy all along the way. In the world we live in with schools and businesses requiring the use of devices, social media, and laptops, stubborn withholding of any devices would be unwise. All of the boundaries and rules I have discussed here are simply my philosophy to give the best support possible while preparing your kids for the world and their future careers, relationships, and lives. A philosophy that I have seen echoed in the research time and time again.

If all this is leaving you a bit overwhelmed (although I hope it's not), you would not be alone in that feeling. During one of my talks on this topic, a mom raised her hand and said, "This sounds like a lot of work."
I chuckled, and responded, "Well, yes, I'm afraid it is. So maybe you shouldn't give your kid a device or phone just yet."

The reality is that all these ideas and suggestions require a lot of work over a long period of time. It's not like this is our fault. The culture has just sped away with our family, our children, and our peace. We have

259

been thrust into this digital landscape with very little resources or understanding ourselves, and phones are not just phones anymore. That is a big part of my point here. Our 3-pound, head-sized phones didn't pose the same risks as our kids' phones do now. Even the more recent Nokias or flip Razrs – no YouTube or TikTok, no Instagram or Tinder on those guys.

Yes, smartphones were the chicken that came before the egg, and devices obviously play a massive role in our exposure to content, but open access to the internet, different apps and social media are the parts of the phone that really pose the greatest danger. I know it's scary to think of all the ways we must protect our children – in person, on devices, their physical and mental health. Being a parent is no easy feat. It is not for the faint of heart. But I promise tackling all these issues is not only possible, but also not as complicated as it seems. The world has just made us think there is only one way to operate, which is to let our kids use their devices however and whenever they wish. To save our kids and future all we have to do is push back against the ways our society is blindly walking off a cliff in regard to technology.

Protection from phones, and the scarier monster of social media, is not a complicated or convoluted plan that has to be drawn out with a sharpie and red string in your basement.

The ways we can protect our children are fairly simple, and yes, require some work, but over great periods of time and in small ways that don't have to be overwhelming. With devices, maybe that means waiting a bit longer to allow them to use a phone of their own and providing more structure and oversight than other kids' parents. Difficult, but not complicated. The information and solutions related to social media are similar, but I still think those deserve their own discussion. If you're anything like me, I need all the help I can get with all the apps and "trends" that seem to crop up with each passing day. I am sure that many will change as I write this book, but hopefully the spirit of the ideas will not.

Reflection & Discussion

1. When did you get your first phone? What was the phone, and what was that experience like?

2. If your kids are young, had you thought about a plan for introducing smart devices to them? If they are older, what are the smartphone rules in your house?

3. If your kids already use their own devices, how are they using them? Do you think their mental health has been affected at all?

4. Consider discussing family rules about smartphones that everyone comes to agree on and that everyone has to follow, even you as the parent/caregiver.

18. Social Media Sickness[123]

*Modern technology isn't changing us. It's changing society.
The attention economy has commoditized our time and turned us into
products to be bought and sold.*
-Mark Manson

I thought a lot about this chapter and what to call it, and this is where my editor and I landed. Not because we wanted to be provocative or "click-baity" but because we both felt this best expressed what every social media user is going through, at least to some degree. If phones and devices are dangerous tools when used improperly, social media platforms are viruses that can be fatal if we aren't inoculated against them. What would be the vaccine for Instagram anyway? Let's dive into how these various platforms for "connection" are *actually* affecting us and our children.

Here is a vignette of the average person in our current society. Many of us have suffered trauma and pain in our childhoods, often unaddressed even into adulthood. We have attachment issues and deep insecurities passed down from imperfect parents with their own negative experiences. Some of us have trauma and abuse that was passed down from those very same parents. We have been shaped by negative gender stereotypes, a broken educational system, and a world that values us based only on our performance and external qualities.

Unresolved trauma and constant self-doubt have made us desperate for affirmation, affection, attention, and approval. Those desperate needs have blinded us to the need for authenticity and vulnerability and we chase whatever makes us feel good. We are dying for connection and to

---

[123] I urge you to look this phrase up in Google…you will be amazed at all that comes up.

be seen, known, and loved.[124] We are searching for answers to life's scariest questions and working hard to just survive. If all this describes our world's adults, I don't even have to describe what is going on within the hearts of our children. I say all of this because I want us to understand what is going on for the human beings around us. They are in lots of pain. Constant pain. Many of our nervous systems are messed up due to being in fight, flight or freeze most of the time.

Bearing all this in mind, social media waltzes through the door. Just like many tools, the smartphone included, social media in and of itself was not the problem in the beginning.

Let us go through a little timeline to understand just how quickly things have gone downhill.

MySpace hit the scene in 2003. This cool new site was a way for people to post pictures, songs, and short stories about their lives with the idea of helping people stay connected. Many college students and adults would take time to build their "social profile" and express their unique styles and beliefs. I remember getting back from Afghanistan that same year and creating my first profile. Lets just say it took hours to update or change anything and was such a headache, but man was it cool and even came with a built in friend! I call him "MySpace Tom." [125]

Tom

":-)"

Male
32 years old
Santa Monica,
CALIFORNIA
United States

Last Login:
10/22/2007

Mood: busy 😊
View My: **Pics** | **Videos**

In 2005, along came Facebook. I bet some of you will remember this vividly. I was in college at the time, and I remember that you had to have a .edu email to sign up at the beginning. The

---

[124] Tim Keller's lovely quote from *The Meaning of Marriage* comes to mind: "To be loved but not known is comforting but superficial. To be known and not loved is our greatest fear. But to be fully known and truly loved is, well, a lot like being loved by God. It is what we need more than anything. It liberates us from pretense, humbles us out of our self-righteousness, and fortifies us for any difficulty life can throw at us."
[125] If you used MySpace, perhaps you remember Tom! He was your automatic friend haha.

students-only platform slowly opened itself up to the public. Before long, everyone was on Facebook, catching up with old friends and family members all over the world. The differences in that original version of Facebook and the current "Meta" we have today are drastic. One major difference being that we definitely weren't accessing it on our phones. It was a site, not an app, because we didn't even have smartphones yet. Not as we know them today, anyway. In the beginning we were not even capable of checking our status or searching profiles instantly. We didn't start out getting our news or our advertisements from social media. The doom scroll had not begun.[126]

With the advent of the first iPhone in 2007, we also gained instant access to social media in the palm of our hands – something we'd never had before. By 2010, companies like Instagram, Pinterest, Friendster, Foursquare, and many others figured out the trends and jumped on board. Between 2003 and 2023, countless other platforms have invaded our phones and brains. As social media has evolved from a few friends and posts on a wall, to now thousands of followers and image/video content, some of the most utilized apps have become the ones most abused: Snapchat, TikTok, Tinder, and Instagram. These platforms, plus many more that seem to cycle in and out, have been instrumental in exposing families, individuals, and children to information and content to which no one has ever had this level of access. We have not only given them that access, we have let that access become infinite, nonstop, and completely private. It does not matter the content, sex, drugs, violence, medical outbreaks on and on we are inundated with information and false news. Misinformation spreads like wildfire and neither our adult or child brains can handle it.

A Netflix documentary came out a few years ago called *The Social Dilemma*. If you haven't already, I would suggest any parent, teacher, or therapist watch it. You will learn some shocking truths about social media from the mouths of the folks who wrote the very apps in question. The platforms we so casually let rule our phones and our time are essentially manipulating and attacking all of us, irrespective of age. The central premise is that social media companies are using targeted algorithms to curate and manipulate what we see. Perhaps this seems obvious, but

---

[126] Thomson, Freya. "What is doomscrolling and why is it bad for us?," *Open Access Government*, 2022.

their methods are more devious than they seem. Apps like Facebook or Instagram were built with addiction in mind: recent posts near the top, the double-tapping for a like, the distances the apps will travel to learn about you.[127] All these aspects of the technology are designed to keep us scrolling longer, all in an effort to increase revenue. We think of ourselves as consumers and social media as the product we are using, but in fact, *we* are the product that companies are selling. And the market for you as a product is enormous. I'm sure you have already felt the truth of this when you are scrolling. Seeing ads for things you searched a few days ago or getting video recommendations for something you *swear* you only talked about with your dad last week.

If I learned one mind-boggling thing from that documentary, it is that the companies that create these apps only stand to profit from you. The longer you and your child stay on the screen, the more profit stacks up. More screen time, more addiction to social media, more ad revenue for their billion-dollar companies. They discuss how games and app interfaces were literally designed to release dopamine and become addictive, even in the way we swipe and press buttons.

The CEOs and CFOs of these companies confess in the show that they stopped allowing their children to use the very apps they helped build, as they saw the damage of the past decade begin to unfold. Big Tech didn't seem to care that marriages were ended, families were being shattered, and children have been trafficked, abused, exposed, and neglected due to the smart device and lack of accountability and safety. It may be argued that this is a low number or that there are other contributing factors, but there's no doubt that the smartphone and social media have been used to negatively impact our society. I do believe that the phone and social media are tools and that those tools cannot be fully to blame, but they are being put in the hands of humans emotionally, spiritually, and communally not supported enough to manage them without dire consequences.

---

[127] Montag, Christian et al. "Addictive Features of Social Media/Messenger Platforms and Freemium Games against the Background of Psychological and Economic Theories." *International journal of environmental research and public health* vol. 16,14 2612. 23 Jul. 2019.

Building Better Bridges

I don't have enough breath in my lungs or pages of ink to list all the examples of how social media has affected our lives, for better or for worse, but I will say that one of the saddest consequences is the breakdown of the nuclear family. As I said, we were already suffering from years of emotional, spiritual, and physical neglect, and now we have social media in our hands. We are imploding. Do you feel it? I know I do. I feel the weight of how social media has affected me, my clients, my friends.

Aside from what I *feel* to be true, here are a few data points and stats related to our social media use.

Let's look first at ourselves. We're the ones raising these kids...so how do we hold up? How is social media affecting our lives and marriages?[128]

> - Heavy social media users are 2 times more likely to contemplate divorce.
> - Online affairs now contribute to more than a third of divorces.
> - 30% of Tinder users are married.
> - 80% of divorce lawyers said social media was responsible for most of the cheating in marriage and that Facebook caused 1 out of 5 divorce cases.
> - Ashley Madison (an app for those seeking an affair) gets over 130 million matches per month producing 40,000 affairs every day.
> - 1 in 10 adults admit to hiding messages and content on social media from their spouses.
> - 72% of adult polled say there is no negative impact on their marriages[129]

I couldn't believe that last one. No negative impact? Maybe that is just how badly we are afraid of the truth, how much we don't want those stats

---

[128] All these statistics come from a site that has pulled in the statistics from various research databases and included direct social media platform data. This page gets updated frequently as new data and polls are gathered. (Referenced in the following footnote.)

[129] Sebastian. "45 Facts How Social Media Affects Marriage: Does It Ruin Or Help Relationships?," *Relationship Advice*, updated 22 April 2023. (https://relationshipsadvice.co/social-media-marriage-statistics/)

to be true. I am guilty of this sometimes as well, but we have let some of the atrocities of social media become normalized. Even our world's digital immigrants are now facing many difficulties and consequences from their heavy social media use. So, what are the kids dealing with?

According to the Pew Research Center, here are just a few data points regarding teens:

- 1 out of 4 minors receive a sexual solicitation through private messages (only 25% told a parent).
- 60% have received a private message or picture from a stranger and 50% responded.
- 41% of people have experienced bullying and harassment.
- According to the eSafety Commissioner, children are being trafficked and sexually exploited through phishing and traps. (Adults pose as children, convince other children to send nude pictures, and then threaten to tell their parents. This can lead to suicide and mental breakdowns in children.)[130]

I also think I have mentioned this stat, but according to research, "There is also a large increase in the suicide rate for teen girls in the USA (up 77% for older teen girls; up 151% for younger teens, when you compare 2017 to the average of 2000-2009)."[131] These stats are decidedly not normal and COVID increased them even more. Does that 2010 sound familiar? That was about the time social media apps started booming, and our children had new and uninhibited access. If we haven't been able to really handle it, how are they going to avoid the addictive pull of social media apps and tempting content?

If you are reading this book and happen to be a young adult with no children yet, I beg you to see what has been happening to you. Possibly

---

[130] Vogels, Emily. "The State of Online Harassment," Pew Research Center, 13 January 2021.
[131] Haidt, J., & Twenge, J. (ongoing). *Adolescent mood disorders since 2010: A collaborative review.* Unpublished manuscript, New York University.

what has been happening to you since many years ago. I know using social media seems like an inevitable part of your life, but I also know there is so much confusion, shame, and exposure to things that you should have never seen or been exposed to. I know you probably got very little support navigating these things. Please take steps to protect your heart, mind, and body. Get help if you need it. If you are a parent to a teenager, get them help. They might be even less okay than they seem, and they are our future.

With the onset of social media, more children than ever are harming themselves, confused about their gender or sexuality, and addicted to pornography. Correlation is not causation, but we need to take a hard look at how this is informing many of the children and adolescents using these apps and devices. The percentages are astounding...and not in a good way. The social media world is filled with manipulation, lies, dangerous adults, and violent or pornographic content. This is across every platform and is truly not that hard to come across. I mean bots will send it to you through a direct message or text even if you don't go looking. These companies' ability to monitor and block this stuff is abysmal. This content sells and gets clicks, which pushes it to more and more viewers, increasing mental health concerns in our adults and children.

In a 2018 forum at Southern Virginia University, Collin Kartcnher[132] offered a few insights on our kids' screen time. In an article discussing the speech, Anna Bowers writes that "According to Kartchner, while spending one half to one hour on social media has minimal effects on someone's emotional

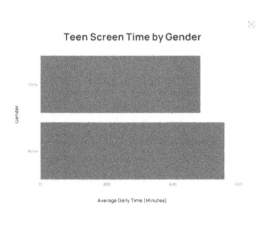

Teen Screen Time by Gender

Average Daily Time (Minutes)

---

[132] Collin was a Utah videographer and internet presence that ended up using his own platform to warn children and parents about the dangers of social media use. He passed away in 2020.

health, spending three to five hours a day results in a 30 percent increase in suicide ideation, and spending over five hours results in a 71 percent increase." Additionally, Collin goes on to note that this generation is spending "nine hours per day" on social media platforms. I also really like the phrase he uses when he discusses his purpose in educating teens and adults. He wants to help restore the "self-love [we] gave away to a stupid machine." I find myself whole-heartedly agreeing with that purpose.[133] Collin's assessment is echoed in the graph on the right, which shows the average minutes on a screen per day by male and female teens, girls on the top bar and boys on the bottom bar.[134]

The thing is, I know that we have a chance to help our children do better than we did and to avoid some of these horrifying statistics, and I know we should be leaping at that chance as early as possible. When it comes to social media, we are quite often the blind leading the blind, but it does not have to be like that.

Like I said, social media is full of lies, and being aware of those lies is half the battle. If we can wake ourselves up to the tricks and snares of these apps, we can arm our children with that knowledge as well.

The lies social media tells us and our children are many, but I will talk about just three of them here. First, though, there is one overarching lie that applies to the whole social media system that we should address. Social media, in all its many forms, preaches to us a sense of connection and community that is *manufactured*, not really there at all. Maybe it started out that way, but as adults, we now know that our Facebook friends and Instagram followers are typically not our real friends. And let's all pray that the people who like our posts aren't really following us. On the flip side of that, the only person I want my children and family to follow is Jesus, certainly not some celebrity or influencer with no real compassion for my boys and my wife.

---

[133] Bowers, Anna. "Collin Kartchner Speaks about Mental Health and the Dangers of Social Media," South Virginia University, 05 October 2018.

[134] Duarte, Fabio. "Average Screen Time for Teens (2023)," Exploding Topics, 09 April 2023.

According to a *Washington Post* article, what these platforms have marketed as a way to stay "connected" has translated into "more than 95 percent of people ages 13 to 17 in the country [using] a social media platform, and more than a third [who] say they are "almost constantly" using one."[135] This means hours a day doom-scrolling, editing their own pictures, or stalking profiles. Between endless filters and 20-second reels, people can't get enough of promoting fake versions of themselves and their lives, thus sending our children into confused depressive spirals when their life doesn't look that way. Lies, lies and more lies.

There is a new-ish TedTalk by Katanu Mbevi[136] where she talks about the impact of social media on our youth, and I want to elaborate on that and expand upon her idea with my own research and personal experiences. I have learned so much from the children and families in my clinical practice as well as learning about social media through countless parenting seminars. Social media is bad enough for adults when not used properly, but our under-educated, under-supervised, highly hormonal, and emotionally immature children surely cannot handle it without help. We have seen the loss of all civility, logic, reality, kindness, and truth in the past decade due to social media. Yet, every year these companies are increasing the ways to manipulate us into falling deeper into sleep, accepting the lies as normal and even comforting. Again social media is a tool, but in the hands of someone untrained and uninformed it is a dangerous one.

In order to wake up to the lies being sold to ourselves and to our children, we first have to know them. I want to talk about each of them a little bit so you can recognize them in your own social media use as well as prepare your children to see and debunk them.

The 3 Lies

Lie #1 – You are not enough.
The message that social media sends nearly 24/7 is that we are not enough. Nearly any time I speak, I love to poll audiences and provide a

---

[135] Velarde, Luis. "How addictive, endless scrolling is bad for your mental health," *The Washington Post,"* 2023.
[136] Katanu's talk is called "The Impact of Social Media on Youth," and it is very impactful if you have time to go watch it!

question-and-answer session at the end of my talks. When I give talks to teenage audiences, I ask the crowd, especially the ladies, how many pictures (aka selfies) they take to get the perfect angle and tilt that hides all qualities that *cough cough* make them *human*. Do you know what the average number of photos is before they pick one they like? *Nineteen*.

This means that our little girls take nearly 20 pictures of themselves before finally settling for a photo they can post. I follow up and ask the girls "What do you say to yourself in your head about the other 18 pictures?"
They usually shout out things like "not good enough – ugly – gross – that ain't the one – ewww." This means that our little girls, and often our boys too, are shaming themselves 18 times before they find a picture they like. Then the winning photo is still not good enough, so they edit it, use a filter, and then finally post. I ask them how many times they do this a day. The answer was 3-5. This means that our daughters and sons are saying to themselves almost 100 times a day that they are unworthy, ugly, not good enough, and less than. Why is it any surprise they feel depressed or suicidal? Or why are we shocked when they are confused, ashamed of their bodies, and always longing to change the way they look? If even adults sometimes struggle to discern the difference between real and fake, imagine how hard it is for teens to do it. They do not understand that they are comparing themselves to everyone else's highlight reel, someone else's highly edited and curated moments. It is no wonder they are chasing the dopamine rush that likes, hearts, and follows are going to provide. No wonder they feel like they have to lie and manipulate. No wonder their life does not compare to the fake lies that everyone else is sharing. They become addicted to the facade. They are chasing a high as much as anyone who has ever done drugs. The high of affirmation and earning what they assume to be love and security. As you read this, you know that this is true, because we do it too. Which brings us to lie number 2.

Lie #2 – Your worth comes from others.
Now that social media has pressured us into taking and harshly judging nearly 20 pictures, the picture gets posted, and the real sadness begins. If a certain, albeit completely arbitrary and algorithm-driven, number of people do not like, heart it, or comment positively on it, they will delete

the post and start the entire process over again. This painful routine comes from the second lie, which is that our worth and value comes from what other people think about us and how those people, mostly strangers, perceive us and our lives. Teach this pattern to a young person, and much of their life will be molded and motivated by seeking the approval of others. This is made worse for anyone with trauma or attachment wounds in their background!

Life is hard enough without having to seek our security, love, and worth from strangers we barely know, if at all, and who wouldn't even show up at your funeral. They won't show up when you get a devastating diagnosis. Or when you have a bad week or lose a job. They won't call whenever you are suffocating from debt or your business fails. Yet, despite all that, these acquaintances or strangers are who we look to for affirmation and approval. At Clint Davis Counseling, our mission statement is "Helping people make internal change for a lifetime of external success." Social Media's mission statement should go something like "Tricking you into getting temporary external validation, for a lifetime of chasing the wind."

Keeping in mind our conversation from earlier, smartphones and social media apps are engineered to keep us sucked in and mindlessly scrolling. So instead of spending time on self-healing, reflection, self-care, and growth, our teenage digital natives are spending more than 4 hours a day on a counterfeit version of themselves in the creation of their various media accounts and profiles. This profile can be whatever they want it to be. Perfectly curated, edited, and filtered. Children model after what they see every day. If we weren't constantly expressing to them how much social media matters to *us*, and if they didn't know social media was an option, they would not value it either. The idolization of this form of media has made our teens believe that is the only way to stay involved and "cool." (Do people still use the word cool?) Which, you guessed it, brings us to major lie number 3: FOMO (Fear of Missing Out).

Lie #3 – You are missing out.
Social media tells us all, especially teens and young adults, that we are missing out, that we will never be as happy, rich, supported, pretty, loved, good looking, fit, or as competent as everyone else. Not to mention that as different influencers make you feel lacking, they will also attempt

to sell you that one makeup product or health supplement or morning routine that will fix all your problems. Not all of this is bad, but most of it is garbage.

I remember when I was a child, I probably knew what *three* of my friends were doing on a Thursday night or a weekend. They were usually neighbor kids or a cousin down the street. Nowadays, social media lets everyone know what everyone else is doing at all times. It is becoming all too common for teenagers to use iPhone tracking, Life360, or social media to locate many of their "friends and followers." This means they will always know when they don't get invited to a birthday party or get left out of the plan to get Sonic slushies after the game. Many kids tell me that even if they didn't care about a particular event or party, they still feel rejected, left out, unloved, and unworthy when they realize they weren't included. You know the feeling...we all do. Being left out sucks at any age. This is what social media is all the time: realizing we weren't included or feeling like someone has a better life than we do. We obviously can't be responsible for how everyone feels and we cannot invite everyone to everything, nor are we always going to be invited to everything. When mismanaged and misunderstood, social media can do lots of damage to our kiddos. Our kids do not stand a chance mentally when they are acutely aware of every single social event, hangout, or party that is available and that if they don't get included, then their life is officially ruined. By the time they get past it, a new day dawns then this whole roller coaster goes up and down again.

So, there you go. Those are the lies. I am sure there are many more. And guys and gals, I am here to tell you not one of those things is true. Including the initial lie that social media will bring us closer to each other...it won't. It has the capacity to do some amazing things, but nothing like a real face to face relationship.

Preach this to your kids, and preach it to yourself. Because you *are* enough, your worth does *not* come from other people, and you are most likely not missing out *at all.* Because of my clinical practice and speaking engagements, I still have many of these apps, but I try my best to use them very carefully. My editor told me she got rid of all her social media accounts a few years ago. She is still recovering from the tendencies she learned from Instagram – comparing herself to everyone, feeling boring and lame, wishing she was different and more "normal." Are you in that boat, too? Sarah would tell you, "Get out of the boat! You don't have to feel that way every day."

One more negative comment, and we will move on to what we can do about all this! This is not really a lie social media tells, but is one of its ugliest qualities. I remember being in 7th grade, and I had two boys who bullied me almost all the time. They chased me around, pushed me, wrestled with me, and would even hit me with senior rings on their fingers. I was miserable. I got knots in my stomach every day at lunch. I couldn't wait for school to end or for the weekend because I could get away from them. Let me tell you – those days are gone. Today children with social media cannot get away from their bullies. The bully can stalk them online, come to where they are, or make an entire malicious Instagram or Twitter post about their private life. Teen suicide due to online bullying has increased tremendously in the past decade in large part because they feel there is no escape. They are damned if they have social media, and they feel damned if they don't.

I point all of this out not to overwhelm you but because I know that there are so many well-intentioned parents who want to do what is best for their child. The world right now, though, is telling you to let your child have total freedom, that social media is not that bad, and that the consequences of entertainment and social apps are few and far between. Screen time keeps them occupied. Instagram keeps them "connected." Many of their schools, churches, and favorite places have Facebook pages and post content or news online. This is all true, and I understand. But the statistical consequences (more of which are emerging every day) are enormous and long-lasting. The juice is not worth the squeeze. The pros are not adding up to the cons, and we all have to make some changes if we want to save our culture and our children.

In some ways, social media has embedded itself into every nook and cranny of our daily lives. I am well aware of how hard change will be, and with two boys headed toward puberty, I am running this difficult race with you. I am also here to say that just because something will be hard and scary, doesn't mean we can avoid it. Those are usually the things we need to face most. If you find yourself willing to try something new or to forge a new path for your family, here are some of my thoughts and insight on how to do that. Although, I share so much of this so you can customize my advice and build the structure and safe boundaries that help your family the most. Armed with these warnings, I hope you feel more prepared to help yourself and your kids in ways that work for your household!

Quite simply, my first big piece of advice is the most straightforward, even if it seems daunting to execute. If you are a parent of a young child and you haven't given them social media, please don't. I beg that you wait until they are mature enough to manage it with wisdom and are guided to be responsible. Maybe wait until they can drive a car. Until they can regulate their own emotions and understand when they are being manipulated. Regardless of what timeframe makes sense for you or your kids, I still hope you will reflect on the various statistics I have shared. Reflect on what the research shows us about social media and its effects on our children. Your kid may be more mature than other kids, but make sure that there are structures and safety guards in place. The truth is hard to face, but just because we may not want to face the truth doesn't make it any less true.

Think about it this way: devices and the social media apps we put on them were never rated for children. Do you know what the R stands for on the movie ratings scale? *Restricted.* A show is rated R and thus is restricted from children under 17 for a few reasons. Sex, violence, language, nudity. These are aspects of a film that we know have a negative impact on children's minds. This is why we have a ratings system at all – to avoid putting images in front of children that will negatively influence their thoughts for years into the future. Well, this, and the fact that film companies do not want to get sued for exposing children to inappropriate content. Phones, devices, and social media platforms don't have this system in place, and none of the "inappropriate content" filters are good enough to protect our kids. Sure, a game or app might be rated for 12+ or 18+, but unlike the movie theater, there is no ticket taker at the door checking drivers' licenses to prevent minors from going in unsupervised.[137] What's more, the things that your child has

---

[137] Case in point, visiting a website for a brewery will often bring up a page that asks "Are you 21 or older?" Which is absolutely hilarious to me considering all you have to do is click "no."

access to on their phone and social media accounts can be much more graphic and appalling than what they'd see in an R-rated movie. Porn, violence against others, rape, suicides, bestiality, child pornography, sex camps, and human trafficking. It is all there, and it seems to be getting easier and easier to find. No need for the illusive dark web anymore. One wrong rabbit trail, and you might find yourself looking at horrible content. Content that should be rated XXX. If you wouldn't let your 11-year-old child see an R-rated movie, you should think twice about letting them have untethered access to their X-rated device or social media account. Children want to use them innocently. Children are innocent, but they can be corrupted so quickly without proper guidance and protection.

Ultimately, tech companies will argue that any monitoring or boundaries should be enforced by and are up to the parents. What should be and what is, are two different issues. I hope and wish that companies like TikTok, Snapchat, Instagram, Android, or Apple would get better filters with greater and more targeted accountability, but at the end of the day, they are doing their job which is to make a profit for their shareholders. We, therefore, need to be doing our job: to act as our children's filters until they are able to do that for themselves. To inform them and keep them protected from the apps that are costing them their mental health. If you ask me, the best way to do that, especially in our younger children, is to avoid giving them the device or the apps at all. Just as an aside, this goes the same for the shows or movies they watch, the music they listen to, the books they read, the artists they love etc. Our job is to know what our children are being exposed to and protect their hearts, minds, and bodies.

For those in a different situation, the parents of kids or teens who already use devices regularly, here is the advice I have for you. Yes, the adults and parents as well. I challenge you and your children to take a 90 day fast from all things social media. If you can fast from the phone altogether, even better. Set these things aside for 90 days. I promise you that it will revolutionize your entire world view. If you have never taken a breather from these various things, then you do not see the lies and tricks that are keeping you trapped, exhausted, and numb. If you are a parent of a teenager and they have already stepped too deep into this world, I beg you to show your child how to step away and find a better way to live. Help them. Guide them. I am not saying it will be easy.

Phones can be an addiction like anything else and therefore are equally hard to give up. You will have to find a support system to help you stand firm and to find people around you who are willing to take this journey alongside you. "What will I do with all that time, then?" you might be asking. Eat dinner together and actually talk, discuss. Play board games. Take walks or bike rides. Spend real time together laughing, crying, and living together again. I guarantee that you will be better for it, even if that journey takes a little while. Your brain and body will reset. It might be painful. It might feel like a drug or alcohol detox. That's because the science shows that it is very similar. So...don't do this alone. Get some friends and families to join you, and make it a group effort. See what comes of your 90-day fast. Then, if and only if, you chose to go back to your device or social media, you will have a better and clearer grasp on its effects on your mental health. Heck, if you feel like 90 days is way too hard to go cold-turkey, just start with 1 day or 1 week and try building up to longer periods, but a reset is due.

Clint's Rules for *Digital* Life

- Daily and weekly phone check-ins where you read your child's texts and go over conversations
- Talk about what was sent to and from your child
- Advice and answers on how to navigate any questionable interactions
- Text forwarding app (clone their phone to yours)
- Time limits for gaming and social media strictly enforced
- Phone lock box
- No phones or devices in rooms
- No open access to the app store (put a password on the store)
- No free roaming YouTube (suggested content and pop-ups can be inappropriate)
- Check Common Sense Media site before allowing them to read certain books or watch certain movies to check for content
- Put a passcode on any device that they will be accessing, especially those with streaming services
- Talk with other friends and family and make sure they are on board with these new rules or get new friends and limit exposure to unhealthy family members
- No smart phone until 9th grade
- No social media until they show enough maturity

Those are my two more major suggestions for how to either prevent damage from our devices and social media accounts, but I realize they are drastic and possibly very scary to implement, in yourself or your children. I still hope you take the leap of faith and try to fully detox from the sad and manipulative world of smartphones and apps, but I have some other pieces of advice too. These "rules," as I call them, are a bit smaller, more manageable, but still very effective in creating a future where your children can avoid abuse, mental health issues, and isolation. I call this list my rules for digital life, because let's face it, so much of our lives are lived out on our phones these days.

I realize some of those rules might sound severe, and I want to make it very clear that every family is different. Every child is different. You will likely have the best idea of what your family needs, how much trust is earned, and what level of maturity they are at. This set of rules is intense. I won't lie about that. But these (mostly) hard rules are what actually have power to limit your family's exposure and abuse. Even put into place, these rules aren't foolproof. Kids can always get another person's phone, buy a burner phone, hide their device, or just flat out lie to you. The ideal scenario would be to set these boundaries early and to build a culture in your home where phones aren't idolized, and therefore, your child won't feel the need to lie or lash out anyway. Despite what you may think, your children want to be like you, or at the very least, they learn many behaviors from mimicking you. If we always have our phones in our hands and spend hours scrolling through social media, then they will want to do the same. The good news is, no matter what bad habits we have started, we can always start fresh and break the phone-addiction cycle. We as parents need this change just as much as our kids do. Having scary conversations, putting new structures in place in your home, and setting up rules that might seem difficult, all have the potential to cause friction in your home. Your kids might not understand, and even if they do, they might be frustrated. What kid hasn't been frustrated with a parent when they try to set boundaries that are good for them? I know this is not the easy road, but I am sure it will be worth it. If you limit their gaming, social media use, and how much they are on their smartphone, you will be giving them the keys to become more successful, engaged, and attentive than all of their peers. Will we see it in their diplomas, their sports achievements, their free ride to college, or their SAT scores? It's entirely possible, but not certain. Plenty of people have been "successful"[138] even with deep mental and emotional trauma. The success we see will be measured in the next decade by how they can function emotionally, spiritually, and physically. The children of today are drowning and need a lifeline. At whatever cost, we must guide them better. Addictive and obsessive smartphone and social media use is mentally butchering a generation, and we have so many tools and resources to stop it. Will you be brave enough to fight this battle with me? I hope so.

There are two conversations that I see play out in my clinical office every single week. As I close out this chapter, I challenge you to reflect on both. Because your child might be calling you to have one of these conversations by the time they turn 21-25. Like many other children who hit adulthood and start to gain wisdom and insight into their parents' actions, your children will similarly start to wake up to the motivation behind many of *your* decisions. They will gain distance from their childhood and childish mindsets. When this starts to happen within them, they might call you and have one of two things to say.

They might call or visit and say, "Mom, Dad – if I gave you a ton of grief about the phone, using social media, and gaming too much, I am so sorry. I see now how you were protecting me and teaching me ways to stay safe. All my friends are addicted, depressed, anxious, and don't know how to be alone or how to manage a relationship. Thank you for being willing to show me a different way. Forgive me for giving you such a hard time."
Maybe it won't play out exactly like that, but it will be close. You might remember calling your parents and apologizing or thanking them for things that you never understood until you were an adult or parent yourself.

Or maybe they will come to you with another conversation. One where they call and say, "Mom, Dad – I am struggling. How could you let a kid, with no clue what they were doing or asking for, talk you into giving them

---

[138] I don't devote any real time to the concept of success in this book, but just a small note that you and your family should definitely discuss what success means to you. Is success climbing a career ladder, changing the world, being kind and impactful towards others, living a life according to God's word? That's something we have to define for ourselves every single day. Check out our podcast episode on the topic for more info!

social media and a phone. Why did you let me stay on my console for so many hours without making me take a break? Did you know what it was going to do to me? Did you know what was happening to me online or about the dangers I would face? Did you realize I was in my room gaming until 3 am with kids saying horrible and nasty things? Did you know I got sucked into watching porn and was living in shame? Did you know I was getting harassed and bullied for 6 years? Did you know the anxiety and pressure I was under trying to keep up with all the other people on social media? I have been living with mental health issues and zero self-esteem or communication skills for so long. If you knew what was out there, why didn't you try to stop me? Why didn't you teach me a different way? I wish I could go back and choose differently."

Again, not a word-for-word version of what you will hear, but many of our current adults have asked their parents these things or at least talked to a therapist about them. Have you ever wondered why your protectors didn't protect you better? Have you had to work through recovery and forgiveness? Would you do it all again with this new information and understanding?

I don't know about you, but I want my kids to call me with that first conversation. I don't want to do anything less than my best to give them the ultimate shot at a full and wonderful life, with a protected mind and a heart that knows Jesus is the only "influencer" with the words of life. If that means they get mad at me while they are kids, I will do my best to handle their frustration as it comes. Sometimes love doesn't look like giving our children everything they *think* they want.

It does not matter if the conversations are from erections to social media, from smartphones to body parts – no matter what the topic, I don't want my boys to be neglected because of my fear to have tough, uncomfortable (for me) conversations, or to set difficult boundaries. I hope you are willing to be brave too, in all the ways we've talked about here and many more. It takes courage to raise children in this new world. Parenting is not for the faint of heart!

Reflection & Discussion

1. What are your personal thoughts on social media? What apps do you use, and how often a day are you checking them?

2. How does your presence on social media make you feel about yourself and your life?

3. What would be your ideal scenario for your children using social media?

4. What lies do you think you have been accepting from social media, news, or the internet?

5. What friends or neighbors in your life would be willing to try out a phone-fast with you?

6. Do you find yourself thinking you or your children are "too far gone" into social media? Why?

19. Finding Hope In the Darkness

We all want progress, but if you're on the wrong road, progress means doing
an about-turn and walking back to the right road; in that case,
the man who turns back soonest is the most progressive.
-C. S. Lewis, *Mere Christianity*

Well...you did it. This is our final chapter together. The End Game.
I realize that this book has been a massive undertaking on your part. I
understand that within its pages there is a lot to chew on, process, and
decide. There are also a lot of action steps that need to take place. Above
all, there are probably many, *many* conversations to have. I find myself
struggling to find a perfect ending to wrap it all up, but I think it's worth
attempting to paint a full picture of what this book has said and what the
research is showing us.

Here is the sum of all that I am trying to say in the form of a story about
the average child in America.

Imagine a little boy or girl who grows from 0-5 years old with a heavy
focus on his/her behavior and not a lot of attunement, affirmation, or
focus on attachment. Imagine that this child's brain starts forming
unhealthy wirings and behaviors to meet those needs.

They have been spanked into submission, their parents constantly fight
and argue, and they are allowed to watch a screen for most of the day,
because it is a great babysitter. Then from 5-12, on those same screens,
this child is exposed to content littered with sex, violence, and toxic
lessons about relationships through movies, video games, books, and
experiences.

This same child has never had a conversation about their body or how to stay safe online or in person. Their parents cringe at saying penis, much less talking to them about sex, porn, or body safety. They are allowed to hear about it from friends, sing about it to songs on the radio, and look at it on their devices, but not given space to talk about it with their caregivers. They have many experiences in private, with their bodies and the bodies of others, that lead to shame and secrets.

This child then goes to sleepovers and lives life with other children who are going through the same thing. These kids live on devices that are full of apps that allow strangers and corporations to access them without their parents even knowing. Remember this is all from the ages of 5-12. Now also during this time, this child has most likely experienced sexual abuse or sexual touch by someone they know. They begin exploring and acting out sexually with other children because of what they have seen, experienced, or because of curiosity. No one knows any of this is happening, and there are no adults who come alongside this child to defend them, process with them, or explain to them what is right or wrong. No one tells this child, "It's not your fault. Let's talk about it together." This child is now full of confusion and shame. They blame themselves and become either hypersexual with warped arousal templates or just completely turned off by all of it and anyone who reminds them of those experiences.

Now imagine puberty hits. The child's devices are now full of social media, porn, and dangerous adults. Their lives are surrounded by other children, who again, are going through similar things at varying degrees. The only sex education they have had was from their peers and the internet or maybe health class. The messages from public school only seem to be confusing these kids. The child in question is now somewhere between 13 and 18 years old. This teenager starts to date other teens and explore their sexuality. They have huge deficits in emotional intelligence, no models for healthy relationships because their parents are in their second marriage, and if they attend church, which is unlikely, the one they attend doesn't talk about any of these topics on Sunday morning or Wednesday night. No one even acknowledges that any of this is happening or has happened.

Building Better Bridges

Did I mention that our hypothetical teen makes perfect grades, is the captain of a sports team, or is the leading role in the school play? They look so successful to all the adults in their lives. Or, in a separate turn of events, they are a drop out. They have failing grades, smoke pot, and get into fights all the time. They are labeled as the troubled kid or worse "bad kid." Either of these options is possible and extremely common. Their outside shell may look different, - one seemingly successful and thriving, the other very outwardly struggling - but their social, emotional, and sexual trauma is the same, the symptoms just look different based on socioeconomic status. This teen then ends their high school career and goes into a life of debauchery or college. Sometimes both of those at the same time. If they survive the college years with more sex, drugs, alcohol and porn, then they finally can move into adult life.

Soon this once-kid, now adult, gets a job and gets married and has a couple of kids. 12 years into marriage, their spouse finds out they have porn, gambling, and drug addictions or are having an affair of some kind. They don't know how to resolve conflict. They live in constant shame, and they have no clue who they are or why they do what they do. Depression and anxiety riddle their lives. At some point they cannot tolerate all the pressure, pain, and stress and then end up hurting their spouse and their children. Now they are sitting on my couch with their head in their hands begging for help. Help which is certainly attainable, but that will take years to achieve. My job as a clinician or pastor is to then help figure out what happened. How did this person get here? What is their story? What is the narrative they have told themselves about this story? What do they need to take responsibility for and what do they need to let go of.

Does this sound familiar to you? This is what the average story I have heard for more than a decade sounds like. It is not an uncommon one. This is not a story that is for the "bad people." This is the story that needs help recovering from all the unaddressed abuse and neglect built up internally for who knows how many years.

We are living in a world where most adults grew up uninformed, uneducated, and ill-equipped to handle the trajectory of sexual content and technology in our society and the world at large. A focus on emotional intelligence and mental health was rarely there. Because of the things I have tried to outline in this book, well meaning people failed to

284

protect generations of children. These generations grew up to be inundated with different levels of technology and increased exposure that created the world we currently live in. Trauma, on top of trauma, on top of trauma. Generation after generation. As aware as we are as a society, as informed as we are about so many things, we still seem to be helplessly lost in the area of sexual health and education. These issues have always been here, but advances in technology and changes in culture have drastically increased the consequences for the humans involved. If we do not adjust and correct, then there will continue to be a massive number of people living with hidden toxic behaviors and brokenness that keep them bound in shame. These behaviors will continue to be disconnected from the root causes that were so preventable if we had only known what to do and why to do it.

I hope that you have learned what to do and why to do it. I hope that you have learned that people are the way they are because they have been neglected and abused in ways that have been swept under the rug for far too long. Ways that we never talk about in a robust and nuanced way.

I truly believe that this is the generation to stop the cycle. We can change things. We can stop letting the trauma and neglect of generations move any further. All these tears in the fabric of our world can begin to be mended and healed, through building better bridges, between loving and kind human beings. Parents or caregivers can learn to lead and teach their children in helpful ways that will change the lives of countless future generations. It starts with us believing we deserve it and taking one small step that will turn into giant leaps!

As I stated in the beginning, this book is about two things. Prevention and recovery. If you are a parent of a teen or young adult, I understand that there can be a lot of grief and heartache. Several people have asked me, "Where were you when we had kids?" or "Where were you 15 years ago?" Many of the problems we struggle with as parents have always existed, but the ways in which they get spread across the earth and within our communities continues to change drastically. I get that you are working from a deficit and that walking some of this back might seem difficult or even impossible. Please don't believe that. You can start your own healing journey today. Your behaviors, proclivities, or unhealthy patterns don't define you and are not permanent as long as you are willing to try something new! You can start having these conversations and changing the boundaries in your home, even if you have missed some opportunities or even if you didn't receive these lessons. Starting now with a teen or young adult can help shape their future tremendously. Children are resilient. They can bounce back from our unintended neglect and mistakes. Please don't give up!

If you are a parent of a young child 10 years or under please share this book and these resources with everyone you know. Buy a copy for your parents, the babysitter, your Sunday school pastor, whoever will read it. Step up and make changes that can save, not just your children, but everyone else's. Stir the pot, make some waves, be a squeaky wheel!! Please build a community of like-minded people who are able to walk through life with you and follow the same lifestyle you are creating. The major problem with surviving this new culture is that we are walking it alone. A strong community is needed now more than ever. Maybe use this book in a Bible study or in a book club, and open up conversations about the risks and rewards of sleepovers, social media, smart devices, and much more. Start teaching about body safety and proper terms for body parts. This will bring up conversations that can lead to safety and health within your sphere of influence. We need to slow down and prioritize true community support to stand a chance.

I know many of you are doing, and have done, the best you can with what you have. When we know better, we can do better. I desperately hope that this book helps many of us to know better. I pray that it gives you concrete examples with research and professional experience to back it up. Ultimately, I can only put my faith in my Lord and Savior, Jesus Christ, and rely on the power of the Holy Spirit to speak light and truth. I do not know what you put your faith in, but I pray that the information is helpful regardless.

I am so thankful that you made it all the way through this book. I know that it is an intense and heavy read. I hope that this has been a very practical and conversational way to talk about a tough and nuanced topic. I hope you can see the big picture now and see how the threads weave together to affect one another. My dream is that we can wake up in a decade or so and have a huge group of families, adults, and children who have a healthy view of themselves and others and know how to protect themselves in person and online.

It would be such a shame if our society collapses all because we did not protect and equip our children. I want to remind you that each one of us has an opportunity to join the fight. We can either get into the work of prevention or recovery. If we do use the resources you found in this book, I truly believe we can reduce childhood sexual neglect, trauma, and exposure to adult content by a massive amount.

I certainly hope that we do not let religion, politics, social status, or awkwardness get in the way of the facts and statistics that I have tried to pull together. After all, if love is not central to everything we do, our actions and words are empty.[139] I pray that we do not let our own insecurity and trauma keep us from protecting our children and their future.

Thank you for giving me the opportunity to talk with you and take you on an imperfect journey. I know by the time I publish this book that things will have changed. New apps and hurdles will be put in front of us. New complications and fears will be brought to light. Regardless, there is always hope.

Lastly, I recommend reaching out to us or someone you trust, for more education and conversation. ***Doing this work cannot be done outside of a healthy and strong community. We are meant to be villages, not silos. We must get back to helping one another and protecting one another.*** I hate that our time together is ending, so I hope you will check out our podcast *Asking Why with Clint Davis* for more discussions and information. Sign up for our newsletter or our Patreon page for more support. There are several printable documents that are companions to this book on our patreon page. We are available now to help you find resources in your area or to walk with you ourselves, through whatever situation and in your own context. One of the best things you can do is

---

[139] "If I speak in the tongues of men and of angels, but have not love, I am a noisy gong or a clanging cymbal. And if I have prophetic powers, and understand all mysteries and all knowledge, and if I have all faith, so as to remove mountains, but have not love, I am nothing." -1 Corinthians 13:1-2

book a speaker at www.clintdaviscounseling.com to have this information shared and processed with your community. I would love nothing more than to come and talk about this information and help you in your own context! Lastly, follow us on social media for daily tips and wisdom around mental health and spiritual living (see, I'm really not anti-social-media.)

Thank you very much for taking the time to read this book. As I walk this journey myself, I will be praying and rooting for you as your path unfolds. This life is not perfect. In fact it is broken. However, this life is important. There is much good to be found in it. We must find a way to live in the duplicity that is this life - good and evil living right next door to one another. Scripture says that the whole earth is moaning and groaning for the return of Jesus. I am confident many of us can relate to this feeling, whatever your values might be. We moan and groan for something better. We know there should be more to life than what we have been given. We are in pain and grief over what we have lost and the ways we know things should be better for humanity. This life is a gift, even in the hard parts, and for Christ followers, that means showing gratitude and fulfilling God's ministry of reconciliation. For humans in general, I think this means doing our best to seek out "better" for ourselves and our families, making things right where we have the ability to do so. And I hope that this book helps you set some things right in your life, the life of your children and their future children.

Reflection & Discussion

1. Check in with yourself after finishing the book. What are your thoughts, and how are you feeling?

2. What things do you feel empowered to implement in your life and in your parenting? What things turned you off or gave you fear?

3. If you involved your children in discussions as you were reading, what were their thoughts and feelings about all this information?

4. Who in your life could benefit from reading this or applying its principles? If you decide to, do you have a community who can do this with you?

5. What are your biggest goals for your children, their hearts, and their future life?

6. How do the people in your family define success?

Q&A w/ Clint Davis

1. What if my kid tells me that they want a lifestyle that I disagree with?
First of all, you always want to listen first. Get support for yourself, as well. Tell them that you love them no matter what they are going through or trying to figure out and that they can always come to you without judgment or criticism. Then you should ask them questions to see if you can understand the root causes of these desires. Consider meeting with a professional or a leader in your community who will walk them slowly through this process and gain insight and understanding. What you don't want to do is to shame them or isolate them. At the same time, however, keep the boundaries and expectations in your home in place. They are minors and need support and love, but they also need structure before the freedom of adulthood.

2. What do I do if I am the single parent of my household?
Find community support. You must have other men and women in your child's life to
mentor them and teach them about what it means to be a healthy human. None of us can handle this life alone, so I strongly urge you to get into therapy and gain your own support and healing. Above all, be patient with yourself and your child.

3. What if I am divorced and my ex doesn't follow the rules?
First try to give them information and inform them of the risks of not being unified in household rules you established. Document your requests and the consequences of the lack of rules and boundaries.
You can also have your child see a mental health professional and document any consequences. Bring this evidence to court and ask the judge to mandate that rules with devices, safety, and exposure to content are followed. Finally, have someone else in your community go with you to be supportive and minimize

conflict.

4. When should I let my child start to date?

Obviously dating in our culture is extremely confusing. Until you have covered all of the rules in this book and built incredibly strong bridges, I recommend dating being held until driving age. Supervision should be paramount until there is confidence that your child can handle themselves appropriately.

Preteens like to say they have a boyfriend or girlfriend. It is important to help them clarify this language and tell them to call the person a friend. When you do start allowing dating, be diligent about talking with them about exclusivity, boundaries, and safety.

5. How do I know when or if my child (or our family) should seek out professional counseling?

Are you human? I believe every person can benefit from a professional and objective third party listener. Someone not connected to your life or your past who can listen to you without bias or judgment. This allows an open dialogue without shame or blame and gives a space for you or your child to discuss and then just leave that in the session. I advocate for counseling often, perhaps I am biased, but I think anyone at any time can benefit from a therapist or counselor of some kind. Certainly don't let yourself fall into the belief that counseling means something has gone wrong. That is the major misconception surrounding seeing a therapist, and it is simply not true.

6. What apps should I use for my child's device?

Here, as well as earlier in the book, is a list of helpful apps to have for your child's phone: Net Nanny, Bark, Covenant Eyes, Ever Accountable, Disney Circle, OurPact.

7. What questions should I be asking myself before I give my child a smart device?

a. Do I want them to have access to the internet or apps?
b. Can I track their location?
c. Do they have access to the app store?
d. Am I in control of adding to their contacts list?
e. Do I have concerns about screen time limits?

f. Do they really need emails and texts?
g. Do I want them to have access to entertainment like music, movies, games etc.?
h. Can they take videos and photos?
i. Can I monitor their communication regularly through my device or through check-ins?
j. Am I confident that my child knows safety rules and will be honest with me when they make mistakes?
k. Am I giving into peer pressure from other parents?
l. Did I train my child on their phone and or the internet and social media?
m. Do I know how to monitor their social media use and educate them on the pitfalls?

8. What are the best alternatives for children who must have a communication device?
a. Gabb Phone or watch
b. Samsung Bark phone
c. Jitterbug
d. The LightPhone
e. T-Mobile SyncUP KIDS watch
f. Verizon Gizmo Watch 2
g. Palm Phone

9. What are some of the most important conversations I should be having with my teen
and preteen around our family values? (not an exhaustive list)
a. What is an *influencer* and how do they affect our mindstate
b. Friends who are different from us
c. The risks and reasons for people using drugs and alcohol
d. What do I do if I or someone I know is bullied online or in person
e. Race and Gender ideology
f. Eating disorders and body shaming
g. How to deal with grief and loss
h. How to use social media properly
i. Modesty and dressing appropriately
j. Body positivity
k. Cancel culture
l. The value of hard work

m. How to deal with money and bills
n. Mental Health issues like depression, anxiety, trauma and where these come from
o. Forming their own faith and belief in God and His love for them
p. Forming mentors
q. The importance of asking for help and asking for their needs to be met
r. Selfless service and community
s. How to handle someone making sexual advances towards you
t. How being mean or being jealous is not cute or funny and doesn't mean the person likes you.

*****

10. You mention Christ throughout your book - what is your understanding of the Gospel?

I believe that God loves you and that He wants to be in a relationship with you. He doesn't judge you or want to condemn you. We are broken and in need of saving, and we cannot save ourselves. God became flesh and blood in the form of His son Jesus. Jesus lived a perfect, sinless life and died to make a way for *us* to be with a Holy and perfect God.[140] Jesus was buried and rose on the third day. It was such a powerful resurrection that scripture tells us over 500 people saw him and walked with Him after that day. Other people were documented resurrecting as well and "walking into the Holy city." The disciples (the guys who lived life with Jesus) who had previously fled in fear on Friday (the crucifixion), started a revival and community that is the largest and most expansive in the world today. All these men and women who had abandoned Jesus were *so sure* that He came back to life and was fulfilling all His promises that they literally gave their lives up to practice His way of life. So dedicated were they to this way of life, they were willing to face a violent death, along with their families, to proclaim its truth.

After His resurrection, Jesus ascended to Heaven to sit by the Father. He lives today as our way to God the Father. He left behind the Holy Spirit to

---

[140] "For God so loved the world, that he gave his only Son, that whoever believes in him should not perish but have eternal life. For God did not send his Son into the world to condemn the world, but in order that the world might be saved through him." John 3:16-17 (ESV)

help us along the way, the spirit that is often called our Helper and Comforter. Everyone who believes in Jesus and calls Him Lord can ask to receive the Holy Spirit to help them through life and to, in the words of Jesus, "do greater things than I."[141] The bottom line is that no one is too bad, and no one is too good to receive this gift. No one can lose the love of God, and no one can earn it. It is the *free gift* of grace that is offered, because God loves every single person on earth.[142] The only choice that any of us have to make is to accept the forgiveness, and salvation that is granted to us forever. Heaven on Earth and in eternity is our reward, as well as constant relationship with a perfect Father. As Christians, our job is to walk in the fruit of the Spirit: love, joy, peace, patience, kindness, goodness, gentleness, faithfulness and self-control.[143] This has all been documented in the Bible, which I believe "all Scripture is breathed out by God and profitable for teaching, for reproof, for correction, and for training in righteousness, that the man or woman of God may be complete, equipped for every good work." I hope that *this* is what you see when you read this book and that these are the things you experience when you run into someone who claims to be a Christ follower.

I pray right now that this little paragraph speaks to your heart and that you would accept the sacrifice and love of Jesus for the first time and run to our Father. He sees and knows you the most and loves you the best.

11. What is your biggest fear as a parent? How do you respond to those fears without being paralyzed into inaction?

I would say my main fear as a father would be my kids not having a deep relationship with me later in life that allows them to come to me for advice or seeing me as someone they can trust. I fear them being afraid to share their struggles with me as they grow into adults. I combat those fears by ultimately just being present with them. In some ways the future affects us now and how I want to parent, but I can't control the future,

---

[141] "Truly, truly, I say to you, whoever believes in me will also do the works that I do; and greater works than these will he do, because I am going to the Father." John 14:12 (ESV)

[142] "For by grace you have been saved through faith. And this is not your own doing; it is the gift of God,
not a result of works, so that no one may boast." Ephesians 2:8-9 (ESV)

[143] "The fruits of the spirit are love, joy, peace, patience, kindness, goodness, gentleness, faithfulness, and self-control, against these things, there is no law." Galatians 5:22-23 (ESV)

only the ways I love them and lift them up right now. I strive to use every present opportunity to love them unconditionally and do my best to do the right thing by them. To answer the un-asked question…the way I control those fears is to attend therapy for myself, learning my own triggers and insecurities that have absolutely nothing to do with my kids. I share my struggles with my wife and get support from her, as well. Above all, I just pray and try to give my boys to the Lord, knowing He will protect them far better than I can.

12. With all the rules and strategies you have mentioned in the book, did you build those structures and rules with your wife? How did you both arrive at an agreement on your parenting?

Yes, definitely, we worked together. I have learned that me and my wife have different red lines or triggers for certain behaviors or rules, so as we have grown together and understood those things in each other, we can build around that. We are obviously both looking out for the best interests of our kids, and if we disagree on something, especially if it's not a major deal breaker or anything life/death, then we have learned to be flexible with each other, particularly if one of us cares about a certain rule a lot, the other one will be flexible with that to show love and grace about that issue. Deciding on rules together, though, is very important to us so that we can be consistent with one another as well as with our boys. Many parenting strategies we discussed prior to having kids, and many come up at random. Something massively important for us is also not letting other parents influence our parenting. We are doing what is best for each of our particular boys without trying to meet the styles of other families. Ultimately, when both spouses want the best for the child, getting to an agreement out of selflessness is not too hard!

13. Throughout the book, you discuss many techniques you have implemented in your home for your children. How do you feel they respond to these?

Ha - well. They respond like children. They often respond inconsistently, sometimes in surprising ways. They can be difficult. Overall, though, I think focusing on the long game is working for us. If I were to take any individual moment, I start to feel like maybe it's not working, but when I look over time, it definitely is. What I tell people all the time is that your child doesn't need you to be a perfect parent. They just need to know what they are going to get from you 8 out of 10 times. That consistency is what will make the difference in "building the bridges" of trust with your kids that allow your relationship to face trials or heavy things over time. Of course this means that sometimes they don't understand our rules or what I am doing, but consistency is the key.

14. What has been the most powerful or helpful part of your own journey of healing?
Many things. Therapists have allowed me to see that healthy relationships are possible, that my feelings and experiences are valid. I have learned (am still learning) how to take responsibility for the areas in my life that I do have control over and to let go of those areas that are out of my control. Learning to forgive where and when I need to forgive, while at the same time honoring my own boundaries to avoid getting hurt in meaningless or purposeless ways. Those have been some of the most impactful lessons I have learned on my path, and many of those things I will be learning for years to come.

Appendix I: Tips Regarding Human Trafficking

Despite not discussing human and/or sex trafficking in depth throughout the body of this book, I feel the topic definitely deserves some time here. More human trafficking goes on than most of us ever think about. That being said, preventing human trafficking requires a concerted effort from individuals, communities, governments, and organizations and should be a priority for us. Here are some tips to help combat human trafficking and child abduction:

- Raise awareness: Educate yourself and others about the signs of human trafficking and its different forms, including forced labor, sex trafficking, and child trafficking. The more people are aware of the issue, the more likely they are to recognize and report suspicious activities. This will also lower unnecessary fears.

- Support anti-trafficking organizations: Get involved with reputable organizations that work to combat human trafficking. They often provide support to survivors, conduct awareness campaigns, and advocate for stronger anti-trafficking policies. In my city, Shreveport, Louisiana, our anti-trafficking ministry is called *Purchased, Not for Sale*, a fabulous organization I have been part of for many years. Find the one in your area and see how you can get involved!

- Report suspicious activities: If you suspect human trafficking is occurring, don't hesitate to report it to law enforcement or a human trafficking hotline. In many countries, hotlines are available for anonymous reporting.

- Be cautious online: Human traffickers may use social media and online platforms to lure victims. Be cautious about sharing personal information online and report any suspicious online behavior or advertisements.

Building Better Bridges

- Support fair trade and ethical businesses: Choose products and services that support fair labor practices. Avoid purchasing goods and services from companies with a history of labor exploitation.

- Promote safe migration: Encourage safe migration practices and be aware of the risks associated with illegal immigration. Support policies that protect vulnerable migrants and hold traffickers accountable.

- Educate vulnerable populations: Reach out to communities and individuals who are at a higher risk of becoming victims of trafficking. Provide them with information about their rights, potential dangers, and available resources.

- Strengthen laws and policies: Advocate for robust anti-trafficking laws and policies at local, national, and international levels. Support measures that focus on prevention, prosecution, and protection of victims.

- Engage with businesses: Encourage businesses to adopt anti-trafficking policies and supply chain transparency. Holding corporations accountable for their practices can help reduce the demand for exploited labor.

- Support survivors: Offer support to survivors of trafficking by donating to organizations that provide resources such as counseling, housing, education, and vocational training.

- Involve the media: Work with media outlets to raise awareness and promote responsible reporting on human trafficking. Accurate and sensitive reporting can help shape public opinion and encourage action.

- Encourage school involvement: Schools can play a crucial role in educating students about human trafficking and teaching them about their rights and how to protect themselves. Make sure your school, church, or place of worship has policies in place and follows them.

Remember, preventing human trafficking is an ongoing effort that requires collaboration and vigilance from everyone in society. By taking these steps, we can work towards a world where human trafficking is eradicated. Until that day comes, however, there are also some steps you can take in your family to prevent any of these tragedies occurring in your own household.

Here are a few important family rules (in addition to many of the conversations we have already discussed) that will help reduce the risk of abduction:

- Stay Together in Public Places: When in public areas like malls, parks, or busy streets, ensure that family members stay close together and never wander off alone.

- Use the Buddy System: Encourage children to have a buddy or a family member with them when going to places like the restroom or playing outside.

- Know and Trust Adults: Teach children to only go with trusted adults, like parents, relatives, or designated caregivers. Make sure they know whom to approach for help in case they get separated from the family.

- Avoid Sharing Personal Information: Teach children not to share personal information, such as their full name, address, school name, or daily routines with strangers or on social media. Do not post nude pictures of your child online.

- Discuss Strangers: Educate children about stranger awareness without causing unnecessary fear. Stranger danger can teach them the wrong ideas. Teach them to recognize and avoid potentially dangerous situations and people without fearing everyone. Most people are not out to get them, even strangers.

- Safe Routes and Places: Discuss safe routes to school, friend's houses, and other frequented locations. Identify safe places they can go to if they feel threatened. Have a list of contacts they can call.

- Verify Identification: If someone claims to be an authority figure (e.g., police officer, school personnel) and requests to take your child somewhere, verify their identification and call their office to confirm. Teach your child to do the same.

- Open Communication: Keep open lines of communication with your children, encouraging them to share any concerns or unusual encounters with you without fear of judgment or punishment.

- Code words: Use private words that only safe people will know and teach your children to never go with someone who does not know these code words or phrases.

- Scream fire: If someone ever tries to take you or your child, scream help and fire as loudly as you can.

- Self Defense: Consider having your family go through a basic training of self defense at a local Jiu-Jitsu School so that they know how to make it extremely difficult to be taken or harmed. Remember that these rules should be discussed regularly and reinforced through age-appropriate discussions. It's also essential to lead by example, demonstrating safe behaviors for your children to follow. Additionally, consider involving your local community in safety initiatives and staying informed about any recent incidents or safety concerns in your area.

Appendix II: Conversation Starters/Topics

➤ Staying Safe Online:

Does your child know how to connect safely to the internet?

How and where do you connect to the internet? Let's learn more about how that method works. Find a video on YoutTube to watch together about risks and dangers of connecting poorly or on an unsafe computer.

Why do you think sharing personal information, like credit card numbers or addresses over an unsecured network is dangerous?

Why is it important to be careful about sharing our family's Wi-Fi password with anyone?

Do they know about privacy settings while browsing? Talk about privacy settings and walk them through these on their devices.

How do you use privacy settings to protect your information or being exposed to certain content while browsing?

Did you know that images may contain metadata telling when and where they were taken? Let's make sure that you turn that off on all your devices and block this from websites.

Do you always check into places on social media? What are the risks to telling everyone where you are and when you go out of town? Let's be mindful of sharing our location with apps and on social media when it is unnecessary.

➤ Passwords/Privacy

A strong password is so important. Many Apple or Android devices can store your passwords for you so that you can make complicated and difficult to hack passwords without fear of forgetting them.

Have you ever shared your password with someone out of peer pressure or a threat?

Why is it important to have a different password for every account?

Do you feel like you have the tools to keep you safe online?

How do we minimize sharing our personal information? Context matters when it comes to sharing information. Make sure your teen knows how to validate who people are and to filter people's desire to have access to your personal information before sharing. There are lots of scammers out there.

Do you know what personal information is risky to share online? How do you know if a website/platform/person is safe to share info like credit cards, address, personal information with?

What can you do if someone you know violates your trust and information?

What do you do if you are being scammed or blackmailed online?

➤ Physical Touch

How far is too far with certain types of physical touch? And at what ages or relationship stages?

Help your child set limits and boundaries about physical contact before the choice ever comes up in their lives. Be frank about the potential dangers and pitfalls that come with various types of touching, how it affects our hearts and minds and feelings.

Go through all different types of touch to help guide them on what is appropriate: hand-holding, hugging, kissing, someone touching their breasts or private areas, tickling, napping together, and many others. Anything from hand-holding or tickling all the way to sexual intercourse or masturbation should be discussed prior to your child experiencing it in an unfamiliar or unsafe way. Visit our patreon page for printable resources for teaching healthy biblical sexuality to your children.

The things we want to teach our children can feel endless. If you still have things you want to address, check out this site for more conversation help on topics that can be scary or difficult to address with your children: https://axis.org/resource-category/parent-guide/
Obviously these are just guides. I am not promoting a specific version of these conversations, but pointing to the fact that these conversations have to be had. Remember to always pick and choose and adapt to your family values.

Appendix III: Handling Difficult Questions

We discussed this earlier in the book, but here are some specifics about what to do when your child places something heavy on your bridge, something you might not know how to handle in the moment. So here is a little run through of what to do/say when your child comes to you with a question like, "Hey, mom/dad, what is _____?"

This could be something like, "Hey mom what does 69 mean?" or "Hey mom what is lube?"

You have to realize that this might be an innocent math question or question about a sign they saw at "Jiffy Lube." It might not be worthy of a full blown panic attack. But, they could be referring to something like porn, penis, sex, blowjob, or any list of topics that would usually come out of left field or that you know is sexual and not age-appropriate to discuss in detail.

First step? Do *not* react out of anger or disgust.

Try not to say something like "Why the heck are you asking me that!" or "That's disgusting and dirty, never say that again!" This only shames the child and burns bridges instead of building them. They will not come to you in the future if you respond in this way.

Instead:

Remember it is important to respond in some way and not to brush off this conversation entirely, but also don't go into more detail than necessary. Here are some steps to find balance, create confidence, build a safe space, and do no harm. (Go back to chapter 4 to review the content on talking to the "right" brain)

1. Stay calm, take a deep breath, repeat: "This is not a crisis"

2. Vet the information with safety as your first priority. Ask questions casually and not like a machine gun or interrogation. Maybe something

304

Clint Davis

like: "Interesting, what do you think that means?" or "Where did you hear that"?
Keep your questions light and open ended. How did that make you feel inside? Did you share that information with anyone else?

3. See some example responses below when your child asks about something sexual or a term they shouldn't be saying at their particular age:

- "That is something that only adults do with one another. You are not old enough to know about that or worry about that, and we can talk about it some time later."
- "You are not in trouble for asking and will never get in trouble for asking mommy or daddy, but your brain, body, and heart are not ready for this conversation yet."
- "I'm so glad you came to me to check what that is, and it's not really something that others should be telling you about because it's an adult topic/conversation."
- Answer the question as best as you can, stay general and clinical, and ask if they have further questions. Give as much information as you can write on a post-it note. If you over share, pause and say, "I think that's as much as you need to know for now, but if you have other questions, feel free to ask." You know your child. Watch them and look for signs that they are satisfied and feel confident to move on.
- You can ask your child if they remember the body safety rules around private parts and ask if everyone they spend time with follows those rules (you can ask about it generally, like, "At school or church does everyone respect yours and each other's bodies, especially private parts?" "Does anyone make you feel uncomfortable?" "Does anyone do things that you know are not our family rules?" "Do all your teachers make you feel safe?")
- Use this as an opportunity to *calmly* talk about the fact that you're always a safe space to share anything and to ask questions about anything related to bodies and private parts. Remind them that you're always the first person that they should ask about anything related to body safety, private parts, or sex and that they will never get in trouble.

Building Better Bridges

- Remind them that your family has special rules and values that not all families follow. There may be friends who do not do the same things or follow the same rules and that it is okay for you to stick to our family rules that are safe and secure. When someone does not follow our rule and tries to talk you into doing something else, it is important to tell mommy and daddy.

Appendix IV: Resource List

Overall Book Recommendations:

Good Pictures Bad Pictures
Kristen Jensen

Tech Wise Family
Andy Crouch

Take Back Your Family
Jefferson Bethke

Habits of the Household
Justing Whitmel Earley

Redeeming Your Time
Jordan Raynor

God Made All of Me
Justin and Linsdsey Holcomb

God Made Boys and Girls
Marty Machowski

ABC of Body Safety and Consent
Jayneen Sanders

Whole Brain Child
Dr. Dan Siegle & Tina Bryson

Families and Forgiveness
Terry Hargrave

God Made Your Body
Jim Burns

Beyond Behaviors
Dr. Mona Delahooke

How to Talk So Kids Will Listen & How to Listen So Kids Will Talk
Adele Faber

Raising Good Humans
Hunter Clarke-Fields

Parenting
Paul David Tripp

Parenting from the Inside Out
Dan Siegel & Mary Hartzell

Brain-Body Parenting
Dr. Mona Delahooke

The Coddling of the American Mind   Greg Lukianoff and Jonathan Haidt

Parenting with Heart: How Imperfect Parents Can Raise Resilient, Loving, and Wise-Hearted Kids
Stephen James and Chip Dodd

Building Better Bridges

Additional Books About Science-Based Parenting:

Wildhood
Barbara Natterson-Horowitz

Positive Discipline
Jane Nelsen

The Gift of Failure
Jessica Lahey

Raising Your Spirited Child
Mary Sheedy Kurcinka

No Bad Kids
Janet Lansbury

Books to Read If Your Teen Struggles with Pornography:

The Porn Trap
Wendy & Larry Maltz

Treating Pornography Addiction
Kevin Skinner

Sex Addiction 101
Robert Weiss

Your Brain on Porn
Gary Wilson

Facing the Shadow (and workbooks)
Patrick Carnes

13 Ways to Ruin Your Life
Jarrod Jones

Here are a few other titles related to body safety and sexual development, especially tailored for young children, and there is good information in all of them. None of them, however, covers the information perfectly, and I recommend only using the tools you find helpful:

Let's Talk about Body Boundaries, Consent & Respect
Jayneen Sanders

It's Not the Stork
Robie Harris

Who Has What?
Robie Harris

What's In There? All about Before You were Born
Robie Harris

What Makes a Baby?
Cory Silverberg

Clint Davis

*Amazing You! Getting
Smart about Private Parts*
Gail Saltz

*An Exceptional Children's
Guide to Touch*
Hunter Manasco

CALL TO ACTION:

If you felt that this book was helpful, I would be extremely grateful if you left us an honest review on Amazon and Goodreads. This helps people get a look at what this book is about and how it was helpful to other parents, caregivers, or professionals.

If you want your community to implement some of the things in this book, please reach out and book some training with Clint or buy a copy and give it to everyone you know. I truly believe we can change the future if we will just act and engage together.

Lastly, please go on social media and do a post, reel, or story about how this book impacted you and your family and join us in spreading the message of hope and protection!! See I am not anti-technology!

For printables and resources to apply things you learned in this book sign up to our patreon page: *Asking Why with Clint Davis*

- Family Device Contract
- A Guidebook to talking about healthy biblical sexuality
- A smart device rules list
- Body Safety Checklist for your child's daycare, sitter, nanny, or anyone keeping your young one while you are away.
- And much more.

May Yahweh bless you and keep you; may Yahweh make his face shine on you and be gracious to you; may Yahweh turn his face toward you and give you peace.

-Numbers 6:24-26

The End.

(Actually, the beginning.)

Clint Davis

Clint Davis is an Army veteran with a bachelor's in Psychology and a master's in Marriage and Family Therapy. He is an ordained minister and a Licensed Professional Counselor, trained in trauma and certified in sexual addiction recovery. He has worked for many years in ministry to help find freedom for those stuck in human trafficking and poverty. Clint owns Clint Davis Counseling and Integrative Wellness where he has a team of licensed mental health counselors, biblical counselors, and other medical professionals who help people recover from trauma to the mind, body, and spirit. Clint also hosts the *Asking Why* podcast. He is married to Jacie with whom he has two sons, Grady and Jude. Clint enjoys reading, podcasting, Jiu Jitsu, and talking about Jesus.

To inquire about booking Clint Davis for a speaking engagement, please visit our Book a Speaker page at clintdaviscounseling.com.
Visit us on social media @clintdaviscounseling or @buildingbetterbridges

Garrison and Mitcham Press
Shreveport, Louisiana 2023

Made in the USA
Monee, IL
18 November 2023

46874996R00175